ADD: *THE 20-HOUR SOLUTION*

TRAINING MINDS TO CONCENTRATE
AND SELF-REGULATE NATURALLY
WITHOUT MEDICATION

MARK STEINBERG, PH.D.

AND

SIEGFRIED OTHMER, PH.D.

ROBERT D. REED PUBLISHERS • BANDON, OR

Robert D. Reed Publishers
P. O. Box 1992
Bandon, OR 97411
Phone: 541/347-9882 • Fax: -9883
E-mail: 4bobreed@msn.com
www.rdrpublishers.com

Book Design by Marilyn Yasmine Nadel
Cover Design by Julia Gaskill

3rd Printing 2005

ISBN: 1-931741-37-9
Library of Congress Card Number: 2003097732
Produced and Printed in United States

Table of Contents

Dedication

*We dedicate this book
to the memory of
Brian Othmer and to
Sue Othmer and Pearl Steinberg,
who know about
raising difficult children.*

Foreword

As a physicist and a psychiatrist, I find it extremely gratifying to see a book made available on Attention Deficit/Hyperactivity Disorder that is written with an emphasis on the rapidly developing field of neurofeedback training. It is timely and badly needed for several reasons. First, the medical community and the general public have finally become aware that ADD/ADHD is unusually common and is tremendously detrimental to those afflicted. Likewise, mental health professionals have accepted that a substantial fraction (perhaps half) of children with ADD/ADHD remains significantly impaired throughout adulthood.

Furthermore, neurofeedback as a treatment modality for a wide range of psychiatric disorders has attained an increasingly sound stature in the scientific and clinical communities. Research has established the legitimacy of both its neurophysical basis and its clinical efficacy in studies over the last three decades. In addition, current practice allows neurofeedback techniques to be used concurrently with more traditional pharmacological approaches.

Finally, there has been ongoing success in treating several co-morbid conditions that have been refractory to traditional approaches. These include: Conduct Disorder, Oppositional Defiant Disorder, a range of learning disorders and of brain injuries — the latter often either resulting from ADD/ADHD or exacerbating the symptomatology. Since these frequently devastating conditions have been resistant to traditional approaches, neurofeedback's success with them represents a tremendous advance.

For these reasons, adversarial attitudes on the part of traditional practitioners toward neurofeedback are, at present, ill-informed scientifically, clinically, and practically.

In sum, the present volume is an unusually seminal and timely contribution to our approach to ADD/ADHD and related conditions.

Andrew Abarbanel, M.D., Ph.D.

As a child psychiatrist, I have been treating children and adults with ADD/ADHD for the last 30 years. There have been many successes with combined approaches of medication, dietary changes, and psychotherapy. However, four years ago, my older son went through a regimen of neurofeedback for his ADD and learning problems. I saw changes in him that could never have occurred with only medication, diet and/or therapy. Since then, I have learned and incorporated the neurofeedback technique into my practice, and have applied it with great success to patients with ADD/ADHD. Some still require small amounts of medication, but, overall, their functioning is at a much higher level than it could be with the traditional approaches alone.

In addition to helping with focus and concentration, neurofeedback goes much further. It improves emotional self-regulation, sleep patterns, organization, planning, and anxiety problems associated with ADD/ADHD. I have found that neurofeedback does this 24 hours a day, rather than simply when the medication is in the patient's system. This augments my tools as a physician and the independent resources available to my patients.

Hank Mann, M.D.

Introduction

As the distraught mother related the nature of her child's difficulties, her pain was palpable. In great detail, she described her son's distractibility, behavioral problems, social ostracism, difficulty finishing schoolwork, and chronic impulsivity. Alternating between blaming and vindicating her son, she portrayed her life as "a living hell." Despite the distress her child's behavior was causing, she repeatedly defended the nine-year-old as "basically a good kid, very bright, who just can't sit still, doesn't follow directions, and resists everything he doesn't want to do."

The litany of misdeeds was extensive. Matthew continually provoked and fought with his older brother and younger sister. He was constantly in motion, made inappropriate comments, and was reckless and often insolent. The mother's attempts to get her son to do his homework met with continual resistance and triggered predictable daily battles and confrontations.

Matthew's teacher shared the mother's frustration and exasperation. She reported that the third grader incessantly fidgeted in class, disturbed the other children, and needed constant supervision. For no apparent reason, he would often get up from his desk and begin wandering aimlessly around the classroom. Because of his erratic behavior, the other children made fun of him, shunned him on the playground, refused to play with him after school, and excluded him from birthday parties.

Matthew's mother bitterly complained that her husband provided little emotional support. Returning home late most evenings, he was preoccupied with his own work-related concerns and tensions. The ritual was scripted. As soon as he came through the front door, she would recount the crises of the day. He would then shake his head with exasperation and accuse her of overreacting. "What do you expect?" he would intone. "He's a typical active boy. My mother tells me I was the same way when I was his age." With this fuel thrown on the fire, she would usually respond with indignation. "It's easy for you to justify his behavior. You don't have to deal with it everyday!"

To protect their sanity, both parents had become somewhat inured to their son's continual acting out behavior. Neither had a clue about how to handle the situation. Matthew's mother resented her husband's seeming indifference and was particularly vexed by his apparent lack of empathy. She felt that he dismissed her feelings and offered simplistic solutions to the problems she had to face everyday. As the challenges of dealing with Matthew took their psychological toll, she felt alone and abandoned. It infuriated her that her husband could conveniently escape to his office while she was forced to do daily battle with an ADHD child. "My husband is in denial about Matthew's problems, and he denies being in denial!" she exclaimed with indignation.

Matthew's father, in turn, had his own shopping list of grievances. He felt misunderstood and wrongly accused of not listening and not being empathetic. Moreover, he believed that he was the one being denied a receptive and sympathetic ear.

Both parents resented the damage that Matthew was doing to the family and the constant stress he created wherever he went. He was nine years old, and his parents had serious apprehensions about the future. "How is he going to succeed in school and in life if he can't concentrate for more than five seconds?" his mother asked plaintively.

This book is about helping kids like Matthew: ADD/ADHD children who possess the potential to succeed, but who chronically function below their abilities because they cannot regulate themselves. *ADD: The 20-Hour Solution* describes and examines a revolutionary hi-tech methodology called EEG biofeedback (also called neurofeedback) that has unequivocally demonstrated its efficacy in helping chronically inattentive, distractible, impulsive, and hyperactive children regulate themselves. This treatment offers a viable and highly effective alternative to children having to ingest large doses of psychotropic drugs every day.

Using digital computer technology and advanced software, EEG biofeedback unlocks the brain's ability to manage the tasks of daily living that are daunting to those struggling with ADD/ADHD and other neurological-efficiency related conditions. As the ADD/ADHD child's brain is methodically retrained to function more efficiently, problems such as chronic impulsivity, distractibility, hyperactivity, and disorganiza- tion dissipate, and academic performance, self-confidence, and social skills improve commensurately.

Over the years, clinicians throughout the United States have reported remarkably positive results with thousands of clients. Children who were treated with EEG biofeedback learned how to sustain their concentration, control their bodies, and focus on at-home and in-school tasks. As these children acquired the capacity to regulate themselves, they began functioning at levels equivalent with their true abilities; in so doing, they avoided potentially life-long patterns of underachievement, frustration, and demoralization. These clinical results have been reinforced by research that objectively documents the efficacy of the methodology.[1]

Thousands of children like Matthew have been successfully treated with neurofeedback. As they train, children of all ages function more effectively in school and at home, and their counterproductive behaviors, inattentiveness, impulsivity diminish. In approximately twenty hours of "brain time" on specially configured computers, the underlying causal factors for the concentration and self-discipline difficulties are resolved and the negative symptoms eliminated.

The pluses of EEG biofeedback training in treating ADD/ADHD children are extensive. This quick and painless treatment:

Provides a viable alternative to psychotropic medication

The technology frees children from the merry-go-round of side effects, dependence, dosage-specific limitations, counterbalancing drugs, and potential addiction. For millions of parents who have legitimate concerns about using powerful drugs to alter cerebral chemistry and suppress the symptoms of ADD/ADHD, this emancipation from reliance on daily doses of time-released medication is a godsend.

Trains children to self-regulate naturally and safely

Unlike psychotropic drugs, EEG biofeedback is a natural treatment. Negative side effects are rare and minimal. Only a small percentage of people react negatively to biofeedback, and these individuals are typically less hypersensitive to biofeedback than they are to medications, foods, and environmental conditions. Because the treatment increases brain awareness and capability, even atypical side effects are usually resolved quickly and naturally by the brain itself.

Trains children to adjust automatically to changing demands and conditions

Through systematic computer-based training, ADD/ADHD children become more flexible, adaptable, independent, and behaviorally appropriate. At the same time, they become more resistant to the errant environmental stimuli and distractions that can undermine their abilities to

---

1 John K. Nash, "Treatment of Attention Deficit Disorder with Neurotherapy," *Clinical Encephalography.* Lynda Thompson and Michael Thompson, "Neurofeedback Combined with Training in Metacognitive Strategies: Effectiveness in Students with ADD," *Applied Psychophysiology and Biofeedback.* David A. Kaiser, and Siegfried Othmer, "Effect of Neurofeedback on Variables of Attention in a Large Multi-Center Trial," *Journal of Neurotherapy.*

focus and remain on task. These capacities are vital to adapting success-fully to a stressful and frenetic world.

Emancipates children from continual professional supervision

Because children are no longer dependent on biochemical medical man-agement, their parents can avoid the on-going expense of prescription refills and, in many cases, the inconvenience of weekly visits to a psy-chotherapist or behavior management specialist.

Creates a synergistic effect that can help other treatments work more effectively

EEG biofeedback is routinely used in conjunction with protocols that may include medication, educational therapy, behavior modification, exercise, nutritional modification, psychotherapy, and physical, occupa-tional, and speech therapy. In cases where medication is part of treat-ment, neurofeedback can make medications effective at lower dosages.

Permits parents to become involved directly in the treatment process

Parents may prefer to have a professional supervise the biofeedback at a clinic. Some clinics, however, permit parents to lease or purchase the equipment so that they can continue the EEG training at home with minimal professional consultation. This option, of course, requires that parents receive intensive preparation before they administer the EEG training to their child.

ADD: The 20-Hour Solution offers two unique perspectives. The book is co-authored by a licensed psychologist with more than twenty-eight years of clinical experience (including neurotherapy) in treating children and adults and by a physicist who, in tandem with his wife, a neurophysiologist, has developed the neurofeedback instruments, refined the techniques, launched a world-wide movement, and trained thousands of professionals to administer this life-altering intervention. The tragic personal experiences of Susan and Siegfried Othmer with their own neu-rologically impaired children and with ADD/ADHD propelled them into the unrelenting pursuit of a viable intervention. As you will discover, this revolutionary technique takes us beyond traditional psychological explanations and into the realm of scientifically-based models of brain function and brain self-regulation derived from neurophysiology and neurophysics.

In this easy-to-read and easy-to-understand book, we will methodically:

1. Examine the dynamics and symptoms of ADD/ADHD.

2. Review how the brain functions and malfunctions.

3. Explore the origins of EEG biofeedback.

4. Describe the therapeutic procedures in detail.

5. Relate how EEG biofeedback has improved lives and altered the outlook and practices of many professionals who treat ADD/ADHD children.

ADD: The 20-Hour Solution also chronicles the parallel paths that we, the authors, have taken in our quest for a viable alternative to psychotropic drug treatment for children and adults who struggle to concentrate, regulate themselves, and function commensurately with their full potential.

You will learn how EEG biofeedback teaches the brain to know itself and control itself according to conditions that are continually changing inside and outside the person's psychobiological interface with the environment. You will also discover how the methodology trains the mind to "drive at the right speed for the existing conditions." In response to life's ever-changing demands, EEG biofeedback tunes up brain function. Performance and efficiency are enhanced. Stability is developed and maintained. Control becomes automatic. Collisions are avoided. Desired destinations are reached.

After reading this book, you will understand how EEG biofeedback has created a new paradigm for helping the brain function more efficiently and effectively. This new paradigm for wellness, mental fitness, and personal development could profoundly affect your child's capacity to prevail in a highly competitive world that can be harsh and unforgiving toward those who are unable to sustain their concentration and self-regulate. One fact is certain: EEG biofeedback is literally transforming the minds of ADD/ADHD children and adults throughout the world.

ADD/ADHD Demystified

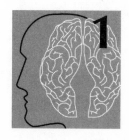

THE ADD/ADHD ENIGMA

Almost everyone has heard of ADD/ADHD*. Most people have opinions about it; some have very strong, even stubborn, opinions. It is common to know people with ADD, or to find out that someone you know has ADD — perhaps even someone in your family. Whether communicated by relieved announcement or decried through hushed whispers, ADD tends to stir emotions and attitudes in those who live with it or around it. This condition — presumably a deficiency of attention — draws ironically to itself a remarkable amount of attention, as if to make up for its namesake. There are ADD organizations, ADD pharmaceuticals, laws about ADD, treatments for it, diagnostic guidelines — yet, there is little agreement (in the broad consensus) about what ADD is, how to diagnose it, and how to treat it.

Though the medical mainstream would like to present a unity about ADD, this condition eludes easy categorization and cure through medicine. In recent years, the pharmaceutical monolith has prevailed, justifying the prolific use of drugs to counteract an imputed biochemical imbalance. Despite the impact of the pharmaceutical approach (along with its convenience and its staggering profits for the drug manufacturers), there is little evidence that ADD can be pinpointed as a unitary disease of enzymes or neurotransmitters or microorganisms, easily targeted and controlled by external (and patented) substances.

The conglomerate of behavior problems, mood and learning irregularities, and nervous system fluctuations that characterize ADD have been evident for a very long time, subsumed under different labels and targeted by numerous and sundry attempts to control it, deny it, or minimize its impact. At times, ADD has been called "MBD – Minimal Brain Dysfunction," "Cerebral Dysfunction," and other medical buzzwords. When its symptoms became severe, ADD has morphed into other medical or mental conditions, easier to label and more recognizable by prominent symptoms in familiar disorders.

Attempts to pin down ADD as specific biological mechanisms or intrinsic character anomalies are a bit like fitting the fabled naked emperor with our preferred clothes: It's obvious that something is not

---
* Throughout this book, we use the abbreviation ADD to denote Attention Deficit Disorder and Attention Deficit Disorder with Hyperactivity (ADHD) interchangeably.

right, but a majority agreement system will minimize the problem, at least in the minds of onlookers. However, this is neither science nor reality, and our good sense dictates that the emperor should get dressed. Similarly, when the mind is not working right, it needs fixing. Efforts to affix labels, excuses, or temporary patches simply shortchange those involved.

When it comes to the mind and the workings of the brain, we note that "the brain that heals itself is not of much interest to the medical community."

In this book, we describe ADD and its solution in terms of the brain's ability to heal itself. The essence of ADD (as described below) lies in glitches in the brain's ability to consistently *self-regulate,* and the solution lies in providing the brain with a catalyst (in the form of EEG neurofeedback) for learning or re-learning its own self-management.

Our approach to treating ADD problems bears remarkable parallels to the constructs of traditional medicine and psychological behavioral methods. We address brain chemistry, behavior modification, and physiological response mechanisms. The difference is that EEG neurofeedback training is a self-contained solution that allows the brain to heal itself, thus reducing or ending the constant need for biochemical supplementation and environmental modification required by other treatment modes.

The brain that can heal itself transcends both the limitations of lockstep diagnosis and the negative cycle of maladaptive behaviors and dissatisfying interactions with the world. Such a solution — implemented through EEG neurofeedback — has enabled thousands of people of all ages[2] to disembark from the ADD merry-go-round.

WHAT IS ADD/ADHD?

Attention deficit disorder (ADD) and Attention deficit hyperactivity disorder (ADHD) are conditions listed as developmental disorders in the classification manual for psychiatric, psychological, and mental disorders (*DSM-IV, or Diagnostic and Statistical Manual, Fourth Edition*). The DSM-IV is a categorization of mental disorders listed by types, sympto-matology, and diagnostic criteria. It is a "common language" agreed upon by experts to classify, interpret, and communicate about psychiatric and psychological illnesses and disorders.

The details of the DSM-IV medical criteria for ADD/ADHD are listed in Appendix B. For present purposes, we suggest a more penetrating description of ADD/ADHD that is tied to a practical solution for its maladaptive characteristics.

---

2   This book is written with a primary focus on children and adolescents. Thus, the language style is addressed to parents, and the case examples are children. However, the efficacy of neurofeedback for adults with ADD and other conditions is well-established through the experience of the authors and other practitioners, as well as thousands of successfully treated adults.

The problem with defining and identifying ADD is that the brain has little regard for our attempts to classify it. It simply does not follow the rules of publication in the psychiatric manuals. Symptoms, behaviors, and personality patterns "leak" and "creep" across brackets of diagnoses and categories. This recognition is fortuitous; aside from its fidelity with the reality of individual differences and brain functions, the cross-migration of symptoms across diagnoses parallels the discovery that treatments designed for one condition are often very effective for others. This holds true for many mental and developmental conditions, as well as for treatment interventions including pharmacological, behavioral, neurocognitive, and energy-based approaches.

WHAT YOU REALLY NEED TO KNOW ABOUT ADD

ADD doesn't care what you call it. Those afflicted just want to feel better and function better. Fortunately, a model exists for understanding and simplifying ADD in a manner consistent with and true to its essential characteristics. This characterization lends uncanny accuracy and practical utility without compromising medical theories, oversimplifying the diagnosis, or generalizing the disorder to the point of over-inclusion. Happily, the model also lends itself to practical solutions for the problems of ADD.

This model is known as the *disregulation* model. The essential common denominator that characterizes all ADD/ADHD and that manifests in such a variety of seemingly disparate symptoms and diagnoses is *disregulation*. This term refers to the uneven, inconsistent, sporadic, or irregular management by the brain and nervous system of the internal housekeeping functions of the body and mind.

Disregulation is the touchstone for the relevant and distinguishing characteristics of ADD/ADHD. It is also the fundamental underlying mechanism by which we can control and improve mental functioning and behavior. The core characteristics of ADD/ADHD (underpinned by disregulation) can be relieved — and the brain regulated — through the vehicle of EEG neurofeedback training.

Let us first examine the five core characteristics of ADD/ADHD:

1. Disregulation of the arousal system

Just as the human body has systems for respiration, digestion, circulation, cell rebuilding, etc., it also has a system for managing arousal. Arousal refers to states of excitation and relaxation that are in constant relationship with each other. Think of picking up a cup and then setting it down and letting go. Your muscles must tense to grip the cup, and must relax to release your grip. The nervous system performs similarly with regard to excitation and relaxation. This continuous feedback loop is described technically in terms of the activity of the central nervous system, in particular of the voluntary nervous system. This is aided and abetted by the involuntary, or autonomic nervous system, involving both the sympathetic and parasympathetic branches. Collectively, this regulatory activity controls states of attention, wakefulness and sleepiness, impulsivity, mood, awareness, and also contributes to behavioral inhibition and disinhibition.

The arousal system manages or regulates a person's appetites, perceptions, and abilities to control, soothe, gear up, and modulate oneself. It may be likened to a biological thermostat that regulates internal housekeeping. When this thermostat malfunctions or works only intermittently, the resulting glitches in the continual and automatic adjustment of arousal functions give rise to unpleasant symptoms and functional disruptions.

This fluctuation and irregular management of arousal is at the core of ADD, and it results in a variety of behavioral, emotional, and physical symptoms (such as anger, moodiness, difficulty concentrating, anxiety, sleep problems, etc.). It also leads to inconsistencies in performance.

The aspect of arousal regulation is so important that all of ADD revolves around it. Indeed, a more precise term than attention deficit disorder would be *arousal disregulation disorder.*

Neuroscientists describe brain function in terms of activation. A brain that is calm, alert, and processing functionally is said to be activated. A de-activated brain exerts less differentiation over its electrical activity, its neurotransmission, and, consequently, its self-management and outward responses. A disregulated brain has trouble activating and resting, recognizing cues for change, and shifting from a de-activated state to an activated one, and back again.

ADD is characterized by disregulation in brain activation, often reflected in the inefficient activation management of the EEG. Although the EEG may not typically show morphological abnormalities (marked deviations in the type or structure of the brainwaves), the EEGs of ADD people are often less differentiated, less activated, and less responsive to internal and external cues requiring shifts in activation states.

2. Poor integration with environmental demands

A common complaint about ADD children is that they do, in fact, pay attention, but mostly to what interests them. Usually they can sustain attention for prolonged periods when they are engaged in activities of their choice. Perhaps you've heard or echoed the refrain, "It's amazing how he can sit and play video games for hours, but he can't pay attention to his work for more than two minutes!"

Disregulation of arousal predisposes people to become drawn to (possibly fixated or "stuck" on) highly stimulating, novel, and even risky activities because the activity stimulates their brains and makes them feel involved, even more normal. (This is also why stimulant medications work to make people pay better attention.) When the nervous system is underaroused, substances or activities that boost arousal become desirable, and may become addictive.

People with ADD have atypically inconsistent performance. This is due to fluctuations in arousal management. By contrast, what is notable is their consistently better performance on tasks they select and on time schedules that suit them. Realistically, most of us are more interested and involved in activities we prefer. The difference with ADD folks is that their performances on tasks they choose are markedly better than on those delegated to them. This selective attention factor (so entwined with arousal) also reflects in the difficulty ADD individuals have with schedules, deadlines, timeliness, and conformity. People with ADD tend to function at much higher levels when they choose what they will do and when they will do it. Schedules, specifications, and demands imposed from the environment (even routine cues like bed time and waking time) can present huge problems in handling daily life.

Parents and teachers often notice that ADD children have trouble transitioning or shifting from one activity to another. This, too, is a manifestation of disregulation — taking cues from the environment and integrating its demands requires fluidity of arousal. The brain has to shift gears and modify brainwaves — something usually quite difficult for the ADD person.

3. Perceptual focus problems

A hallmark of ADD is distractibility, the faltering of attention and its ready disruption by random stimuli unrelated to the intended focus. Many ADD people are overly sensitive to sounds and other stimuli that intrude in their consciousness and vie for their attention.

Whether or not distractibility is an overt problem, the disregulation that underlies it invariably causes perceptual differences that throw the ADD person off-track. Thus, novel stimuli or unique components elicit selective attention. While this can result in refreshing creativity and original perspectives, it frequently leads the ADD person to focus on unconventional, less relevant, and less productive aspects of a situation or problem. This leads to greater peripheral activity and reduced goal attainment.

Disregulation sponsors idiosyncrasies in perception that make less important details seem salient. It promotes a perceptual style that predisposes the ADD individual to attend to the urgent rather than the important. It can cloud judgment and boost impulsivity. Perceptual anomalies can also color information processing and make it more arduous and inefficient.

Perceptual distortions are much more likely when you study postage stamps from across the room, or you watch a movie with your nose pressed to the big screen. Though these may seem like metaphorical exaggerations, they typify the perceptual idiosyncrasies to which the ADD mind is prone.

We refer to this phenomenon as the "zoom lens malfunction." On a video camera, the zoom apparatus allows you to zoom in for detail and zoom out for the bigger picture. Our brains have to do this, too. Otherwise, we lose perspective, over-focus, miss important details, miss social and nonverbal cues, and leave ourselves exposed and vulnerable. Get the picture? Most ADD people struggle mightily with the zoom lens function.

4. Stressed brain syndrome

A very familiar scenario routinely occurs for those with ADD: The person applies himself to a task… and gets stuck! Some people freeze up, some become frustrated or angry, some give up easily, some redouble their efforts. The effect is ironically similar: The harder the person tries, the more his brain stresses and the less efficient his performance becomes. (This has been documented repeatedly by medical imaging studies of the ADD brain under challenge conditions.)

This inordinate brain stress response is indeed a defining characteristic of ADD. However, since the average person can't see this relationship, its repeated occurrence often brands the ADD person as lazy. This is both tragic and inaccurate. The reality is that normal brain function depends upon the intermittent recurrence of the resting response within a period of exertion or challenge. Because the ADD brain has not learned to rest when challenged, it goes into overdrive and stalls or freezes. People who recognize this episode sometimes term it "brain lock." Most ADD people simply experience the discomfort, restlessness, and shame of not measuring up to the challenge. Then, the avoidance or release mechanisms kick in, and the task gets abandoned while the person gets criticized.

5. Compromised flexibility

Flexibility involves the ability to change set or perspective, to view things from different vantage points, to shift gears when necessary, to vary one's repertoire. It is essentially "the ability to drive at the speed appropriate for the conditions."

By definition, flexibility involves making adjustments; and, making adjustments presupposes a functional frame of reference and adequate monitoring and evaluation. Disregulation throws a monkey wrench into these works. When the gearshift gets jammed, it's hard to make timely adjustments. This is the situation that poorly regulated ADD people face every day.

One tool and one speed will only carry you so far in a world with plentiful variation, complexity, changing circumstances, and demands. Compromised flexibility is a liability that the ADD person can ill-afford, but often harbors.

THE ADD MERRY-GO-ROUND

As you read the following story of Matthew and his family, notice the features, pitfalls, and negative cycles of the ADD merry-go-round. See if you can recognize the five core characteristics described above as they operate in the travails of Matthew and his family — and, perhaps, in the lives of others closer to home.

Then, in Chapter 3, we will see how EEG neurofeedback successfully addresses and corrects these underlying problems.

The ADD Merry-Go-Round:
Matthew's Story

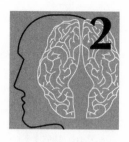

As his teacher slowly turned down the aisle where Matthew sat, the child's body contracted, as if he wanted to make himself invisible. He dreaded the inevitable scolding, knowing what was coming and yet somehow recoiling in surprise. This time — based upon the previous two dozen rebukes of the day — Matthew could sense that the hammer was about to fall again. He had just leaned out of his seat to tell William to shut up, and the teacher was glaring at him. William, who sat in the next aisle, teased him constantly, yet the reprimands always seemed to fall upon Matthew.

"Stay in your seat, Matthew!!"

The teacher's voice thundered mercilessly as she stood above him like a storm of clouds gathered in fury. There was no escape. With undisguised irritation and an unmistakably insulting tone of voice, she would assault him with her frustration for transgressions he only partially understood. Actually, it could be argued that most of Matthew's "education" consisted of his teacher's inflamed public proclamations of his many transgressions and infractions. Though a video replay would have proven far more effective in helping the nine-year-old understand why his behavior pressed his teacher's "buttons," Matthew received no such feedback. Instead, his teacher simply castigated and demeaned him in front of his classmates in the misguided hope that this would somehow magically alter his behavior.

"How many times must I tell you to stay in your seat and keep your hands to yourself?" Matthew sat still. Under great duress in these moments when he was on the receiving end of his teacher's harsh glare and undisguised hostility, he was able to control his hyperactivity temporarily; this added to the consternation of those who dogmatically believed he could actually sit still, control his impulsiveness, and be quiet all the time, if only he so desired.

In this no-win situation, Matthew simply went limp with contrition and surrender.

"Do you hear me?" the teacher demanded.

"Yes, ma'am," Matthew murmured.

"Then why don't you follow directions and stop interrupting the class?"

The question, which seemed to invite reply, instead dangled heavily unanswered in the haze of Matthew's humiliation.

Matthew felt a momentary surge of anger, followed quickly by a rush of thoughts about the kids who teased him, how unfair it was, how the teacher always blamed him, and his parents never took his side, either. He smothered his impulse to complain to the teacher about William, who wouldn't leave him alone. Alas, even this silent act of self-control passed unrecognized. Matthew himself failed to recognize the irony in which his forlorn childhood was enmeshed: He was verbally exuberant when others wanted him to be quiet, and he was withdrawn and often clueless when people demanded answers.

Matthew barely understood the cause-and-effect link between his misdeeds and the scripted reactions to these misdeeds. He had no inkling about these effects upon his unhappiness and continued misbehavior. He was a nine-year-old, and children — especially children with a diagnosis of ADD — didn't think in such objective and analytical terms. Matthew was simply lost in an internal maze of jumbled, intense feelings, sporadic mood shifts, changes in energy level and focus, and incomplete thoughts. He acted, (or, more precisely, reacted) in a play written by others and performed on a stage not of his design, his clumsy entrances and poorly delivered lines often drawing unwelcome laughter and jeers from his audience.

More surprising, however, was the failure of adults in Matthew's world to empathize with the pattern of rebuke and castigation that deluged Matthew without offering pragmatic and applicable hints about how he could respond more acceptably. No one showed him, in concrete terms, how he might control his impulsiveness and rein in his inappropriate behavior, and no one seemed aware of this glaring omission. Were it not for this collective obliviousness, it might seem like a deliberate plot to foil the child — the lack of instruction, practice, and reinforcement of socially acceptable behavior. A recipe, in fact, for delinquency.

Matthew, however, could never articulate how the adults in his world were letting him down. He was a scattered, frenetic, poorly organized and poorly regulated kid with an array of disheveled and aggravating behaviors. A lot of people construed these behaviors as conclusive proof that he was hopelessly wicked. Matthew was among those holding such an opinion, although he harbored some ambivalence. Matthew wanted to believe that, deep down inside, he was good, though misunderstood. His soul-wrenching belief that he was deserving lent him some semblance of esteem and the will to survive. Yet, his dignity and existence were regularly under attack.

The teacher scowled at him and continued her tirade.

"Where's your book?" She ruffled the mess on Matthew's desk, emphasizing her displeasure. "Of course, if you had done your homework, you might be able to drum up some interest and follow the lesson instead of disrupting the class."

The teacher would make her points in a series of verbal stabs, punctuated by trips around the room with flashes of fiery remarks directed at Matthew. As she strode toward the front of the room, still ranting, Matthew became aware of his classmates timorously stealing nasty glances at him. When the teacher bore down on him, the other students politely looked at their books or stared ahead.

Allowing one disruptive pupil to assume the feature role held numerous dynamic advantages. Other students could hide their distractions and misadventures. The cumulative frustrations that accrue along the course of a school year could find an easy target by scapegoating a vulnerable student. The victim's reactions would often justify the blame. Most children squeal when they hurt; ADD children usually squeal louder.

Under the intense scrutiny and reproof, Matthew's squirming resurfaced. The teacher continued her tirade, wandered around the room in widening concentric circles, commanding the net of obligatory gazes from the students.

Matthew cowered in embarrassment as the teacher blared her refrain.

"I don't know how your parents put up with you… I can't put up with this behavior. You need help — your family needs help." Privately, the teacher had spoken with his family and urged them many times to give him medicine and to get counseling. This made Matthew squirm and feel sad that there had to be something very wrong with him.

Matthew again became distracted by a torrent of thoughts. He felt pressed to go to the bathroom, but thought this would be an unwelcome time to ask. The teacher was winding down from her lashing, preparing to re-engage the reading lesson. Relief visited Matthew temporarily, only to be displaced by a room full of reminders that his torment would continue at recess — if the teacher let him go to recess. Matthew was often "benched" during recess — he had to sit on the bench in the principal's office — due to any one or several of a long list of missing assignments, disruptions, and other citations for misconduct. Matthew hardly understood the particular offense for which he was being punished; he just knew there was a lineup of them, an ongoing debt that never got fully paid.

Sitting on the bench was difficult enough; sometimes, just the sheer effort of *sitting* there (it was *so boring!*) made him antsy enough to call out or get up without realizing what he was doing. That would earn him another day's penance on the bench. Matthew didn't see himself as victimized — he hadn't yet acquired the vocabulary or indignation required for embodying victimization — but he did feel trapped. The main way he expressed his frustration and his feelings was through his behavior — loud, impulsive, uninhibited, demanding, self-centered and often disrespectful — which brought more of the painful, provoking, and alienating experiences he was accused of formatting in this vicious cycle of transgression, retribution, and frustration that sculpted his young life.

The bench was hard time, and it made Matthew reel with restlessness. Though he felt isolated and deprived, he reminded himself that, here in the protection of the office, peers could not tease him (at least, not openly). Disapproving glances from passersby weren't fun, but they were innocuous compared to the aggressive taunts hurled at him daily on the playground.

Matthew was excluded from games. His attempts to join were rebuffed, and he was teased without remorse. His callow bids for attention caused him to be regularly ostracized, and his initiative often escalated into quarrels.

Because Matthew had little sense of future time and lived almost exclusively in the now, he defended himself against the demands of the world by unconsciously denying and avoiding the unrelenting exigencies that were continually being imposed on him. Chief among his unwitting tormentors was his mother, to whom he would have to answer for his poor performance and misbehavior in school. The afternoon and evening beckoned with promises of yelling, teasing, blaming, and restriction.

At home, there were other injustices. Matthew detested the way his brother and sister managed to blame him and get his mother to buy their stories. The anger welled up inside of him just thinking about it. What stinkers the two of them were!

To make matters worse, his siblings made fun of his reading, and needled him about his homework and poor attention. Matthew was confused about this; it was hard to pay attention, but, God, most of it was so boring! As if it were his fault! He tried to do the work… but, most of the time, he just kind of drifted away.

What always got his attention, even more reliably than a call from his bladder, was the piercing sound of his own name:

"MATTHEW!!"

Many people sounded the call, but none as shrilly and constantly as his mother.

MATTHEW'S FAMILY

The lineup of cars trudged toward the school's main entrance where a sputtering, then a gush, of students heralded the afternoon dismissal. Matthew's mother, Julie, nudged her car in dutiful procession. She was always uneasy driving up to the school, and the reasons were understandable. Matthew and school were like oil and water, a combination that wouldn't mix, despite all the circumstantial shaking. Almost daily, Julie was confronted with Matthew's legacy of misdeeds; these ranged from outright scuffles to missing assignments, disrespect, and social blunders. Julie felt that she was being personally denigrated when the teacher or the principal reported Matthew's latest transgressions. She reminded herself that these were professionals, and that it was their duty to inform her of her son's activities. The reports, however, felt more like a reading of charges against *her*. Once, while the principal was recounting Matthew's latest offense, Julie tried to listen, but had to suppress laughter as she entertained the errant thought that the principal would soon ask, "And how do you plead?"

She was never asked for her views, however, or even given a chance to discuss her frustrations about the ways the teacher was handling Matthew. She felt coerced into accepting the educators' disapproval and pressing concerns about Matthew. What was she doing about his ADD? Had she seen a doctor? When was Matthew going to take medication so the school could do its job of teaching? What about counseling? *"Many families have problems, you know, and the children act them out."*

These scenarios made Julie cringe. They also made her angry — angry at the school, angry at Matthew, angry at her husband, Dave, who had the freedom to escape the daily battles with Matthew and his world. Julie was also a bit angry at herself for putting up with the accusations and demands, and for not expressing herself more forcefully. She had talked to a number of close confidants about this, and they had comforted, encouraged, and pushed her to be more assertive. Julie appreciated their support, but realized that Matthew was not *their* problem, and that she would have to find some solutions on her own. *But how?* These inner conversations left Julie feeling alone and increasingly despondent. She was responsible, and strong — indeed, a good wife and mother, and minister to needs of an entire family. But she was wearing out and approaching desperation.

She loved Matthew, but he made it hard. Taking him (actually, dragging him) places was loathsome; he was a constant reminder to her and a symbol to others of perceived defects in parenting. Julie reflected with distasteful irony that Matthew represented her scarlet letters: ADD.

She felt she wore them on her sleeve, as Matthew constantly pulled at her to get his way. Everyone could see it. Most had comments and criticism. Few suggestions even remotely addressed constructive and realistic fixes to the awful state of disrepair that characterized Matthew's interactions with the world.

Julie parked her car in the school lot and approached the dismissal area. She hoped that Matthew would just come to the car like other children; but, she knew from experience that he was likely to become distracted in some scuffling or teasing, and she had best be there to intercept a likely negative outcome. Waiting for Matthew was a habitual and aggravating routine — the less of it done in public, the better.

She spotted him and called his name. Mercifully, he noticed her, and it took only her methodical march toward him and a grasp of his arm to head him toward the car. Julie tensed and prepared to screen out the customary teasing that followed Matthew. She didn't want to hear the childish name-calling, didn't want to exert the energy to figure out whether she imagined or actually heard the taunts. Reminding herself that she was a mother picking up her child from school, Julie bit her lip and fought the encroaching tears, the anger, the embarrassment — and the powerlessness. Preoccupied with her self-consciousness, Julie only gradually heard Matthew yammering at her. They entered the car, and Matthew pitched his complaints in earnest: The teacher yelled at him; William punched him, Carlos teased him, and when he protested, the teacher scolded him for that; he got another detention; could they please stop at McDonald's, he's so hungry...

As Julie looked at her hapless, animated son, she noticed an envelope scrunched into his backpack, sticking out like an afterthought. She mentioned this to him.

"Oh, yeah, Mom, this is for you." He thrust it at her. Julie fumbled the envelope, then ripped it open. It was a short note from the teacher, reminding her that Matthew should see a doctor and get some medication.

Julie felt a flash of irritation. She was ambivalent about this whole medication business, and she reacted defensively when people (especially people at school) pushed it. Who were they, anyway, to insist that medication was the solution? Julie hated the pressure. She'd read something about how educators' insistence on medication was a violation of civil rights. A friend told her that another parent had filed a complaint after being harassed about medication — this parent had accused the teacher of practicing medicine without a license! Reflecting upon this made Julie more overwhelmed. She was not militant; no, thank you, she had quite enough conflict in her life already. She was tired of fighting *everybody*. Matthew was gradually turning her into a defeated warrior. She knew he needed help, and, though she hated the way the school hammered the medication drumbeat constantly, a part of her couldn't blame them. Something had to be done. Narrow though it was, medication seemed a ready solution, a bandwagon on which many were jumping.

Julie wasn't so sure. She worried about side effects. She'd heard and read about too many cases where medication made things worse. There was even a new problem to worry about — she believed it was called "polypharmacy management" — children taking additional "medications" to control for the side effects of previous ones. In many cases, the children's lives were overtaken by the effects of the drugs, thereby diminishing or overshadowing the good they were supposed to do in the first place.

She had brought such concerns up with her pediatrician. He reassured her that these drugs had been thoroughly tested, and were safe, effective, and non-addicting. Julie had wanted to believe him — it seemed so easy. But her doubts lingered, even grew stronger. Nobody had provided a satisfactory rebuttal to the concern that medicating children with narcotics (yes, indeed, that is the classification for most of the commonly prescribed ADD drugs) predisposed them to a pattern of addictions and dependence upon chemical controls to make their brains work. These were the children who were most vulnerable, most impulsive, most heedless of consequences, and most at risk in the first place. To Julie, using psychotropic drugs with kids seemed illogical and eerie.

The avoidance of medication was a desire Julie shared with her husband. Ironically, Julie thought, that was one of the few topics about which she and Dave lately agreed. Their relationship was becoming more fractured and certainly less compassionate and loving. Dave was distant, caught up in his own world and his own concerns. His presence raised the level of tension in the household. He shouted regularly at Matthew and continually griped about his misbehavior. In her moments alone, Julie thought about Dave and wondered if she was handling the situation as badly as her husband. Maybe she just couldn't see it. She tried to be the peacemaker. She labored in the homework battles. Dave mostly complained.

All the while she hated his carping, Julie agreed with his points. Matthew was not "up to speed," as Dave put it. He was struggling academically, making enemies at school, and avoiding virtually all of his responsibilities. He seemed to have an uncanny knack for getting under people's skin. Julie knew Matthew didn't enjoy being singled out, picked on, punished, criticized, and ridiculed. But it was only a matter of time before most people became exasperated with him.

Dave shared similar frustrations, but these were far from joyous bonds with his wife. He thought she was much too impressionable and indecisive; thus, Matthew took advantage of her. He deplored Matthew's manipulative wiles and undisciplined habits. Dave reasoned that Matthew was smart, but had not learned how to use his ability and translate his intellectual gifts into common sense and productive behavior. Though he maintained publicly that Matthew was just "exercising his right to be a boy," Dave inwardly brooded about the obvious differences that Matthew showed. Most of the time, Dave could abide the hyperactivity, but it really bothered him that Matthew carried many things too far. What could have been an aggressive competitive edge seemed to Dave like a death wish featuring consistently poor judgment. This puzzled Dave, for he saw clear indications of high intelligence in Matthew, yet the boy did stupid things with amazing regularity. It was as if his son was intent on willfully sabotaging himself.

Dave berated himself privately for his impatience. He resolved over and over again to take Matthew under his wing and lovingly, methodically, and patiently teach him better ways. All his good intentions crumbled, however, each time he encountered the irritating effects of Matthew's behavior. Dave would drive home rehearsing his positive approaches, only to be confronted with the latest series of crises, emergencies, and antics. Usually, he arrived home to a family of frayed nerves and combative arguments. Not particularly comfortable or calm in the role of administering relationship triage, Dave found himself retreating to his home office or bedroom to avoid hostilities. When he tried to help Matthew with homework, the situation escalated into a full-blown confrontation replete with angry words, unproductive interrogation, resentment, reiterated demands, intractable defensiveness, chronic denial of responsibility, evasiveness, and manipulative behavior. All too often, it would happen like this:

"Matthew, let's see your homework. What are you supposed to do?
"I don't know."
"Whaddya mean 'I don't know'"?
"Like I said, 'I don't know'."
"Come on… you know. You have to know!"
"I *don't* know!"

And it would degrade from there. If Dave continued, Matthew (feeling cornered and desperate) might throw a tantrum, and often would lie. This gave his dad something specific to pursue, and so the "conversation" would continue:

"Why did you lie?"

"About what?"

"Oh, you know!"

"I don't know!"

"Yes, you do!"

At this point in the immaturity spiral, Julie would enter and disapprovingly separate the two of them. Her choice of lines was often regrettable.

These engagements did little to spare the erosion of family harmony and dedication Julie and Dave had to each other's and their children's well-being. Everybody in the family was suffering, and the general consensus (as announced periodically by his brother) was that it was all Matthew's fault.

They tried to squash any overt blaming of Matthew (the experts had assured them that blaming would cause damage), but Dave and Julie silently colluded in their growing resentment of their son's negative impact on the family. Dave had once sarcastically referred to Matthew as "Dennis the Manic Menace." Julie found it hard to get that phrase out of her mind. On the surface, they denied and ignored as much as possible. Inwardly, they brooded, prayed, and rationalized.

Julie felt isolated, overwhelmed, helpless, and dismissed by Dave's simplistic solutions. She believed that Dave minimized the seriousness and urgency of Matthew's problems. Dave, in turn, felt misunderstood and wrongly accused of not listening and not being empathetic. Moreover, he believed that he was the one being denied a receptive and sympathetic ear.

They had even tried marriage counseling and family therapy. At first, it was aimless, then pointless; eventually, they discontinued. Therapy was expensive, and Matthew continued to act in a dysfunctional manner.

Dave didn't like the invasiveness of family counseling. He was open to talking, but he was convinced that he and Julie weren't the problem. After all, the problem was Matthew.

Indeed, Dave was confused. At heart, he really didn't think there was anything wrong with his son. He found it difficult to trust the professionals. At the bottom of their fancy theories, he suspected that there was blame, and that, somehow, it had to be directed at his family. He was worldly, and had grown up in a family and an environment where people blamed each other. To an extent, he had survived well by learning to point his own finger quicker. His tough veneer barely disguised the wellspring of his love and compassion for Matthew. It grieved him, even choked him up at times, that his son behaved idiotically in front of others. Dave covered it with reprimands, but each time Matthew acted out inappropriately, Dave died a bit inside, forfeiting more of his pride and hope for his son's future. Dave was psychologically sophisticated enough to understand the conflict with which he grappled: He loved Matthew, felt bound to protect him, and envisioned his potential. Yet, the realist in him begrudgingly agreed that the world's reproof of his son was justified.

As the crises and despair mounted, both parents became somewhat inured to their son's continual acting out behavior. Neither had a clue about how to handle the situation. It was especially frustrating that such little assistance was offered by the educators and other professionals in the way of treatment options. And, the insinuation that not medicating Matthew showed that they were negligent parents in denial — well, that was simply infuriating.

In her relentless search for answers, Julie heard and read about a treatment for ADD called EEG biofeedback. The procedure involved training brainwaves to improve concentration and behavior. Supposedly, by playing video games while attached to special computers, children could learn to control themselves, pay sustained attention, improve their behavior, and maintain the gains they made over the long-term. This intrigued Julie, but, at the same time, she wondered if the claims were too good to be true. Was she just grasping at straws, or could the program really help Matthew? The more she found out, the more EEG biofeedback began to make sense: It was natural, non-invasive, fun, and promised both quick and long-lasting results.

Julie had heard enthusiastic commendations third-hand about the positive effects of biofeedback. Not knowing anyone personally who had experienced it, she decided to find out for herself. Through experience, she had become wary of the arguments and counterarguments expounded by experts and professional pundits, and she had come to rely on her own instincts and her abilities to evaluate what she found. She scoured the websites of the EEG Institute (www.eeginstitute.com), EEG Directory (www.eegdirectory.com), the Brian Othmer Foundation (www.brianothmerfoundation.org), and EEG Spectrum International (www.eegspectrum.com) — respected sources of information about EEG biofeedback. From these organizations, she obtained the name of a highly reputable licensed psychologist in her area who was extensively trained in EEG biofeedback and who had been affiliated for many years with the EEG biofeedback professional community.

After perusing the psychologist's website, Julie called and made an appointment. Following years of frustration, they were about to embark on a radically different approach to handling Matthew's problem. Like so many families in the throes of dealing with ADD, Matthew and his family hardly knew what to expect. Despite this uncertainty and a degree of justifiable trepidation, Julie felt, for the first time in years, that there was actually hope. Just maybe they had stumbled onto something that could transform their son's life and remove the black cloud that hovered above their family.

A PREVALENT PLIGHT — AND A PROPER SOLUTION

Matthew's plight is a wrenching example of the anguish of ADD/ADHD. This nightmare is played out every day in thousands of classrooms throughout the United States. Children who are "different" are continually being castigated, segregated, socially ostracized, rejected, and demeaned.

The differences that make ADD/ADHD children conspicuous also predispose them to a childhood (and beyond) of interactive torment between them and the surrounding world whose standards, tempo, and conventions they find so difficult to meet.

Marching to the (often hyperactive and erratic) beat of their own drums, these children typically do poorly in school and establish marginal or unsatisfying relationships. They are often involved in unruly manipulations, either as aggressors or victims.

Though not a uniform group, some eight million American children are currently diagnosed as having Attention deficit disorder or Attention deficit hyperactivity disorder (ADD/ADHD). Each year, more than ten million prescriptions are written for psychotropic drugs to treat what appears to be an epidemic whose symptoms include distractibility, inattentiveness, hyperactivity, behavioral problems, forgetfulness, social conflict, difficulty finishing schoolwork, impulsivity, anger and moodiness, aggression, daydreaming, avoidance, procrastination, disorganization, insolence, and erratic performance.

These children often have problems and vulnerabilities associated with the condition stereotyped as ADD/ADHD. Many struggle with mood disorders, learning disabilities, or other neurological irregularities. Because of their difficulties, this population is highly at risk — for achievement failure (both in every day expectations and in fulfillment of their potential), social acceptance, legal difficulties, addictions, and health problems.

The prevalence and effects of this trend are alarming. Ten percent of American school children are being medicated every day for two purported reasons: To help them learn more effectively and to make them more manageable at home and in the classroom. Many physicians, educators, mental health professionals, and parents are apparently convinced that, without aggressive pharmacological intervention, ADD/ADHD youngsters are fated to struggle academically, suffer psychologically, alienate their parents, teachers, siblings, and classmates, and function below their abilities.

The families of those afflicted are caught between the proverbial "rock and hard place." Spurred by disruption and conflict to remedy the problem, they often find little recourse but to drug their children and/or migrate to a new classroom or social circle in the hope that a tarnished reputation will vanish. However, they have many misgivings, and face ambivalence and uncertainty about their children's maladjustments and the consequences of chemically and environmentally controlling them.

Fortunately, a better option for resolving the pernicious aspects of ADD/ADHD is available. Along with thousands, Matthew and his family are emerging from the haze of suffering to the welcome relief of the 20-hour solution for ADD/ADHD.

How EEG Neurofeedback Addresses ADD/ADHD

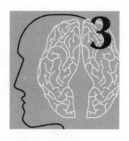

We have suggested a framework for understanding ADD/ADHD that recognizes disregulation as the underpinning problem spawning the core characteristics of ADD/ADHD and that must be corrected in order for its symptoms to resolve. We have also intimated that the human brain is capable of "self-healing," by which we mean the ability to learn or re-learn the self-regulatory mechanisms that are basic to its normal design and function.

In dealing with ADD, it is vital to correct the disregulated condition. When the brain becomes organized and self-regulated, symptoms from seemingly disparate origins ameliorate. Behavior improves, concentration and focus increase, sleep normalizes, and moods become more even.

What a marvelous testimony to the innate flexibility and plasticity of the human brain! These inherent capabilities can be activated through brainwave training, known as EEG biofeedback or neurofeedback.

Neurofeedback improves brain function and self-control in many ways, but the underlying mechanism involves the refinement of self-regulatory mechanisms necessary for effective functioning.

Let's review the real-world problems the ADD/ADHD child experiences and tie them to the disregulation and core characteristics they reflect. Then, we will show how EEG neurofeedback addresses and resolves these problems.

1. Disregulation of the arousal system

In Chapter 1, we introduced the notion that our bodies and minds have a system for managing arousal — that is, the states of excitation and relaxation that are in constant relationship with each other.

This continuous feedback loop of central nervous system (sympathetic and parasympathetic) activity controls states of attention, wakefulness and sleepiness, impulsivity, mood, awareness, and behavioral inhibition/disinhibition.

The arousal system is the "thermostat" that senses changing conditions and manages our adjustment to those conditions.

Remember how Matthew (in Chapter 2) had trouble staying in his seat and keeping his hands to himself? Note that he was "verbally exuberant when others wanted him to be quiet, and ...withdrawn and often clueless when people demanded answers... Matthew was simply lost in an internal maze of jumbled, intense feelings, sporadic mood shifts, changes in energy level and focus, and incomplete thoughts." These are hallmark signs of disregulation.

Matthew's difficulty staying seated, his wandering attention, difficulty concentrating, and inconsistent performance all reflected the underlying disregulated state of his nervous system. His brain was not in charge, even though it may be very capable. That's why his teacher kept prompting him to re-focus and his mother must remind him of routine things. If we could look inside Matthew's head (and, in a way, we can, by looking at the electrical signals generated by his brainwaves), we would probably see a de-activated EEG. This would signify a brain that isn't utilizing all its cylinders, so to speak – and, in this state, Matthew would be less able to differentiate things happening within and around him. Therefore, he would be less likely to notice important clues that would tell him how to act — clues like the teacher giving instructions or, perhaps, that someone next to him was becoming annoyed.

Poor Matthew was riding on the ADD merry-go-round — an up-and-down, on-and-off again cycle of fluctuating brain activation that robs him of the ability to automatically control his own brain and its levels of arousal. It's not a fun ride, really a "not-so-merry-go-round," this carousel of a brain activating and (mostly) de-activating around the irritating and seemingly random prompts and intrusions of others in a demanding environment.

This fluctuating, irregular "arousal-go-round" produces other effects that lead children like Matthew off-track. As we shall see, EEG neurofeedback enables the brain to self-correct arousal fluctuations so that children can stay on-task and on-track.

2. Poor integration with environmental demands

When disregulation prevails, children find it very difficult to remain in step with others. Although they may seem distracted by novel stimuli or mesmerized by some entertaining activity, they are actually more focused inside themselves and less attuned to subtle changes and shifts in the conditions and events around them. This is because the lack of automatic self-regulation requires a rather constant energy to manage things internally. As a natural consequence, such children falter in perceiving and responding appropriately to the world around them on a consistent basis.

Matthew "was able to control his hyperactivity temporarily," frustrating those who "believed he could actually sit still, control his impulsiveness, and be quiet all the time, if only he so desired."

Matthew paid attention sometimes to the communal or important focus. Often, he didn't follow directions, interrupted the class, or engaged in (neurologically) stimulating conflict behavior that tended to boost attention and involvement, even if it was unproductive.

Matthew "had little sense of future time and lived almost exclusively in the now… he defended himself against the demands of the world by unconsciously denying and avoiding the unrelenting exigencies that were continually being imposed on him." Thus, Matthew's fluctuation in arousal and his selective attention reflected a classic difficulty ADD individuals have with schedules, deadlines, timeliness, and conformity. As mentioned, people with ADD tend to function at much higher levels when they choose what they will do and when they will do it. Schedules, specifications, and demands imposed from the environment require arousal management in order to integrate what goes on inside the person with the demands from outside.

Like Matthew's parents, you may notice your child's lack of smooth transition from one activity to another. This can become obvious in the child not wanting to leave one activity or in "forgetting" important materials or cues for the next activity. Matthew "forgot" to give his mother the teacher's note until she saw it scrunched in his backpack and mentioned it. He forgot what he was supposed to do for homework when his father asked him. For the ADD child, "out-of-sight, out-of-mind" holds truer than for most people. In this manifestation of disregulation — noticing, remembering, and integrating cues from the environment – the fluidity of arousal necessary for the brain to shift gears and modify brainwaves often is erratic or insufficiently developed.

The difficulties in shifting, remembering, integrating, and adapting to schedules and outside demands are also bound up with problems of perceptual focus, brain stress, and inflexibility.

3. Perceptual focus problems

An accompaniment to disregulation is the perceptual distortion and dis-tractibility that interfere with the ability to maintain focus and complete goal-oriented behavior. Whether it is distractibility, over-sensitivity, or foggy and disconnected thoughts, many ADD people have thinking patterns that cloud clarity. These patterns tend to distract them, compel them to react to the urgent rather than persist with the important, and result in atypical perceptions and distortions of interpretation. We compared this in the first chapter to a "zoom lens" malfunction in which control over the mix of attention to detail and the bigger picture becomes impaired.

Matthew's selective attention, his forgetting, his likeliness to become distracted in some scuffling or teasing on the way to his mother's car after school, his minimal sense of future time, the anger welled up inside of him just thinking about his siblings and the injustices heaped upon him — these are all examples of the exaggerated effects that perceptual focus problems bring.

By training the brain to self-regulate and focus, EEG neurofeedback organizes thinking, promotes flexibility in shifting the "zoom lens," and regulates the emotional excesses and narrow focus that tend to entrench people in idiosyncratic and "stuck" patterns of thinking. By reducing impulsivity, neurofeedback also allows children to better evaluate circumstances and consider conclusions and consequences before acting. Improved focus and brain communication result in better apprehension of social and environmental cues and less likelihood of negative feedback in response to precipitous or inappropriate behavior.

4. Stressed brain syndrome

There is a very familiar and unnerving pattern to which the ADD child is predisposed: Ineffective or inappropriate behavior, negative response, sanction, or punishment by others, stress and defensiveness, and reinforcement and repetition of the inappropriate behavior.

Effective performance, efficient learning, flexibility of response, accuracy, and sustained attention and effort all depend upon the brain's ability to rest. Just as our lungs (and brains) require a steady supply of oxygen to function, our brains must alternate between work and rest, even during the actual time we perform tasks. This happens so automatically for most of us that we only notice it when we are either really stressed or fatigued or when we are in that special state (sometimes called the "zone") where everything seems to go well effortlessly.

The ADD child, however, is more susceptible to stress because his brain is not in the habit of active resting. The ADD brain often responds to challenge (a demand from the environment) by shutting down (avoidance) or by over-reacting and staying in the "on" (adrenaline) mode. This is not only ineffective — it leads to burnout, emotional turn-off, and a cycle of underachievement and poor self-esteem. For the ADD person, ordinary tasks incur extraordinary stress and hardship — a brain reaction most of the world does not seem to understand.

EEG neurofeedback solves this vicious cycle by teaching the brain how to automatically and integrally rest as it meets the challenges of imposed demands. It's as though the brain learns to pace itself and bring forth that second and third wind instead of hyperventilating or choking. With brainwave training, children learn fairly quickly that they cannot force or sprint to effective brainwaves; they have to observe and repeat the cycles of effort and rest. This neurological habit then generalizes to whatever they do. Neurofeedback teaches the brain to adapt and pace itself to demands and challenges.

Incidentally, the "bored" brain is a very stressed brain. Many ADD children are chronically bored. Often (as with Matthew), they attribute this boredom to properties of the task — as in, "schoolwork is so boring." The experience of boredom is actually a combination of under-stimulation of the brain (a de-activated EEG) and avoidance of over-stimulation by a task (like reading) to which the brain overreacts by trying too hard and not adequately resting within the task.

When children learn how to regulate their brain activity, they learn to rest automatically, and they become noticeably more involved and less bored. It's amazing how much more interesting tasks become when the brain gets involved!

5. Compromised flexibility

Flexibility is so integral to responding appropriately and effectively. It is an interactive cause-and-effect cycle of making adjustments, shifting gears, and modulating our behavior in order to fit in and to achieve desired outcomes.

Remember that Matthew and school "were like oil and water, a combination that wouldn't mix." Matthew's flexibility was severely compromised by his poor self-regulation. Like many ADD children, he had trouble shifting perspective, attending to what was relevant and important, adjusting his mood and his reactions, and evaluating cause-and-effect in order to make adaptive adjustments.

The feedback Matthew received from his environment was mostly negative — it told him when he was doing something wrong, not when he was doing something right or how to correct himself. Thus, Matthew could not develop the habits of self-modification, adjustment, accurate evaluation, and flexibility because he was not getting adequate and constructive feedback. His true brain abilities were dormant.

This is the situation that poorly regulated ADD people face every day. However, EEG neurofeedback is ideally suited to providing the interactive feedback method for alleviating these deficiencies and teaching the brain how to regulate and maintain its proper functions.

HOW EEG NEUROFEEDBACK ADDRESSES ADD/ADHD CHARACTERISTICS

With this understanding about the underpinnings of ADD symptoms in disregulated arousal, it becomes apparent that developing and maintaining better self-regulation is the key to overcoming ADD. Toward this end, EEG neurofeedback (biofeedback) is an elegant and effective solution.

EEG neurofeedback is a technique in which people learn (by means of real-time computer feedback) how to produce more of the brainwaves associated with desired behaviors — such as concentration, attentional focus, relaxation, cooperative behavior, and reduction in irritability, pain, bad mood, hyperactivity, and sleep disturbance.

This technique is remarkable in that the results are so obviously generalizable; this is because the procedure teaches people specifically to modify brainwave activity — it addresses no specific symptom directly, yet it has profound and enduring effects on a wide variety of symptoms. This is because EEG biofeedback very efficiently modifies the control mechanisms responsible for producing and maintaining the symptoms. The struggles and inconsistencies people have with learning, paying attention, modulating moods, pain, and alertness are largely caused by irregularities in the way the brain self-regulates its "housekeeping" and higher-order functions. EEG biofeedback trains the brain to produce more waves in the bandwidths associated with better self-regulation.

EEG biofeedback is a training regimen in which the client reinforces himself — often 2000 times or more during a 30-minute session! It is a relatively pure learning paradigm with no punishment, negative reinforcement, or emotional content. It does not require talking. The client's cortical EEG is simply displayed in a way that allows him to change it, earn rewards, and see and hear the results of his efforts, moment by moment.

Specific descriptions and details about how the procedures work are given in Chapter 4. Now, let's review how the application of neurofeedback addresses each of the maladaptive characteristics of ADD/ADHD:

A. How neurofeedback corrects disregulation of the arousal system

Arousal functions and their regulation are closely tied to brain-body, bio-physiological electrical signals. These are measured through the EEG (electroencephalogram) or brainwaves. An underactivated or overactivated brain reflects its irregularities in the EEG. By challenging and modifying the EEG response, we can influence brain activation and, ultimately, the brain's control mechanisms for regulating itself.

EEG biofeedback presents the brain with a continuous stream of challenges. By feeding back to the client information about what his brain has been doing in the last few seconds, this training system challenges the client's brain to adjust, modulate, and maintain brain activity within specific parameters. In effect, the brain is asked to "juggle" different brainwaves by making more of certain waves and less of others. This is done on a "real-time" basis where the parameters for success are externally set and may be changed over time. Thus, the brain learns to target the goals based on the direction of the goal (in electrical activity) relative to where the brain has just been. This process is very different from a conscious process of analyzing, figuring out, or describing the solution. It is problem-solving at its most instinctive and visceral level.

Just as a thermostat must sense (measure) temperature and send adjustment signals based on a continuous sensing, the brain relies on similar mechanisms to maintain balance and make adjustments. Though the adjustments are not based upon feelings (per se), the effects of those adjustments will result in different feelings as the temperature rises and falls — or, in people, as the arousal level increases, decreases, or shifts in balance.

By practicing these constant adjustments, the brain not only becomes more adept at making them, but it also establishes new reference points (or settings) for its recognition of normal or "home base." Through this process of excitation and relaxation, the brain gradually learns and accepts induced states of arousal as normal and appropriate.

Thus, the child who is underaroused (often showing symptoms of inattention, crankiness, distractibility, lack of motivation, etc.) can be neurologically taught to naturally stimulate his neurotransmitter functions (much in the way that stimulant medications do this artificially) so that his brain eventually functions that way independently, having discovered and ingrained a more useful setting in its repertoire.

Similarly, the child who is overaroused (possibly angry, anxious, impulsive, overreactive, "wired") develops new brain activity patterns that maintain calmness, attentiveness, reflectiveness, self-observation, cheerfulness, and patience.

Importantly, because the human brain is so adaptable and able to conform itself to new and changing demands (this is known as plasticity), these new arousal levels are maintained, as they are more rewarding and functional.

B. How neurofeedback fosters better integration with environmental demands

We are constantly monitoring, exchanging, negotiating, and re-negotiating the give-and-take between ourselves and the outer world. We give and we get; we meet the needs of others and the demands made upon us, and we make our own requests, demands, and expectations. To be successful (or even reasonable) in this on-going process, we need to constantly monitor and make adjustments. Failure to do so adequately makes us out-of-sync with others and with the requirements of varying situations. This is true at all levels of development, from a toddler who is tired, frustrated, or hungry to an adult faced with overwhelming demands and stressors.

Inappropriate arousal levels or rampant fluctuations in arousal breach the delicate interplay our nervous systems must maintain to meet inner and outer demands. Continual adjustments are necessary, and they should, for the most part, be automatic. Neurofeedback trains the brain and nervous system to make these adjustments automatically and consistently. It conditions the brain to achieve and maintain states of quiet activation.

When the brain is quietly activated, it is easier to attend to and recognize environmental signals and to adjust one's responses to demands of the situation. During and after the training, children who have had great difficulty transitioning between activities or breaking away from activities they like show much more flexibility and adaptable compliance to demands and schedules not of their own choosing.

For example, the child no longer experiences a parent's request to follow a direction as an intrusion. The tendency to over-focus (such as to become absorbed in TV or video games) evaporates under the incipient warmth of the brain's newfound ability to relax.

When arousal is regulated, learning becomes more efficient and performance more consistent. Attention to detail, accuracy, and reliability improve. The considerable energy that was formerly devoted to self-soothing (keeping arousal from "boiling over") is now available for environmental demands.

People become more competent and comfortable with outward focus.

C. How neurofeedback improves perceptual focusing

Putting things in perspective is a combination of many factors: Maturity and experience, knowledge, attention, temperament, practice, and… a calm and focused mind. When the mind is cluttered, preoccupied, distracted, stuck, or foggy, it is difficult to see things as they are.

When the brain is in a state of balance, perceptions and reactions are less constrained by the priority of modulation; therefore, we can attend much more calmly to what is really happening, rather than to internally projected needs for stimulation or calming. This state dramatically improves vigilance, accuracy, and the ability to shift between details and the larger picture — the mind's "zoom lens" works better!

As neurofeedback establishes modulated arousal, people tend to become more goal-oriented and less tangential. Impulsive reactions to urgencies and crises give way to concentrated awareness of the truly relevant and important aspects of tasks, events, and people. There is a reduction in compulsive preoccupation and an enhanced integration of verbal and nonverbal messages.

D. Neurofeedback's reduction of brain stress

We have all experienced being "stressed." Interestingly, the stress seems to come from "out there" — something outside of ourselves that invades or imposes — at least, that is the subjective experience. Many of us have also enjoyed the converse of stress, the sense of being "in the zone," when everything works well and effortlessly.

Actually, both of these experiences are inside us; they are brain states, and, of course, they exert internal and external consequences. The difference between feeling stressed and feeling on top of things is in the way the brain and nervous system manage challenge and relaxation.

There is a natural biologic interplay between gearing up for response and resting between responses. When the rest periods are insufficient, the brain is stressed. In a state of stress (lack of proper relaxation/effort balance), the harder one tries, the more stress that results. It is, indeed, a vicious cycle.

Neurofeedback corrects this malfunctioning cycle by teaching the brain how to acquire the goal by relaxing at the proper times. The brain achieves this balance by continuously combining effective neurologic electrical activity during the session. Each moment of such effective activity is rewarded.

In the EEG biofeedback process, the stress reaction is simply not rewarded. This teaches the brain to relax and rest in the face of constant challenges. A rested brain is a smarter, happier, less irritated, more effective brain.

E. How neurofeedback improves flexibility

Since flexibility involves making adjustments, the EEG neurofeedback model is ideal for conditioning this "flex-ability." By responding to the continuous challenges the video games present, each person trains his brain to make adjustments "on-the-fly" based on moment-to-moment changes in conditions of brain activity relative to environmental demand.

The driving analogy captures the essence of flexibility in a simple manner comparable to the brain-training model. In driving a motor vehicle, you must make constant adjustments. These adjustments are dictated by ever-changing conditions, as well as by the interplay among the road conditions and the driver's skills, frame of mind, and the vehicle's capacities. Just as safe and goal-oriented driving necessitates the ability to drive at the speed appropriate for the conditions, effective responses to life situations depend upon flexibility. Indeed, human development is thematic in its reliance upon flexibility as cells and tissue progressively differentiate (become more specialized) with maturity. Life experiences, learning, and the right kind of practice help us add on options and variations to our repertoires of answering life's challenges.

Improved flexibility yields better and faster learning because it allows the individual to try different responses, thus improving the odds of positive reinforcement. More flexibility allows the ADD person to escape the vicious cycle of frustration and criticism.

Self-monitoring and evaluation — which are bedrocks of flexibility — are inherent in the continuous adjustment process by which EEG neurofeedback fosters self-regulation.

DRIVING IT HOME

A true personal story ironically illustrates the effects of limited flexibility in the context of driving:

In college, I (Dr. Steinberg) had a friend who became quite excited about getting her driver's license. Though happy for her, I had mixed feelings when she enlisted me to accompany her as she practiced driving around the city. We spent a lot of time together and, because of our relationship, I felt duty-bound to meet her request. As a new driver, she wanted encouragement, and she was sensitive to criticism. She did, however, exhibit a quirk with regard to driving flexibility: She felt uncomfortable with left turns, so she didn't make them.

As you can imagine, this limitation in flexibility lengthened many commutes, errands, and arguments. Over the years, I have reflected back upon that experiential learning, as I have gained new understanding about the role of flexibility in relationships and task accomplishment and powerful tools for augmenting flexibility. Exercising the brain's plasticity develops fitness and behavioral agility in everyday life.

Neurotherapy: Training the Brain with Computers

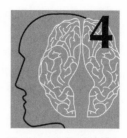

AN UNRECOGNIZED PROBLEM

To describe Jennifer as special would be an understatement. She wasn't like other children, even those who were themselves different and difficult. This explained her mother's extreme stress when she tried to describe Jennifer's problems to doctors, teachers, and friends.

On one level, the litany of symptoms was typical: poor concentration, lack of follow-through, and a seeming unconcern for the needs of others. These were attributes Jennifer shared in common with many "troubled" kids — small consolation for a parent desperate for answers about why her child was *different*. However, Jennifer was quiet — too quiet – and that led adults to look at her mother quizzically when she complained about "the problem." They probably thought she was fussy, too demanding of her child, and that perhaps her parenting needed improvement. Such judgments could easily arise in the minds of onlookers who had not struggled with Jennifer as her mother had, trying a variety of approaches that yielded frustration and tension instead of improvement.

What others didn't see (or at least failed to perceive as critical) was Jennifer's lack of *connection* with others and her *lackluster motivation* for just about everything. Jennifer was not hyperactive; she didn't yell or tantrum. She didn't make herself the center of attention in inappropriate ways. Instead, she muttered — a continual undertone of sighs and complaints about how frustrating and unsatisfying her life was. This drove her mother to the brink of exasperation.

Jennifer struggled in school, and she had virtually no close friends. She was seldom included in peer activities unless some adult in charge made a fuss. She took the longest time to complete even the most basic activities, such as getting dressed or brushing her teeth. Jennifer seemed perennially *stuck*. And unhappy.

She blended in as long as very few demands were made upon her. When she voiced her opinion, her comments were negative. She simply seemed not to care. Her world was narrow and uncomfortable, and she kept mostly to herself, preferring not to consort with others or become involved with them. If she harbored any passion or commitment, these were not clear to others, as she rarely expressed strong feelings, except for the low-key carping that portrayed her as a victim.

Teachers, relatives, and friends all had advice for Jennifer's mother. But the advice was short on practical success, and much of it implied that Jennifer had low ability and that her mother failed to accept this and live with it peaceably.

Jennifer was not doing well in school or in life. She was unpleasant company, yet her mother loved her dearly, and agonized in loneliness over her "shut-down" daughter for whom there seemed to be no proper help.

By the time Jennifer's mother divulged these concerns to a neurotherapist, she had little hope of validation, much less help for Jennifer's substantial dysfunction. She had heard good things about EEG neurofeedback, and she wondered if Jennifer might have some condition this treatment could help. She'd read that ADD often occurs without the hyperactivity, that it can also exist in conjunction with other conditions, like depression and anxiety, and that it frequently is misdiagnosed or misrepresented as laziness or other character traits. In researching EEG neurofeedback, Jennifer's mother discovered that it works with multiple and varied conditions, since it deals with the whole brain – unlike many medications, which target specific brain chemistry, cause unwanted side effects, and result in a rollercoaster of biochemical and personality adjustments.

Besides, they had tried medications, and that was a disaster. Jennifer's complaints had increased, and her mother added this and her worry about side effects to the mountain of woes.

A RECOGNIZABLE SOLUTION

Jennifer's mother decided to take action. She would have her daughter try EEG biofeedback, a treatment process also known as *neurotherapy*. The neurotherapist they visited didn't seem surprised by what Jennifer and her mother presented. In fact, Jennifer didn't present much in the way of insight about her problems, nor did she seem interested in "fixing" things. She liked the therapist, who spent lots of time with her and gave her some unusual tests. She thought the electrodes and the video games were cool, actually "way better" than most of the stuff her mother made her do.

Jennifer's mother was surprised — by the matter-of-fact way that the therapist talked about Jennifer's condition — which he described as "ADD characterized by slow neuroprocessing with accompanying depression" — and by the confidence he expressed that EEG neurofeedback would help.

After five EEG sessions, Jennifer was definitely more talkative. Her mother thought she might be getting sick, since an onset of illness usually made her complain more. But she wasn't really *complaining*; she was communicating. In her own way, Jennifer was asking for her mother to relate to her. Only she was doing it differently; she seemed to care what her mother thought.

Although she shrugged it off at first as her hopeful imagination (not the lightheadedness of an incipient flu), Jennifer's mother noticed after 10 EEG sessions that Jennifer seemed livelier. She stayed at the dinner table after she ate, and she even offered twice to help with the dishes!

Several weeks after starting biofeedback, Jennifer's mother walked past her room. Something was out of place, but she couldn't quite put her finger on it. Then, it dawned on her: Jennifer was reading a book — on her own!

The improvements continued — a better test grade here, a new friend there, a gradual but undeniable reduction in complaining, and a newfound interest that Jennifer showed in people. Her mother was secretly thrilled, but hesitated to talk about it for fear that the bubble would burst. Though others — her teacher, her relatives — noticed and commented upon Jennifer's recent "maturity," only the neurotherapist could openly acknowledge these strides as expected and attributable to neurotherapy.

Of course, there were hindrances and backsliding, and Jennifer even became more demanding of herself and others as her awareness and self-esteem grew. But, these conflicts were typical and normalizing, the kinds of episodes that enable children to resolve ambiguity and meet the challenges of growing up.

Jennifer's mother was quite grateful for the process that liberated her daughter's mind, and she began spreading the word about EEG neurofeedback.

IS NEUROTHERAPY FOR YOU?

Using computers rather than drugs to help children concentrate is a viable alternative for parents who have reservations about relying on medication to alleviate maladaptive behaviors and enhance their child's capacity to pay attention and learn efficiently. Perhaps you, too, are enticed by neurofeedback's extraordinary track record, and perhaps you believe that this non-psychotropic-drug intervention could be the solution you've been seeking.

But, just how does neurofeedback work?

Let's take a step-by-step look at the process, beginning with a glimpse at why this approach makes sense, explaining the steps in the process, and concluding with guidelines for selecting an EEG training program or clinician, asking meaningful questions, and evaluating progress and results.

WHAT DOES NEUROTHERAPY INVOLVE?

In previous chapters, we have reviewed key elements of ADD/ADHD and portrayed its symptoms as examples of the condition of disregulation that underlies this disorder. This disregulation causes the brain to be inconsistent in its "housekeeping" functions and to wander into activity that does not suit the demands of the situation. Neurofeedback uses the brain's own natural bio-electrical rhythms to self-correct.

You can think of the process as teaching the brain and nervous system to stay within a lane consistently while driving or, while riding a bicycle, balancing automatically while navigating different speeds, terrains, and conditions. These capacities are not induced by verbal instruction or logical thinking. Rather, the capacities are developed by training the brain to monitor and conduct the business of focusing attention on the relevant events, both inside the mind and outside in the environment. In so doing, the person makes necessary adjustments — automatically, continuously, and without strain — just like steering a car or a bicycle. The process becomes a natural interplay of subconscious and conscious influences.

The vehicle for actively training these "steering" mechanisms of the brain is a computer system that allows children to see the effects of their brainwaves on video games and to control the game operation by producing more of certain brainwaves and less of others. The "how-to-make-different-brainwaves" learning occurs as the child's brain adjusts and interprets the cause-and-effect relationship between its own activity and the resultant video game responses.

Through neurofeedback, this cause-and-effect relationship is made intuitively observable and accessible; it is as simple as noticing when geometric shapes on the screen become bigger or smaller, when objects are higher or lower, when sounds are on or off. We develop these basic perceptual skills by the age of two.

The brain activity that makes critical differences are the various brainwave frequencies. They "carry" information from one part of the brain to another, much like radio signals carry information from the antenna to your personal radio. There is a natural ebb and flow in this activity, which we detect with our sensitive computer instrumentation. The information about the preferred brainwaves is simply represented in the form of geometric figures on the video monitor. A larger brainwave shows up as a larger box or a wider bar on the screen. The child is simply asked to make the box bigger, or the bar wider, just by watching the screen and wishing it to be so! Eventually, the brain learns the task. Yet other brainwaves show us how the brain goes out of control at times, and we display that information back to the child as well. "Make this box smaller," one might urge the child. Eventually, the child achieves control of his brainwaves through making these changes happen on the computer screen. This improved control translates into more appropriate and functional behaviors in everyday living.

This process of training the brain experientially is called operant conditioning. We assimilate, process, and react to feedback. A child, for example, quickly learns in kindergarten that he is expected to raise his hand before he speaks. He also learns that he will be chastised or punished if he doesn't conform to this rule. In effect, he is conditioned to form behaviors that rapidly become automatic and continue through the internal process of self-regulation. This is the same process by which we learn just about everything that is not evoked by pain or instinct (such as not touching fire, by contrast). We use operant conditioning to learn all kinds of habits, such as automatically brushing teeth before going to bed, stopping at red lights, waiting for the walk signal at intersections, and to develop skills, such as spelling, cooking, fixing things, arguing, and avoiding arguments.

The distinguishing features of neurofeedback are that it:

- Initiates learning at a neurological level. We are training brain behavior, for which the child does not particularly feel responsible, and to which he may not feel strongly connected. But, when brain behavior is normalized, the child's behavior follows. And, eventually, even the child senses that life has become more manageable, without any additional effort on his part.

- The child becomes the witness to his own brain in action. He sees it meander from success to struggle and back again. The neurofeedback process teaches him about his own visible behavior while, simultaneously, the brain is learning about itself in a unique and replicable way.

- Accelerates learning and modifies behavior more rapidly and efficiently (producing up to 4,000 reinforcements per hour).

- Develops brain abilities that translate to other situations in life. This is because these abilities are fundamental, allowing the brain to remain calm, organized, and focused, whereas otherwise it might have lapsed into too much excitability.

HOOKING UP FOR TREATMENT

Neurofeedback training is administered by having the child play a video game solely with his brain, with information provided by brainwaves that are monitored through electrodes attached to his head. There is no use of hands. There is no joystick or GameBoy console. This may sound strange, but it is not. In fact, most children find the hook-up fun. While playing the game, the child's brainwaves are monitored by an amplifier and a computer-based instrument that processes the signal and provides the proper feedback. Gradually and cumulatively, the brain responds to the continual feedback cues and makes adjustments, and cognitive performance, attention, and self-control improve.

Like any other intervention, neurotherapy involves an alliance between practitioner and client (and, of course, the family, even though the child is being treated). While EEG neurofeedback is not a verbal treatment, the treatment *process* involves communication with clients about what to expect, how the treatment works, what is required, etc. Typically, the process begins with an assessment (discussed in Chapter 5) that includes a lengthy interview, some testing, and hooking up the child to examine his brainwaves.

These "intake" procedures vary among practitioners, but certain essential groundwork should be covered before treatment is initiated. This input involves an exchange of information between you and the therapist about your child, your questions and expectations, and the manner in which treatment will proceed.

Either before or at the first appointment, you should know the practitioner's qualifications and experience. Professionals in many disciplines practice EEG neurofeedback. Although psychologists traditionally study operant conditioning, many professionals administer the EEG training and provide the competent clinical care (such as supervision, assessment, and consultation) that goes along with effective treatment. This range of professionals includes (but is not limited to) psychologists, educational psychologists, nurses, social workers, marriage and family therapists, medical doctors, and educators.

In our experience, there are three factors that determine whether the neurofeedback experience is likely to be a good one for you and your child:

1. **Training and experience in neurotherapy** — where has the therapist trained, how long has he/she practiced neurotherapy, and how does he/she keep up with developments and advances in the field?

2. **Therapist training and experience overall** — what are the credentials and training of the therapist besides the field of

neurotherapy? Education, kinds and amounts of experience, and what types of clients and problems the therapist has worked with all count toward the likelihood of a good outcome. Some therapists specialize in certain disorders, while others treat a wider variety of problems. The important factor is whether the therapist has been successful with people, using the modes and methodologies he/she has employed.

3. **Your comfort level with the therapist** — the personality, office location, ambience, and décor, and the manner of the therapist will not determine the effectiveness of neurofeedback for your child. However, these factors may determine your willingness to openly share, confront, and continue with the therapist and the process. After all, the therapist is working with your child's brain, and your commitment will be to follow through for multiple visits.

Reasonable Questions You Might Want to Ask the Neurotherapist

- What is your training?

- How long have you been a practitioner?

- What role do you see neurotherapy playing in eliminating my child's problems and causing improvement?

- How many clients have you treated?

- How many sessions do you expect will be needed?

- What is expected of me and of family members at home?

- Should I inform my child's teacher that he is receiving help?

- Will you be in contact with the teacher or the physician?

- Will I receive progress reports?

- Will we be having regularly scheduled conferences?

- How do I explain the procedure to my child?

- Do you have a brochure that provides answers to the typical questions people may have?

When you arrive for your child's initial appointment, the practitioner will probably ask you what you know about EEG neurofeedback and why you are interested in pursuing it. The professional doing the intake wants to learn about your child's symptoms, problems, and history, about your experience with other interventions, and about your expectations. This information helps the professional neurotherapist outline parameters for treating and succeeding with your child. The initial conference also, of course, offers you an opportunity to ask questions, get clarification, clear up uncertainties, and come to an understanding about what strides your child will make and what gains you can expect him to achieve during and after the training.

The initial intake assessment provides baseline data and direction for the treatment, and it also lays the groundwork for communication, trust, and comfort between you and the therapist. It is a time to establish rapport and also to define what can be expected.

Most practitioners spend between one and two-and-a-half hours on initial intake assessment. Depending on the age and nature of the child and on scheduling contingencies, the intake may require one or two sessions. Some practitioners include a "practice" period of having the child play the game while hooked up to the neurofeedback instrumentation.

When the initial intake assessment is completed, you should know:

- What will take place when you arrive for a session.

- The duration and frequency of sessions.

- What kinds of changes and effects you should look for and when you might see them.

- The format for communicating with the therapist and evaluating progress.

- Other services the therapist may provide and/or how communication with other professionals is handled.

- Financial arrangements.

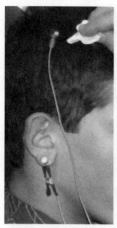

Fig. 4.1
Attaching electrodes
to the scalp

THE NEUROFEEDBACK EXPERIENCE

Most clients enter the treatment room without much knowledge about what to expect. The client has been told that he will be playing a video game using his brain (without hands), and that this is supposed to help him. Some children have insight about their problems (e.g., difficulty with behavior, paying attention, listening, reading, doing homework, fighting, etc.). Other children are unaware about why they are coming for treatment. Much to the surprise of parents, it really doesn't matter whether the child is conscious of or conversant with his "problems." This is because the neurofeedback causes changes at levels much deeper and more basic than conscious awareness, rationalizations, or defense mechanisms. Like antibiotics, the EEG training addresses malfunctions independent of the individual's opinions or attitudes. (Indeed, we might go so far as to say that the training modifies the underpinnings of what forms the child's opinions and attitudes about himself in relation to the world.) All that is required is for the child to sit in the chair, look at the computer screen, intend the game to go, and not disturb the electrodes.

The child will soon learn that moving around, squirming, talking, and activity involving muscle tension or daydreaming diminish his success with the video game. During the first session, he is hooked up with several electrodes and given very basic instructions about how to play the video game.

There are earring-like electrodes that clip to the child's ears and flat electrodes that affix to the scalp. The therapist or technician smears some non-adhesive conductive paste on the electrodes to help conduct the electrical signal. This paste also helps the electrode(s) stay on the scalp. After the session, the technician wipes the paste off with rubbing alcohol, and any remaining paste or stickiness washes away with water. There is no pain involved in this process and no piercing of skin.

Fig. 4.2 Space Race, a neurofeedback game

Occasionally, children (especially young ones) are a bit apprehensive about having electrodes attached. Our experience has been that this fear soon dissolves with explanation, reassurance, and exposure. The preliminary of hooking up becomes a familiar ritual, like suiting up for a sport; children anticipate and cooperate with what they know will be a routine but interesting encounter.

It should be emphasized that no electrical signal is transmitted via the electrodes into the scalp. Nor do we "stimulate" the brain electrically or directly in any other way. (There are such treatments, but they are not EEG neurofeedback!) The effects are caused by the child's responses to the transformed display of his brainwaves that are carried through the wires away from his brain, then amplified and displayed as various elements of the video game (colors, shapes, movement, sounds, points).[3] The child is instructed to make certain shapes (and their corresponding colors) bigger and other shapes and colors smaller. In one game (Space Race), the child is told that he or she is the pilot of a rocket that is flying between two other rockets. He is told to make the middle rocket go ahead and the side rockets stay back. When he does this, he gets points, encouraging sounds, and "space gems" collected by his rocket. We re-emphasize that the child exclusively uses his brain to control the action.

---

3 We offer the example of television broadcast stations whose signals are transmitted out and received by your TV set. You monitor the signal, and you adjust (filter) channels, volume, brightness, etc. However, you don't transmit back to the broadcast stations. Thus, the brain is like the broadcast station, and the neurofeedback equipment is what allows us to see, filter, gauge, and adjust.

There are no "joy sticks." As the child maintains consistency, additional game rewards accrue. The feedback is provided in real time, and the child gets to monitor his on-task performance and his consistency over 30-minute sessions. The middle rocket represents the desirable brainwaves, and the other two rockets represent adverse brain activity that should be minimized or suppressed.

HOW DOES IT WORK?

Because our brains and nervous systems are continuously generating electrical activity across multiple frequencies, the video game functions more like a dimmer switch (for instance, making a light either brighter or dimmer moment-by-moment) than like a discrete toggle switch (where something is either turned on or off). Indeed, through EEG training, we are teaching the nervous system to exert more precise and deliberate control over the ebb and flow of those brainwave frequencies. It is not a matter of turning brainwaves on and off, but of adjusting their predominance, mixture, and influences over periods of time. (This is how we learn to drive, steer, and control at the right speed and location for the conditions.) Therefore, in keeping with our biophysiological make-up, the EEG video games will "play" (that is, represent electrical states) when we are concentrating, daydreaming, trying hard, or even *disattending*.[4] For this reason, children often notice that their conscious activity does not predict or match what happens on the screen.

Sometimes, the middle rocket will accelerate (a successful event) when the child thinks he is daydreaming. He might exclaim, "But I'm not even thinking about the game, and I'm scoring points!" (Yes, just like the car or bicycle is moving and you are subconsciously self-correcting for the road conditions, even when your conscious attention is somewhere else.)

We live in task-oriented environments where most actions have associated discrete reactions. For example, we punch our pin code and proceed to the next screen on the ATM. Even typical video games require mouse or keyboard movements to produce specific effects. Our adult computer tasks had better be discrete and predictable: Type a letter on the keyboard, and that letter should appear on your screen. Brainwave effects are predictable, but, because they are continuous and internal, the cause-and-effects are not quite as discrete or obvious as everyday tasks. The process of EEG training makes them more so. However, there is a learning curve, though it is fortunately short in using the EEG training technique.

---

4   Perhaps you've had the experience of driving and suddenly wondering how you could have safely driven during the preceding few minutes when your mind was somewhere else. This example of the continuous and shifting nature of states of arousal and consciousness provides insight into the process of self-regulation.

Fig. 4.3 Child playing Mazes, a neurofeedback game

For most clients (even ADD/ADHD children, who often need more repetition), the learning curve is mercifully quick and efficient with EEG neurofeedback — hence the "20-Hour Solution for ADD/ADHD." Despite this efficiency, the beginning stages of training involve learning to recognize relationships. In this case, the pivotal relationship is the one between the video game activity and the heretofore unrecognized brainwave activity that causes it. (Parenthetically, like many relationships that are "on-again, off-again," inconsistent brainwaves can result in much confusion, frustration, and anxiety. As in human relationships, better communication, awareness, and flexibility improve brain-behavior relationships, too!)

At the beginning, the therapist may encourage the child to see what happens when he moves around: If the child flails, shouts, bites down, or blinks his eyes excessively, the game stops its rewards, and the *inhibit element* expands (in the Space Race game, the yellow side rocket zooms ahead while the middle target rocket falls behind, and the sounds and points cease). Although certain child behaviors cause the games to slow down (and this is specifically demonstrated), the procedure operates on a continuum. Like the dimmer switch, the child makes the game work on a greater or lesser basis, continuously for 30 minutes at a time. The child's efforts are positively reinforced for target attainment and for consistency. Goal-setting becomes a secondary (but nonetheless important) reinforcer, as the child becomes interested in and competitive with his point totals. This encourages motivation. Neurofeedback games like Mazes, Highway, and Chomper each have unique and compelling feedback indicators to rivet attention and participation.

ANYBODY CAN DO THIS!

ADD/ADHD children are challenging, and they often test limits. Telling the child that moving around will cause the game to stop usually results in the child deliberately trying to make the game stop. This is acceptable, and it will likely resolve very quickly in the child establishing an understanding of the cause-and-effect relationship between his activity and the performance of the video game. It is actually a learning set induced by the neurotherapist under controlled conditions. Using an oppositional child's high-probability behavior (doing the opposite of what he's told) to foster EEG self-control is a natural technique which works well with neurofeedback because of the brain's ability to observe itself and self-regulate through adjustments. (Imagine the dangers in a similar scenario where you tell the child he MUST NOT take more pills!).

An adroit and experienced neurotherapist can engage the child in the neurofeedback experience without being victimized in a power struggle. Errant behaviors are simply not rewarded. The child soon discovers that the way to win is by letting his brain do what is asked of it by the task.

This process is facilitated by adjustments the therapist makes on the computer showing the scrolling brainwaves. (The more sophisticated EEG systems use two computers: The therapist computer, which shows the scrolling brainwaves and allows the therapist to make adjustments, and the game computer, the one the child watches.) The therapist can adjust the difficulty of the game "on-the-fly" (moment-by-moment) by adjusting the thresholds for rewards and inhibits.

Fig. 4.4 Screen from Highway, a neurofeedback game

Fig. 4.5 Screen from Chomper, a neurofeedback game

The EEG software separates, or filters, the EEG signal coming from the child's brain and scrolling across the screen into separate "bandwidths" or frequency ranges (cycles per second). The therapist can then set the goals to specify how much of certain brainwave frequencies the child has to make to earn rewards and, simultaneously, the extent to which the child must inhibit (make less of) other brainwaves to keep the game operating well and rewarding him.

You can think of the reward bandwidth as the accelerator and the inhibit bandwidths as the brakes. The goal for the rewards is typically set to reward the child about 80% of the time, so that the child is encouraged by lots of "yes" feedback when he is producing sufficient brainwaves within that frequency range and at that location in his brain. Concurrently, the inhibit goals are typically set to withhold rewards when the child is producing brainwaves within those ranges about 20% of the time.

Since the disregulated brain often does not distinguish among nuances of brainwave frequencies, this process teaches it to do so automatically. In effect, it teaches the brain to operate the accelerator and the brakes independently.

Though the child is unaware of percentages — he is not even looking at his scrolling brainwaves — he understands when he is within or beyond goals for the reward and inhibit bands on a moment-by-moment basis. This information is conveyed by the game operation. This is the feedback, and it consists of digitally transformed representations of the child's electrophysiological brain activity displayed within sight and sound parameters that tell him when he is on-track. There is no penalty

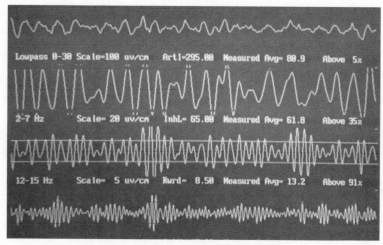

Fig. 4.6 Therapist brainwave screen with adjustable thresholds
for reward and inhibits

for being off-track — just the dimming of the game that signals to the brain an opportunity to DO SOMETHING ELSE to get back on-track and earn rewards. Brains are remarkably adept at taking such hints.

ANY BRAIN CAN DO THIS!

Bear in mind that some of the original research on EEG biofeedback was done on cats (by Dr. Barry Sterman at the UCLA School of Medicine). You can well imagine the difficulty of explaining biofeedback instructions to a cat! Yet, cats learn very well how to make certain kinds of brainwaves — when given the right feedback.

Considering this fact, it is understandable (though no less remarkable) that brainwave training is effective with toddlers (as young as three years) and with nonverbal children (yes, even severely autistic children!).

Although we are addressing the constellation of symptoms and characteristics that comprise ADD/ADHD, it is worth some digression here to appreciate that the mechanism by which neurofeedback works also succeeds with a conglomerate of symptoms ranging from "executive stress" to significantly impaired brain function.

The remarkable quality of self-regulated healing becomes evident when very impaired and observably chaotic individuals attempt EEG training. It is a compelling moment when an acting-out autistic person watches the feedback monitor with a regard that clearly signifies his communion with the process. *He knows that the activity on the screen is a direct reflection of him!* This phenomenon occurs with such striking contrast to the beliefs and experiences of many who think they "know" autistic behaviors. How can a very impaired person — one who communicates minimally or can barely attend to people or tasks for more than a few moments — become immersed in the seemingly abstract process of biofeedback? The answer is empirical — it happens with routine effectiveness. This fortunate and practical discovery allows people of all backgrounds, natures, and levels of development and functioning to benefit from a simple, natural treatment, and to improve a multiplicity of functions, regardless of entering levels of behavior.

It is an uncanny experience to watch very impaired children adapt to and *desire* EEG biofeedback. At first, we hedged when asked by parents of prospective clients how their children would cope with this treatment, or even sit still in a chair. Experience taught us that such clients not only sit in the chair and tolerate the treatment, they enjoy it and anticipate it! Indeed, for the very impaired child, EEG biofeedback training elicits a relatively high level of cognitive behavior: Concentration and tracking occur for lengthy periods, the anticipation (asking to do biofeedback, appearing eager, complying) formulates goal-orientation, and the cooperative assistance reflects distinct contrast with the struggle, fearfulness, resistance, and general noncompliance that characterize treatment interventions for this population.

Observing how the EEG training affects the overly hyperactive, distractible, non-communicative, or otherwise "disconnected" client redefines our preconceived notions about several important things: That person's abilities and potential, the possibilities for treatment not precluded by the person's limitations (and the therapist's methodological limitations), and the nature of meaningful interactions that can occur between the individual and his environment.

DIFFERENT KINDS OF "SMART"

The other side of the coin is that functional and exceptional people can improve their performances through neurofeedback. By nudging the brain into higher ratios of adaptive responses, EEG training develops the mental fitness and peak performance of higher functioning individuals as well.

To the uninitiated, the rapid positive responses of impaired clients to the benefits of neurotherapy occur with marked contrast to the hesitant and tentative reactions by more sophisticated children and adults. Cognitively advanced people tend to rely on logical analysis to interpret and adapt to new situations. However, EEG training requires brain responses that are different from the logical subroutines so well developed in the repertoires of "smart" people. Some people quickly adapt to this new demand, while others struggle with it.

Some comments echoed by "smart" clients:

"I'm not doing anything; that computer is beeping on its own."

"How do you make this work?"

"This is frustrating; I can't figure it out."

"I think about paying attention, and the game stops. Then, I think about how much I hate school, and it goes. This doesn't make sense."

"When I let my mind drift, I score more points."

"What a waste of time; this isn't doing anything for me?"

"Oh, I get it! You have to multiply by sevens in your head in order to get it to go."

"Feelings? What feelings? I'm not feeling anything."

As you may suspect by now, traditional concepts of intelligence do not determine the success of EEG neurofeedback training. We are talking more about working with states of *being* than states of *doing*. The process is more about our unconscious control of brain states than about processing information. In some ways, then, this is easier for the cat to learn than for the executive mind that is used to figuring everything out. So, what can you expect with your child? And how long does it take to see improvements?

THE FIRST SESSIONS: FIVE HOURS OF RE-ORGANIZATION

When the brain is faced with new circumstances and contingencies, it must make adjustments. It compares notes by trying to match the current problem with similar events, stimuli, and solutions in its memory bank. The speed and efficiency with which this occurs depends on many factors, including flexibility. (Ironically, those whose brains are more flexible catch on quicker, thereby reinforcing their mental flexibility along with the other benefits that neurofeedback provides; those who are less flexible take longer, but they also develop more flexibility, which their brains invariably need.)

For most people, the first 10 neurofeedback sessions (five hours of "brain time") lay the foundation for re-organizing patterns of brain response and flexibility. They are acclimating to the training, the routine procedures, the flow and rhythm and cadence of developing a harmony with the feedback computer. While the science of operant conditioning transpires, the individual is working out his "dance," his relationship with the training. Some children are learning they can't force it, that they must be patient and consistent and careful; some are learning to relax and stop "efforting." Others are being consistently reminded to WAKE UP!

Children respond differently to these initial sessions, and the variation is significant. A common reaction to the first few sessions is fatigue and increased appetite. This is not universal, but it is frequent. The training gives the brain a workout; most people are mentally tired for a few hours right after the first sessions. This is usually transient on the days of the sessions, and the fatigue tends to disappear as the child acclimates to the training. A sharp increase in appetite after the first few sessions is also not surprising. This, too, usually diminishes or disappears.

For children who are hyperactive or underweight, these transient side effects may be welcome! However, it is important to remember that the training tends to normalize self-regulated arousal functions like appetite and wakefulness. The first hours of training mobilize the brain and nervous system to re-adjust. The temporary changes in fatigue and hunger are reflections of these re-adjustments.

You may notice some subtle changes over the first five hours of "brain time." Most people sleep better. This may manifest itself as less of a struggle getting your child into bed; or, he may arise with progressively less grouchiness.

Moods tend to brighten. The child given to moodiness or mood swings ususaly becomes less extreme. Changes are gradual and progressive, but often they are striking. Many parents report that their obstreperous children have shorter tantrums, argue less vehemently, and "lose interest" much more quickly in prolonging arguments. (This diminished intensity and interest in controversy is not a reflection of abbreviated attention; it is a fundamental shift in the loss of internal reward from inflamed arousal.)

Children who are anxious or cranky become less so within the first five hours of training. Again, the changes are gradual and cumulative. Many parents notice unmistakable surges in their children's cooperativeness.

By the way, if this seems too good to be true, you are not alone. Many parents reflexively fear that they will "jinx" their child's new behaviors if they comment positively upon it.

Remember that, as your child forms new patterns of response, the interactions between him and others are bound to change. Since neither of you is sure of these new developments, the more familiar negative and self-protective reactions are likely to surface. These, too, will change as time passes and new adjustments are made. Thinking that you will "jinx" improvements by calling attention to them is a misinterpretation of your influence and of the nature of positive reinforcement. You can enjoy these budding improvements without compromise!

SESSIONS 11-20: REGULATION EMERGES

Once the brain adapts to the challenges of recognizing and modifying its own activity, it has a better basis for developing a reference point or "home base." Through the practice of adjusting brainwaves, your child forms and recognizes the brain state experience of clarity, focus, and "even-keeled" mood and perception. In addition to this being a pleasant and functional experience, the brain now has a new response set added to its repertoire. You might think of it as your child's learning the directions to a friend's house where it is calm and non-threatening, not boring, and a fun place to be. Not only can he follow the directions for getting there — he now has developed cues for when to go.

For most children, the period between the tenth and twentieth session is a time when the central nervous system is adapting to newly learned ways of responding to stress and challenges. Their brains have learned to act more flexibly, but this is still new. Therefore, what often emerges are fledgling and different behaviors that seem rough around the edges: New inflections, subtle mood shifts, and newfound (though tenuous) consistency in task persistence.

Typically, parents report after about 10-20 sessions that their children don't argue as hard or as long. It's as if the wind goes out of their sails very quickly. A noticeable upswing in cooperation often occurs and remains after about 10-20 sessions. Parents are understandably astonished that when they announce to their child that it's time to go somewhere, the child no longer complains.

Because the brain has become more activated after about 20 sessions, an amazing shift occurs: Your child will be less bored![5]

SESSIONS 21-40:
CONSOLIDATING AND INTEGRATING ADAPTATIONS

During the first 20 sessions (approximately), your child has adapted to the repeated challenges presented to his brain. Just as our muscles adapt to the challenge of physical exercise by becoming stronger and readier for increased demands, our brains respond to structured challenges by increasing the capabilities of handling these challenges.

In the case of muscle and physical fitness, changes occur in tissue structure and cardiovascular capacity. Often, these result in increased workload capacity, resistance to fatigue, quicker recovery, and increased confidence.

---

5   Dr. Steinberg often jokes with children at the beginning that, since EEG neurofeedback helps kids become less bored, he is known as the "boring doctor."

In mental fitness training, the changes occur in learning — that is, in the responses the brain makes to a given set of stimuli — to produce different and more adaptive outcomes.[6] Specifically, during the first 20 or so sessions, your child has learned subconsciously which brainwave responses will make the video game work better. He has learned a certain degree of control over and relationship between how his brain behaves and how his world (the video game in microcosm) acts in response.

Gradually, this cause-and-effect relationship and your child's newly developed control generalize to the world beyond EEG video games.

The brain states practiced during the EEG training occur spontaneously beyond the training sessions. Your child's brain has, quite plainly, matured to the point of greater sophistication, control, flexibility, and capability. His brain now has more varied and appropriate responses, and can sustain these responses in a more stable fashion. He is better able to recognize changing conditions, to respond to them more adaptively, and to weather temporary inconveniences and setbacks.

These changes manifest in a variety of ways. For example, many ADD children notoriously resist change or transition. They become "stuck" in what they are doing, and attempts to divert them from immersion in a task to another imminent demand ("Time to turn off the TV and …") elicit maladaptive reactions ranging from nonresponsiveness to rageful tantrums.

After about 20 EEG sessions, however, many children "hear" the cues to change activities or follow new directions. They respond more appropriately to the changing conditions and demands of the situation. They appear less "put out" by complying and more aware and acquiescent of what's expected. No wonder they seem more cooperative — much to the amazement and delight of their parents and teachers!

This is because their brains have been conditioned by the EEG neurofeedback training to look for a good response and recognize a successful outcome.

Each time your child's brain does this, not only does his collection of experiential "medals" increase, but so does the likelihood that he will do so in a similar situation again! This is the natural, scientific, and glorious consequence of learning through positive reinforcement — using EEG neurofeedback to operationalize this process at the rate of 4000 times per hour!

As your child acts with new capability upon the world, he will get desirably reinforced in areas where he was previously inattentive or unavailable. This will result in a catapult of growth that parents often interpret as growth spurts or maturation. Not coincidentally, such

---

6   It could be argued (and measured) that the "learned" responses of our neural networks result in better brain oxygenation and a variety of concurrently improved neurophysiological responses

developmental changes characteristically accelerate between the twentieth and fortieth neurofeedback sessions. For most children, mood stabilizes as their internal "thermostats" become more consistent and functional with the demands of self-regulation. Thus, they appear more considerate, tolerant, and even empathetic. These changes win them more approval, more inclusion, and more opportunities to show competence.

The period between sessions 21-40 often accompanies a better accommodation of task demands. Children tend to do more homework, complain less, accept limits more easily, and accomplish tasks more routinely and with greater thoroughness and regularity. Many children report that they feel better able to pay attention. Parents may notice the signs of increased task orientation and accomplishment, or even the absence of previously predictable occurrences of crises.

Eventually, as your child becomes receptive, acceptable, and successful more of the time, he will learn, through the accumulation of life experiences, that he can succeed. His expectations will again conform to and lead the expectations of those around him — but now they will be expectations brimming with approval and confidence.

SUCCESSFUL NEUROTHERAPY: AUSPICIOUS SIGNS AND HALLMARKS OF PROGRESS

We have reviewed the rudiments of the neurotherapy procedures and the essential process by which the brain — yes, your child's brain — can learn and adapt to more functional internal (self-regulatory) and overt (observable) behaviors.

The changes described are gradual and approximate; each brain and nervous system is different, but almost everyone eventually responds to the EEG training process.

Many people ask how to know whether EEG neurofeedback is successful. This seminal concern is best addressed through a combination of measures:

- Your observations.

- Observations of others, including immediate family, relatives, friends, teachers, and the neurotherapist.

- Your child's direct comments and behaviors.

- Neuropsychological tests and assessment measures.

- Rating scales.

- Reduction in medication, where appropriate

Though you can expect to see significant changes relatively early (within the first few weeks to two months), remember that EEG neurofeedback is a learning process that deepens with time, even after the training is discontinued. The "20-hour solution for ADD/ADHD" is more aptly a 20-hour introduction to more successful living through better mental fitness. It is a new lifestyle, generated by the experience of the brain's increased capabilities. Though witnessed as initial symptom relief, the training improvements set in motion a process of growth that is discovered and recognized over time.

Given the proper information, the brain heals and improves itself. However, competent neurotherapy entails procedures, standards, guidelines, and checkpoints that ensure the process remains on-track.

The adept neurotherapist assumes responsibility for the administration of training, evaluation of progress, and guidance as the family enters new phases of experience. Meetings, communications, and re-assessments facilitate the monitoring and evaluation of progress. You should offer the therapist reports and information throughout the treatment (many practitioners have daily or weekly evaluation forms). Moreover, consider that incidental details of your child's behavior or your observations can be very significant precursors of changes. The therapist needs to know this information in order to make adjustments and to advise you.

In the big picture, successful neurotherapy invokes a transition from disorder to order. This is new, if not entirely palpable, for those involved. Paradoxically, the mind is not always ready for the journey it has already accomplished.

One of the most typical, yet uncanny occurrences during neurotherapy training is the subtle transformation of the child/family "problem" from derogative and overly stressful to positive and manageable.

Families and individuals vary in the ways they experience and represent this shift. For some, the changes are dramatic and consciously attributable to EEG neurofeedback. Others are more cautious, less aware, or less inclined to admit that EEG neurofeedback has reliably caused the improvements they recognize.

It may seem curious that parents hopefully engage their children in EEG training, yet some of them harbor reservations even in the face of obvious improvement. This aspect of human nature isn't limited to neurotherapy, although it becomes more prominent in circumstances where understanding is limited and novelty prevails. Perhaps some folks hedge cautiously against disappointment; some take time to adjust, and that adjustment period precludes the accommodation of stark and rapid changes.

The oblivious response to positive changes from neurofeedback typically reflects in a phenomenon known as the *apex problem.*[7] This refers to the mind not functioning at its peak or apex. This takes one of two forms:

1) Either the person admits that a substantial improvement has occurred, but attributes it to something other than the treatment that caused it;

   or,

2) The person denies or minimizes the original nature or existence of the problem.

Thus, when children improve after EEG training, some parents chalk the improvement up to "maturation" or any combination of efforts in which the family has engaged. Sometimes (astoundingly), parents whose lives were in extreme disarray because of an ADD child will retrospectively "normalize" their view of the situation by asserting that the child "did not really have ADD after all — he just needed some time to grow up."

Regardless of the psychological nature of the shifting attitudes throughout treatment, such changes in perspective are expected and common. They are hallmarks of rapid, effective, and predictable behavior change from a powerful intervention introduced in the context of the intransigence and stress of ADD. The shift from "This problem is ruining our lives" to "What problem?" is an auspicious marker of normalization.

---

7   We wish to thank Dr. Roger Callahan for his brilliant exposition of the apex problem and other concepts in transformational healing outlined in his books on Thought Field Therapy.

Assessing Children and Monitoring Progress

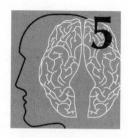

THE CHALLENGE OF CHALLENGES

In embarking upon a program of change or intervention, it is wise to consider several factors:

1. What are the reasons for the intervention?

2. What are the outcome expectations?

3. How good is the "fit" between the program and the participant (probability of success)?

4. By what means will the intervention be tailored to fit the individual?

5. How will results be evaluated?

Determining which (if any) among the array of interventions, programs, and treatments is suitable for your child can be a daunting task, fraught with confusion, uncertainty, and conflicting or vague information. Approaching this task by keeping in mind the factors listed above may guide the process with more sensibility, confidence, and satisfaction.

We have proposed and expounded upon a model of disregulation that underlies ADD/ADHD and the manner in which EEG biofeedback trains the brain to self-correct, thereby resolving this condition (and others). Unlike competing views, our outlook encompasses the spectrum of brain functioning from the perspective of challenge. Although we address deficits, we do not categorize the ADD problem from a fixed-deficit model. Rather, we look at symptoms, strengths, weaknesses, balance, instabilities, tendencies, and vulnerabilities. We see functional problems as expressions of imbalances in these factors; these are excesses, over-extensions, or excursions in brain regulation, precipitated and maintained by varying combinations of habit, environment, and genetics.

We offer a solution that trains the brain to meet its *challenges* — not only to overcome deficiencies, but to function at increasingly higher levels of performance and adaptation. We conceptualize this process as developing *mental fitness.*

There are parallels between mental fitness and physical fitness. (And, after all, why shouldn't there be? The body/mind split is arbitrary.) The exercise model applies to mental and physical fitness with regard to challenge as the fulcrum of improvement. Explaining the physical fitness model helps our understanding of mental fitness.

The desire and efforts to attain physical fitness arise from several motivations. One is analogous to the deficit model: Rehabilitation of injury, illness, weakness, or surgery. Another is the yearning for improved quality of life: More energy and alertness, less fatigue and vulnerability to stress or injury, greater enjoyment and zest. Yet another is the drive for competitive edge: Better performance, sense of accomplishment, greater productivity, and better remuneration and recognition.

People strive for fitness for a variety of reasons, and these may change over time as they improve. The stereotypical 97-pound weakling who resents sand kicked in his face may begin his fitness program out of mortification and resentment; but, his resolve often leads to a more satisfying life with broader rewards and opportunities undisclosed prior to achieving his new level of fitness. The heart attack patient may undertake exercise for recovery, strength, and protection. As he gains fitness, the challenge and mastery cycle claims new manifestations: The once-sedentary coronary patient may eventually run marathons.

These transformations are not uncommon. The principle underlying them is the human body's innate response to structured challenge. Physical exercise challenges muscles, organs and systems; this causes tissue to break down, and the body responds by rebuilding to greater levels of adaptation and resistance.

Such growth and improvements occur across the board, from cardiac patients to athletes. You may have a diagnosis, but you certainly don't need one to go to the gym and improve your fitness.

Mental fitness parallels this process. Arguably, the model applies more broadly to mental fitness since the brain is a control system for other systems in the body, and is more variable, flexible, and "plastic" than other organs. To wit, there are people who cannot exercise physically, but their brains still work. Essentially, the reverse is not true.

So, if physical exercise builds fitness by challenging body tissue, how do we build mental fitness? How and what do we challenge? How do we know if a child will benefit?

Let's answer these questions by defining mental fitness and applying its principles and results to the ailments with which so many children (particularly ADD/ADHD children) struggle.

MENTAL FITNESS

Mental fitness comprises a blending of learned skills, effortless self-regulation, and both automatic and conscious adaptation to the flow of changing conditions. It involves goal-oriented, purposeful, and organized behavior unimpeded by disruptions in the emotional, nervous, or energy system of the mind and body.

The two necessary and interactive components of this process are:

• Learning adaptive responses.

• Eliminating maladaptive responses.

We typically think of behavior and habit changes as functions of acquiring or relinquishing responses. The learning or shaping of new behaviors is elicited by the training (also known as operant conditioning) of responses. EEG biofeedback accomplishes such training elegantly, by shaping neurophysiological behavior with thousands upon thousands of gentle corrections. These small nudges effectively reinforce adaptive behaviors and self-regulatory modifications, building a balanced system that withstands impingements and stressors, and constrains behavior from wandering into maladaptive transgressions.

During the training procedure, the brain is "challenged" by having only specified subconscious activity rewarded (particular frequencies of brainwaves). The plasticity (adaptability) of the brain allows it to learn how to obtain rewards (from the video game), thereby strengthening certain brainwave patterns, as well as goal orientation and attainment.

Several examples help to illustrate this process.

1. The car

Imagine yourself driving a car that has very loose steering. Pretend also that you are tired. You probably can picture the car weaving to either side of the highway lane and occasionally straying into neighboring lanes without your intention. This presents a difficult and potentially dangerous situation of poor control. In order to drive safely and purposefully, you would need to steer the car and overcorrect for random excursions. The feedback would come from observing where you were driving, and the positive reinforcement would derive from seeing when you were successfully staying within your lane, moment to moment. You would be "nudging" your car (and your brain) by using positive feedback. We would not expect you to efficiently "learn" to stay in your lane through the punishing consequences of an accident.

The drift of the car is the challenge to which your brain would eventually find adaptive responses — if given accurate information and rewards for emitting the right responses.

2. The bicycle

Now, imagine you are riding a bicycle. Can you dictate verbal instructions or a formula for keeping your balance? Of course not. The vestibular feedback from your brain (along with practice) tells you how to make adjustments for the centripetal forces of gravity. You do this moment-to-moment, using ever-shifting information from the interaction between yourself and the immediate real environment. Actually, you are constantly "making mistakes," but also correcting these so quickly and automatically that you can ride steadily in a "regulated" fashion. You are self-regulating your balance. Although bicycling involves continuous brain challenges, most people ride smoothly and enjoy it. Once the retinue of skills is compiled, it is adaptable to a wide variety of terrains and environmental conditions (challenges).

3. Strengthening exercises

In the realm of physical conditioning, we can challenge muscles by slightly overworking them and then allowing them to rest. Repeating this on an appropriately structured basis generally strengthens capacity. As coaches, trainers, and athletes know, it is possible to isolate certain muscles and train them specifically. Indeed, this is often necessary to balance the overwork done by certain muscle sets in competitive sports, or to compensate for overuse or injury. The challenged muscles bounce back and become stronger with careful training.

Similarly, neurofeedback isolates particular brainwave patterns for challenge. The process exercises the brain's ability to "steer, lean, or strain" in the service of meeting the challenge.

WHAT'S THE REWARD?

The immediate rewards in neurofeedback consist of audiovisual signals and points. The significant rewards, however, are the conditioning effects that improve the brain's capacity to respond, integrate, and generalize to meet a wide variety of challenges.

Mental fitness comes from achieving the balance and "response-ability" of maintaining self-regulated adaptation and releasing disruptive, interfering responses. Training the brain and nervous system lead to optimal performance and satisfying experience. Mental fitness results in:

- Increased relaxation and reduction in stress and anxiety.

- Enhanced creativity in fluency of ideas generated to solve complex problems.

- Capacity to sustain high workloads for long periods of time.

- Ability to concentrate and reduce error rates (increased accuracy).

- Reduced recovery time from fatigue.

- Increased hemispheric integration, better communication within the brain, greater awareness.

- Flexibility of thinking and facility to shift response sets.

- Ability to weather setbacks and rebound from losses.

- Modulation of arousal and self-regulation.

- Emotional control, sensitivity, and appropriateness.

- Perceptual accuracy.

- Reduced impulsivity.

ELIMINATING MALADAPTIVE RESPONSES

Eliminating or reducing maladaptive responses can be difficult, particularly since conscious or even inadvertent attention tends to reinforce them. The grave paradox of changing attitudes and behavior is that the more one focuses upon undesirable responses, the stronger they tend to become. This is particularly problematic with negative emotions, which exert more influence over us than most of us realize or care to admit. Maladaptive responses quickly become habitual, and they are especially compelling and troublesome for the ADD/ADHD child who exhibits the characteristics explained in Chapter 3 (disregulation of arousal; poor integration with environmental demands; perceptual focus problems; stressed brain syndrome; compromised flexibility).

Steering around the negative excursions is a set of habits and skills to be learned and practiced. The best way to do this is to train by attending to and shaping *adaptive* and *appropriate responses*. We reiterate this because it is so fundamentally important to the development of fitness and self-control. Maladaptive responses are hard to address directly. Typically, they are treated by punishment (which has side effects, and can also strengthen bad behaviors when applied incorrectly or indiscriminately), extinction (the process of systematically ignoring or not reinforcing undesirable behaviors — very tricky, painstaking, and difficult to sustain), or medication (often blunting the person along with the bad behaviors).

The key, then, is to focus on shaping adaptive behaviors. Since neurofeedback does this so efficiently (up to 4,000 reinforcements per hour), the brain is busy attending to carefully selected positive responses, and the process of extinguishing maladaptive responses occurs naturally.

IS YOUR CHILD A CANDIDATE FOR MENTAL FITNESS TRAINING?

Despite our emphasis on positive shaping through operant conditioning, reality dictates that people are driven by negative emotions, negative attitudes and behaviors, and the desire for quick relief from the effects of self-defeating response patterns.

A poignant proverb highlights the tragic consequences of negative focus, assumed to be self-imposed, but often the result of disregulation:

"Vos der mensch ken alts ibertrachten, ken der ergster soyna im nisht vinchen." (What people can think up for themselves, their own worst enemies couldn't wish upon them.)

Since symptoms (maladaptive responses) are so predominant in the motivation of those seeking assistance, let's use those as a baseline to determine if mental fitness training via EEG neurofeedback could be right for your child.

At the beginning of this chapter, we posed several questions to guide selection of an intervention. The first one entailed the reasons for intervention.

The following checklist can help you gauge the degree to which mental fitness training may meet your child's needs.

MENTAL FITNESS SCREENING PROFILE

0	1	2	3	4
Never	Rarely	Occasionally	Frequently	Very Frequently

Bothered by thoughts or worries more than twice a day	
Trouble getting or staying organized	
Sleep not restful and satisfactory	
Gets annoyed or irritated on a regular basis	
Foggy or confused more than occasionally	
Troublesome fears, anxieties, moods, or attitudes	
Routinely overwhelmed or fatigued	
Poor concentration	
Easily angered or upset	
Moody or out of control	
Feels or causes distress in relationships	
Hard to get along with	
Performance needs improvement	
Prone to physical ailments	
Holds grudges, blames others	
Overly inconsistent	
Difficulty moving from one activity to the next	
Avoids or has trouble with schedules or deadlines	
Negative emotions that hamper or restrict participation in and satisfaction with life	
Bored or overly restless more than twice a week	
Trouble coping with frustration	
Hypersensitive or faultfinding	
Impulsive (Ready, Fire, Aim)	
Doesn't finish or follow through on important things	
Chronically misinterprets signals or communications from other people	
Problems learning or executing academic tasks	
Feels wronged or victimized unjustly	
Memory problems, forgetfulness	

Total:

Turn page for scoring interpretation

SCORING INTERPRETATION

After rating each item in the Mental Fitness Screening Profile, add up the total points.

A total above 40 indicates that the person being rated would likely benefit from EEG neurofeedback mental fitness training. A diagnostic evaluation is recommended.

If you assigned a rating of 3 or 4 to only one or two items, please review your ratings. These behaviors tend to occur in clusters. When disregulation is an underlying problem, it tends to manifest across several or numerous symptoms. Isolated high ratings of problem symptoms often reflect either situational/environmental factors or narrow reporting.

The Mental Fitness Screening Profile is helpful both for identifying the need for intervention and for pinpointing desired treatment goals. However, it is not a substitute for professional assessment and evaluation. A good assessment is necessary to achieve proper mental fitness training, and it is invaluable in guiding the provision of suitable expectations, environmental modifications, interactions, and other interventions — these include educational, parenting, therapeutic, lifestyle, and social recommendations. We shall have more to say about this later in the chapter; first, let's look at how to determine realistic outcome expectations for your family's experience with neurofeedback mental fitness training.

INTAKE INTERVIEW

It all begins with a consultation. Whether it's neurotherapy, traditional psychotherapy, or another mode of professional assistance, the outset involves discussion, observation, and exchange of information.

In neurotherapy mental fitness training, the initial interview is a major part of what is known in the field as the "intake assessment." This initial interview usually covers a lot of ground; it is a prime opportunity for you to ask questions, clarify expectations, and gain a clearer picture of how the intervention works. It is also a vehicle for the therapist to form a good working rapport with you and to assess your child.

Assessment involves a number of critical steps and functions. One function is to form realistic goals and expectations about what neurotherapy will accomplish with your child and how that process is likely to unfold. The therapist uses measurements, observations, history, and his/her own clinical judgment and experience to establish direction and goals, set the treatment procedures, and gauge reasonable predictions for your child's progress.

The process should be professional, methodical, and scientific. There is enough established evidence in the field of neurotherapy that we need not espouse the "Forrest Gump" therapeutic method ("Life is like a box of chocolates — you never know what you're gonna get!"). Though there are many incidental positive changes that accrue from this treatment that so efficiently organizes the brain and nervous system, its main effects should be reasonably concrete, specific, and predictable.

However, this does not mean that the therapist, the treatment, and the family are necessarily aligned. People often have overreaching expectations without either realizing or divulging them. When this occurs, disappointment and miscommunications follow. To avoid these pitfalls, the therapist will take notes and perform baseline measures to know your child's strengths and weaknesses, ascertain significant factors or predictors that might influence treatment, and monitor your child's response and progress. It is vital that you disclose information about your child's life and the family history. Items or incidents that may seem trivial to you could be useful to the therapist in making treatment decisions.

For instance, many children have "accidents" that parents chalk up to life's pings and knocks and lessons. However, some of these falls and bangs have resulted in minor brain injury (surprisingly common), and these incidents may influence your child's response to treatment and the treatment protocols that are necessary to overcome the effects of those traumas. Be sure to tell the therapist about any medications taken and responses to them — not only for your child, but for other members of the extended family. Family vulnerabilities tend to have heritable properties. A consequence is that the same or similar medications tend to produce comparable results in family members suffering similar ailments. We can often replicate medication effects quite closely using specific neurofeedback protocols. If the therapist knows that certain medications have produced notable effects in your child or in family members, this may influence decisions about neurofeedback protocols.

KEEPING PERSPECTIVE, TRACKING PROGRESS, AND TOOTH-SHOE-LUMP

Keeping track of progress is important overall, but the initial assessment is critical in establishing reference points for making future appraisals and decisions. The initial interview is an ideal time to highlight the main targets, or goals, for improvement. Most people coming in for EEG neurofeedback have a "headline" list of what they would dearly love to see improved. We generally ask the following questions:

- What are the issues (name one or two or three) that bother you the most, such that, if you saw improvement in these, you would be convinced that neurofeedback was worth it?

- Given what you describe today, how will we observe and verify improvement?

We know from experience that people "forget" what was hurting and how badly it hurt, once their distress abates. This seems to be human nature. We move on from one problem to the next, usually following the order of the urgency with which each problem commands our attention. It is as if nature focuses our efforts selectively, allowing us to experience or minimize problems, according to what is manageable at the time. Standards change in sync with perceptions, progress, and capacity. This gives rise to some interesting perspectives, as illustrated by the following anecdotes:

1. Tooth-shoe-lump

A man with an agonizing toothache called the dentist. Although the dentist was booked, the man prevailed upon the receptionist to grant him an emergency appointment. Nearly delirious with pain, the man donned an old pair of shoes, not noticing that the shoes had shrunk from the rain and were too tight. He arrived at the dentist's office to a full waiting room. The only empty chair had a large lump where a spring was straining to pierce the seat upholstery. The man sat in this chair, and the nurse gave him some painkillers and a cup of water. As the man awaited the dentist, he began to relax, but noticed a strange pinching sensation. Absently, he slipped off his shoes, and immediately he felt relief as the blood circulated back into his feet. He looked down, noticed the old shoes, and wondered how he could have worn too-tight shoes that he meant to discard.

After awhile, the painkillers took effect, and the man's toothache began to mercifully subside. He squirmed around in the chair, shifting away from the lumpy spring. Finally, the man stood up, conscious that he could not sit comfortably in such a chair. With his toothache no longer commanding full attention, he became aware of other discomforts.

2. Heart Attack-Rehab-Marathon

After a heart attack, a fellow underwent physical therapy and slowly rebuilt his strength. At first, he was glad just to be alive. As he improved, he resolved to change his sedentary lifestyle, so he began walking. He continued to exercise and eat more healthfully. Soon, he began to run. Over a period of three years, he entered road races, gradually working his way up to marathons. He trained by running 40 miles per week. Unfortunately, the man was distressed that he had not reduced his marathon time by the number of minutes he wanted. The heart attack was a thing of the past, allowing new goals to emerge.

3. Royal Fishing

The prince and princess were fishing in a lake stocked with fish by their servants. They sat in the rowboat on a gorgeous day, their picnic basket filled with delicacies, awaiting a successful catch. Sure enough, in minutes, a large fish nibbled at the prince's line, and soon the catch was in the boat. The prince was ecstatic.

"This is a wonderful fishing spot!" he exclaimed. "Perhaps we should mark this spot by dropping a yellow ribbon in the water, so that, when we come again tomorrow, we will know exactly where to find fish!"

Of course, it is hard to remember exact circumstances and the way we felt previously. Placing markers can be quite helpful, but only if done with appropriate methodology.

Changes in perspective are natural and common in the course of treatment. Careful monitoring — beginning with initial assessment — can highlight and document the probable positive changes that accrue through treatment, even as attention focuses on newer problems or old ones that were never mentioned at the outset.

It was by virtue of this interesting perspective shift that we learned over time the tremendous reach that EEG neurofeedback exerts over the spectrum of "bracket creep"[8] symptoms. Patients who arrived for ADD treatment reported, after a number of sessions, that they were sleeping better, that they no longer had headaches, etc. A myriad of symptoms were reported as gone or greatly relieved. It was, however, conspicuous, that they had never reported these problems originally, only in retrospect after they had healed.

"You know, it's a funny thing — his handwriting has really improved. He must be going through a growth spurt." (This was an example of many such reports after only two months of neurotherapy.)

"Yes, doctor, my concentration has really improved. I'm getting a lot more done, and I'm no longer depressed."

Depressed? You never mentioned that you were depressed!

Perhaps these patients simply never expected EEG training to affect such troublesome medical symptoms. (After all, neither did we, during the nascent stages of our work.) The logical stretch was too great for them to make the connection. Patients are usually not scientists or trained observers. Maybe these connection glitches and perspective shifts were examples of the tooth-shoe-lump or heart attack-rehab-marathon phenomena.

Or, perhaps we have stumbled upon a revolutionary healing method.

---

8   Bracket creep was described by Peter Kramer in his book, *Listening to Prozac.* This term refers to the cross-migration among symptoms and diagnoses of mental conditions — the "creeping" of one category of mental disorder across the boundaries of others; that is, across once-rigid brackets of diagnostic classification.

STRESSORS, STRESS, AND ASSESSMENT

There is a significant difference between a stressor and stress. A stressor is a stimulus or condition that intrudes and demands a response. Stress is a maladaptive response pattern to stressors that we must deal with routinely in life. Stress is more than being "uptight" occasionally or having a bad day. It is a recurring imbalance resulting in the daily wear-and-tear on the body and mind that leads to dysfunction or breakdown.

The reason stress is harmful is that we are unconsciously creating it, and we become accustomed to sustaining it. Unfortunately, we accept stress as a "normal" part of life, and even rationalize that some stress is good for us. This is a misperception, like thinking that some headaches are good for us.

Much of what we do to cope with this problem focuses on the symptoms, but does little to relieve the underlying condition or cause. This is because stress is not a "thing" like a germ or virus or broken part. It is a pattern of maladaptive responses. Think of the warning lights on an automotive dashboard. When they light up, it signals a condition that has reached breakdown. Pouring oil into the crankcase, for example, will usually not remedy the problem of low oil pressure. The system needs repair so it can maintain regulation.

The same is true with stress. To reduce it, we must restore an internal balance of self-regulation. Specifically, this means a balance between *arousal* and *relaxation*, activation and de-activation, and excitation and inhibition, which are all very basic functions of the nervous system. To the question, "What is the proper speed to drive a car?," the answer is, "It depends on the conditions." Managing stress involves regulating one's internal responsiveness to ever-changing conditions.

Stress is a prison built by maladaptive habits, attitudes, emotions, and response patterns. To relieve and reduce stress, we must modify our internal regulation of arousal and activation, of the excitation/inhibition dynamic. Arousal is the relative state of alertness, stimulation, energy, interest, and heightened emotional and physical responsiveness. Arousal is necessary to interact effectively with people and events around us. It is the mechanism by which we receive and exchange information and action for the functions of living. In the extreme, arousal results in the "fight or flight" response. Its essential and opposite partner is the relative state of inactivity, drowsiness, rest, and relaxation. It is necessary for sleep, digestion, replenishment, and "recharging" of our biological batteries. It is the "reloading" component of effective and purposeful interaction with the world. These two must always be managed in a kind of competitive balance by the nervous system.

When we speak of arousal, we refer to this collective appraisal about the state of the person. Arousal is made up of many specific activations and de-activations of particular neuronal networks, networks that manage more specific brain functions, such as aspects of attention. These networks are, in turn, managed through interactions of many excitatory and inhibitory influences at the neuronal level. Each of these terms looks at the problem of regulation on a different scale. It is our own zoom lens. At the neuronal level, inhibition causes our nerves to stop transmitting messages, as brakes cause a car to slow down or stop.

Just as safe driving requires the coordinated use of acceleration and braking, self-controlled living involves assuming the proper state of arousal, of circuit activations/de-activations, and of excitatory and inhibitory activity. Obviously, this all needs to be handled in autopilot. Arousal is managed by the central nervous system and by the autonomic nervous system, with its sympathetic and parasympathetic branches. The autonomic nervous system is, of course, ultimately also governed centrally. The two branches also inhibit each other. The interplay of these nervous system parts is vital to stress management.

This model of disregulation is implicitly supported by the medical model, insofar as the stimulants and the antidepressants try to address the arousal component of the problem. And, as we know, these medications do not address the entire spectrum of issues.

There is one more over-arching issue, and that is one of nervous system excitability and instability, which can lead to behavioral disinhibition. Arousal disregulation can make these worse; but, even if arousal is well-regulated, there may well still be problems. It is for these problems that the heavy artillery in the medicine cabinet is now being brought to bear: The anticonvulsants and the antipsychotics.

There is an issue, then, of the fundamental stability of nervous system functioning, an understanding of which takes us beyond the arousal disregulation model. We are talking here about rages, temper tantrums, pediatric migraine, seizures and convulsions, asthma attacks, night terrors, motor and vocal tics, etc. These all take us beyond the classical picture of ADD/ADHD, but are frequently seen in association with it. Fortunately, this is precisely where neurofeedback can play a powerful role. Neurofeedback trains the continuity of mental states. It is the very thing needed to address this kind of instability. Fortuitously, then, neurofeedback can be helpful not only with the core issue of arousal disregulation, but with the attendant behavioral inhibition/disinhibition. All of these conditions appear to be described by the disregulation model, and all appear to respond to a significant degree to the self-regulation remedy. Our main concern in this book, however, is with ADD/ADHD and the arousal model, to which we now return.

Various things we do, both intentionally and subconsciously, affect the way our nervous systems manage the braking and acceleration of responses. Habitual mismanagement causes the brake or accelerator responses to get stuck in the "on" position for too long, and this is what we experience as stress. For example, overarousal often results in anger, argumentativeness, difficulty unwinding or relaxing, fear, suspicion, anxiety, restlessness, tension, headaches, and digestive problems. Underarousal may cause attentional problems, depression, pain, PMS, fatigue, and boredom. Many people are chronic victims of overarousal or underarousal, and some people suffer from the symptoms of both — that is, from the disregulation of arousal that can go either way at different times. Besides the obvious unpleasantness of symptoms caused by stress, the continuation of these imbalances leads to disorder and disease. To relieve the discomfort, many people develop unhelpful appetites and habits to compensate the imbalance — substance abuse, overeating, and other addictive behaviors, thrill-seeking, avoidance, "shutdown" — however, these temporary fixes end up reinforcing the imbalances they once relieved.

We believe that the amount of stress one experiences in response to stressors is, in large part, a function of one's mental fitness.

Assessment of stress, however tallied, may highlight conditions or susceptibility for which mental fitness training may be a good choice.

ASSESSMENT MEASURES FOR EEG BIOFEEDBACK

As described, the interview is a critical part of assessment for EEG training. From this interview, observations, and history (which also comes from forms you will be asked to fill out), the neurotherapist will construct a model of how your child's nervous system deals with self-regulation, where it is inefficient, and how best to correct it.

Thousands of therapists have been trained in the self-regulation/disregulation model described in this book, especially those who have trained with EEG Spectrum International or the EEG Institute under the auspices of instruction by Dr. Siegfried Othmer and Sue Othmer. Therapists exposed to this training have been taught a "decision-tree" method of discerning brain and nervous system components of disregulation, especially underarousal, overarousal, and instabilities of arousal.

Testing the brain and nervous system directly, and looking at the EEG are also critical aspects of making protocol decisions. (An EEG protocol is a designation of computer settings on the biofeedback equipment specifying what type of brainwave production will be rewarded by the video game. Protocols are like compass settings for the training.)

Incredibly, the vast majority of ADD/ADHD diagnoses are made on the basis of a questionnaire and brief interview. Whether we are conducting an EEG biofeedback intake assessment or a more comprehensive assessment (see below), we deem that questionnaires and interviews alone are not sufficient, either for diagnoses or treatment. We must test the brain and nervous system directly.[9]

Notwithstanding the relative uniformity of neurotherapists' training in neurotherapeutic procedures (at least, in our network), the field is attracting the attention and practice of multidisciplinary professionals with a range of orientations. Therefore, neurotherapists' training, experience, and comfort with assessment will vary. Different practitioners will administer different tests and measures to get the relevant information to help your child.

From our viewpoint, looking at the EEG and obtaining some direct measurement of the client's performance are necessary prerequisites. We hope to encourage more neurotherapists to acquire experience and competence in the administration and interpretation of neuropsychological tests, and we believe that using such procedures greatly enhances the efficiency of EEG training, as well as contributes to the detection and treatment of conditions that profoundly affect your child's development, education, and general well-being.

However, an abridged assessment aimed at determining the relevant variables for successful EEG neurofeedback should be within the repertoire of those practicing neurotherapy, regardless of their academic degrees or professional disciplines.

One important component of direct assessment is a continuous performance test. This is a type of psychological test that measures sustained attention and a number of variables involved in nervous system functioning. Continuous performance tests have characteristics that distinguish them from other types of tests. They typically present a very simple task that is as free as possible from academic or perceptually complex skills. Continuous performance tests require consistent attention over relatively lengthy time periods.

The continuous performance test we have used for years is the TOVA (Test of Variables of Attention). This test requires the examinee to press a button on a computer input device when a target flashes on the screen, but not to press it when the non-target flashes, nor at any other time. The only difference between the target and the non-target is the position of the box. The task is simple, but it is lengthy and challenging. It reveals useful information about the examinee's brain and nervous system

---

9   Daniel Amen, M.D. has noted that psychiatry is the only medical specialty that does not make a practice of examining the organ that its specialty treats!

Fig. 5.1 TOVA screen

response patterns. Daydreaming, attention-seeking, and attempts to "take a break" are all unavailing; the challenge relentlessly continues. Thus, the test reflects cortical self-regulation and central nervous system problems, and provides important information about independent task accomplishment, adaptation without social or interpersonal cues, and attempts to manipulate a demand situation. Also, TOVA scores are extremely sensitive to slight performance deviations — this is what makes the test so diagnostically useful. The test results give data about inattention, impulsivity, response time, consistency, and neurological perseveration. It is a useful and reliable measure for gaining data and insight about the arousal state of the examinee's brain.

The TOVA was developed by a psychiatrist at the University of Minnesota. Its original use was to titrate medication — that is, to determine the optimal dosages of medications (usually stimulants) given to ADD/ADHD patients. It is still used for that purpose, and has gained more widespread acceptance as a tool in assessment batteries. We use it to measure attention diagnostically, and to monitor and evaluate progress in response to neurotherapy. The TOVA is very sensitive to physiological states. It is a kind of "nervous system blood test" whose results can be integrated into evaluations and treatment decisions, such as when and how to change EEG neurofeedback protocols.

Some neurotherapists use a sophisticated data analysis of TOVA tests called EEG Expert (offered as a service to select professionals by www.EEGdirectory.com). These analyses include:

- Description of the test.
- Summary of results.
- Table of data.
- Bar chart of standard scores.
- Graph of response times.
- Histogram of response data.
- Pre- and posttest comparisons.
- Interpretation of results.

This type of analysis can aid in selecting appropriate neurofeedback protocols and measuring progress in training.

Other measures can be used to assess manifestations of disregulation and brain functioning. Remember from our discussion in Chapters 1 and 3 that ADD/ADHD is characterized by compromised flexibility and perceptual focus problems. There are many tests that yield information about these functions. Some of the better ones include:

- Halstead-Reitan Neuropsychological Battery (HRB)
- Wechsler Intelligence Scale for Children-Third Edition (WISC-III)
- Stanford-Binet Intelligence Scale
- Wide Range Assessment of Memory and Learning (WRAML)
- California Verbal Learning Test (CVLT)
- Bender Gestalt Visual-Motor Test
- Cognitive Assessment System (CAS)
- Reitan-Indiana Aphasia Screening Test (AST)
- Klove Sensory Perceptual Exam
- Developmental Neuropsychological Assessment (NEPSY)
- Delis-Kaufman Executive Functioning System (D-KEFS)
- Rorschach Inkblot Test

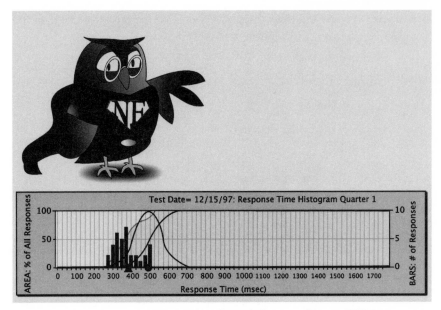

Fig. 5.2 Sample graph from a multi-page EEG Expert report

An intake assessment for EEG biofeedback will not include full administration of these tests as a battery or individually. This is because the purpose of the assessment is threefold:

1. To set EEG training protocols as parameters for training.

2. To establish baseline measures to evaluate progress.

3. To detect notable excesses or abnormalities that may influence training or predict success in the short or long term.

You might think of the intake assessment for EEG biofeedback as a brief screening exam, geared toward a prescription — akin to an eye exam given by an optometrist. Although regular eye exams are recommended, many people visit the eye doctor already aware of their symptoms of vision problems. The eye exam may detect ocular problems or even other health problems, but the imminent practical outcome is likely a prescription for correcting vision. No written reports, no detailed interpretations, just a prescription that will really help.

Neurofeedback intake exams proceed efficiently directed toward a prescriptive solution. Of course, more comprehensive examination may be necessary, especially if anomalies are detected during the screening.

DIAGNOSIS VS. DIAGNOSTIC IMPRESSIONS AND HYPOTHESES

What about the "fit" between EEG neurofeedback and your child? Does neurofeedback require a diagnosis of ADD/ADHD? Does it help the serious cases? The mild cases?

The evidence compiled from over 300,000 sessions indicates that EEG neurofeedback is successful in approximately 80% of the cases. This experience is distributed over hundreds of practitioners worldwide, and it includes many diagnoses, ranging from medical problems through the spectrum of psychiatric disorders and including, of course, a plethora of ADD/ADHD. We believe that the underlying commonality for these cases and their positive response to neurofeedback is *disregulation*.

Such a track record is impressive enough on the statistical merits. The success rate is astounding when one significant variable is considered. Bear in mind that the population of cases is somewhat skewed. Neurofeedback practitioners have tended to attract clients who have not succeeded with other treatments. The attitudes and behavior of mainstream medicine toward this treatment have been largely unreasonable. Physicians tend to refer or endorse neurofeedback only when their treatments have not succeeded. People who are not satisfied or who have had bad experiences with medications are the ones more likely to seek neurofeedback. So, neurofeedback (the treatment that mainstream medicine often dismisses as impotent) is sent to the back of the line while medications (potent toxic ones, indeed) become the first course of action. When the arsenal of traditional medicine fails, neurofeedback may then be considered. It is in this context that we are at least 80% successful. Incredibly, some traditionalists still call neurofeedback experimental!

We should add another perspective. Although success may be interpreted in different ways, we are defining it as follows:

> *Successful neurotherapy means that the client (or client's family) is satisfied that neurotherapy was worth doing, that the client's quality of life is better because of neurotherapy, and that neurotherapy resulted in a substantial alleviation of symptoms or improvement in the condition for which treatment was initiated.*

We believe this standard of success to be generous, practical, humane, and consonant with what most consumers would find sensible and profitable. There are, of course, other standards. There is statistical significance, the veritable religious scroll of science. There are psychometric retest measures, comparative observations, outside reports, client accomplishments and achievements, and so forth. These are valuable and objective, and we use them. Neurofeedback therapists are taught to include follow-up into their practices.

The bottom line, though, is whether the client is satisfied. Appealing to this nonscientific standard will inevitably draw criticism from those whose professional security is bastioned by statistical correlations and double-blind studies.[10] Because of the claims of efficacy and because of the esoteric quality of using computers to modify neurobiology, critics will continue to dismiss EEG biofeedback as a placebo effect. It is a specious allegation.[11]

In evaluating success — whether or not the treatment has worked — we need to account for factors that are not revealed by statistical outcomes. One of these is the tooth-shoe-lump phenomenon, discussed earlier in this chapter. Realistically, one aspect of successful treatment is that the client's standards may shift enough due to progress that he often "forgets" his original problem. (He doesn't become amnestic; he simply no longer relates to originating issue as the huge problem it was.) A shift in focus or priority is a natural positive consequence of problem-solving. It is not the same phenomenon as the apex problem, whereby the person admits that a substantial improvement has occurred, but attributes it to something other than the treatment that caused it, or the person denies or minimizes the original nature or existence of the problem.[12]

After neurofeedback, many ADD/ADHD children no longer exhibit the interfering or maddening behaviors that previously characterized their lives. It is a magnificent and poignant experience to hear a parent say (with a radically different attitude than several months prior):

"Oh, I never thought he was really ADD anyway."

As perspective shifts, and as "bracket creep" shows its brighter face in the move toward normalization, we may consider several aspects of diagnosis, fit, and the appropriateness of EEG training.

Whether one has a diagnosis, or the nature of the interest is simply in reducing certain troublesome symptoms, the brain's response to EEG training will be unfettered by social labels or artificial categories. At one end of the spectrum are people for whom mental fitness means better test scores, gifted programs, outstanding musical recitals, or, at the adult level, perhaps a better golf game. The elegant name for this is "peak performance," and it is really an apt moniker for a process that describes what the brain is truly achieving. At the other end of the spectrum are

---

10   We are reminded of a colleague's definition of a double-blind study: Two pharmaceutical reps studying an EEG.

11   Dr. Roger Callahan, founder of Thought Field Therapy, quips that "a placebo is somebody else's treatment that works better than your own."

12   Also, see Chapter 4, footnote 6.

people whose functioning is so impaired that traditional medicine and society have given them little credence with respect to significant improvement, much less shedding the affixed diagnoses: Autism, aphasia, brain damage, schizophrenia, pervasive developmental disorder, Asperger's Syndrome, mental retardation, and others. Again, the brains of these individuals are unconcerned with diagnoses. Like any human brain, they respond to challenges (and, of course, they vary in responses).

As neurotherapists, we are principally concerned with the brain's response to challenges. It is our operating tool in the language of neurobiology. You might think of this in the way a chef is concerned with heat. To extend the metaphor: Food is unconcerned with the name it is assigned as a "dish." It simply responds to physical and chemical conditions according to its properties.

In the case of a musician or golfer or aspiring student, we need no diagnosis to guide the prescriptive process of challenging the brain to achieve better performance and resilience. Likewise, with autism, success is determined by how effectively we challenge that brain to improve its functioning. Fittingly, the success levels will be appropriately relative.

To harness the power of the brain through neurofeedback, we think in terms of hypotheses and diagnostic impressions, rather than fixed diagnoses. With the scientific method, inquiry is phrased in terms of structured assumptions about causal relationships known as hypotheses. Scientific "truths" are uncovered by testing hypotheses systematically. Hypotheses are formed by gathering observations and facts about events, forces, and matter, and by generating assumptions about their relationships.

In conducting an assessment, the neurotherapist gathers data and forms assumptions about what challenges a particular brain needs to improve its functioning and what computer settings and regimens are likely to achieve this. It is a very pragmatic and operational science. Let's look at some actual examples of how this works in practice:

MATTHEW

Remember Matthew, the boy presented in Chapter 2? Here is a rundown of Matthew's neurofeedback intake assessment:

History and presentation

Matthew — a nine-year-old boy with a history of ADD/ADHD symptoms and behaviors including: Restlessness/hyperactivity, poor concentration, poor follow-through, difficulty getting along with peers and teachers, fights with his brother, easily loses his temper, has difficulty following directions, trouble doing homework, and is a poor reader. He is often hard to get to bed at night (parents see this as typical of his resistant attitude), and occasionally cannot fall asleep for an hour. He is hard to awaken in the morning, and has trouble "getting going," although this is not as noticeable on weekends.

Matthew avoids reading, likes to watch TV and play video and computer games, has difficulty with handwriting (doesn't like to write), does like to draw, plays soccer. Parents describe him as "a smart kid who can be really sweet, but gets on your nerves." He has great difficulty sitting still, and doesn't seem to understand how and why his behaviors annoy others. When impressed with explanations about the effects of his behaviors, he tends to respond by pouting and indulging in self-pity, commenting about how he is "good for nothing."

Parents are reluctant to use medications; family appears tense and greatly worried and ambivalent about courses of action.

Matthew appears distracted at the interview. He has poor eye contact, and often takes several moments to re-orient to the examiner's questions. This is noticeable, as are his answers, which are tangential to the questions. Matthew seems to get lost, even in simple conversations. He asks questions that have little to do with the topic of conversation. He's fidgety, and tries to play with things in the room; he seems surprised when told not to play with certain items, and his attention keeps drawing back to them.

In a one-to-one situation with the examiner, Matthew seems more relaxed than with his mother; however, he is distractible, and seems eager to be done with each task. He has lots of questions, but they have the effect of creating disruptions rather than rapport. In response to examiner denials of repetition on certain test items, Matthew pouts. It's as if he is taking the rules as signs of personal rejection.

Test results

Matthew's TOVA shows a combination of many errors due to both inattentiveness and impulsivity. His response time standard score is at the upper end of the average range; this is higher than his other scores, indicating that he probably is too quick to respond without thinking in many situations. His significant number of omission (inattention) errors suggests an underaroused, inattentive type of ADD, possibly with attempts to compensate by bursts of overarousal. Disregulation is certainly manifest in the TOVA performance.

His scores on the Digit Span (Wechsler Intelligence Scale for Children-III) and Wide Range Assessment of Memory and Learning auditory subtests range between the fifth and the 25 percentiles. The Story Memory subtest showed better performance than the Verbal Learning and Digit Span subtests. This suggests a problem with rote listening and attention, rather than language comprehension deficits. His visual subtests are better, ranging from the 37 to the 63 percentiles. Although his visual functions appear better than his auditory functions, he scores in the mildly impaired range on both Trail Making A and Trail Making B (Halstead-Reitan Neuropsychological Battery); this indicates poor tracking and planning and impaired mental flexibility.

Matthew appears stressed by the short duration of time he is expected to remain on task. His questions about when the testing will be finished are signs of his stress and anxiety.

His sensory-perceptual exam is normal, as is his aphasia screening test. Measures from the Finger-Tapping Test and Grip Strength Test (Halstead-Reitan Neuropsychological Battery) are within normal limits, thus ruling out gross hemispheric imbalance. His Coding subtest (Wechsler Intelligence Scale for Children-III) is at the 16 percentile, and his Picture Completion subtest is at the 37 percentile. His Human Figure Drawing shows average mental development, along with some social immaturity and anxiety.

EEG baseline

Matthew's EEG shows some elevation of theta waves (these are the slower waves, often associated with daydreaming or fogginess in a waking state). His theta-beta ratio is about 3.5 to 1, and there are epochs of rhythmic excursion, particularly in the left hemisphere. These are markers for daydreaming. They are subclinical, meaning that, in all likelihood, on a medical neurological EEG, Matthew would appear entirely normal, according to standard neurology. But we know that Matthew's behavior, his cognitive processing, and, to a subtle extent, his EEG are not normal. His brain and his functioning are paying a price for these brainwave irregularities. They will most likely respond well to EEG training.

EEG Neurofeedback protocols

We prescribe a training regimen of 21 minutes of training at 15-18 Hz at site C3 on the left hemisphere, followed by nine minutes of training at 11-14 Hz at C4 on the right hemisphere.

This is based on the findings of primary underarousal, ineffectively overcompensated with bursts of overarousal and accompanied by anxiety. Matthew's overall picture is one of a boy whose brain is underaroused and

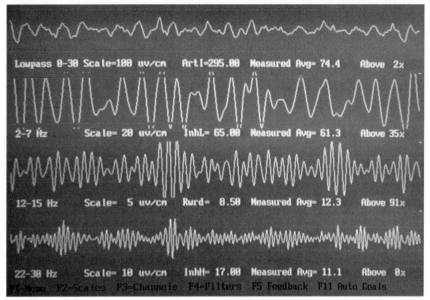

Fig. 5.3 Sample of Matthew's EEG, as seen on the therapist screen

reacts poorly to consistent and varying demands. His brain becomes stressed, overworked, and processes information inefficiently. The affective (attitudinal and emotional) components of his functioning are thought to be secondary to the underarousal and inappropriate EEG slowing, resulting in poor concentration and hemispheric communication.

Matthew will be monitored to assess his responses to this training protocol.

ELIZABETH

She is 12 years old. Her parents are at their wits' end. She has been on many medications, but nothing seems to quell her unsteady moods and eruptive outbursts. Here is the neurofeedback approach:

History and presentation

Elizabeth — 12 years old. She's taking Effexor (an antidepressant), Depakote (an anticonvulsant), and Adderall (a stimulant). Parents are desperate. Many medications and dosages have been tried. She's doing better this last week, but she was violent and was hospitalized two months ago. She went after her mother with a kitchen knife. This was unusual in its extremity — Elizabeth has never done anything like that before — but she has had angry outbursts and rages for years. Her mother wonders if puberty is contributing to this; however, there is a history of Elizabeth's acting out and mood swings for many years. Doctors have prescribed meds and recommended family therapy. She's never had an EEG – health plan wouldn't allow it.

Mother thinks the anticonvulsant has helped quiet the outbursts from what they were — reports that Elizabeth is often very tired. She can get easily excited and argumentative, but sleeps a lot, easily 10 hours a night. Elizabeth does well academically, but has poor attendance. She gets into "cat fights" with other girls. She's very stubborn and manipulative. She can be empathetic and reasonable when she's in a good mood. When she becomes angry, she's described as "fiery."

There is a history of "emotionality" on the mother's side of the family. No formal mental illness reported. Upon questioning, mother reveals that she gets anxious and moody. Father is an angry type; he feels estranged from his daughter, and expresses frustration by blaming her.

During the interview, Elizabeth feigns bored expressions, but is carefully observing the situation. She shows no concern over the severity of her condition and circumstances. When asked about the hospital, she referred to the staff as a "bunch of bozos." She looks physically mature for her age, but carries herself like a child.

Elizabeth emits loud sighs, as if she is nonchalantly bored; however, these expressions reveal significant anxiety. When questioned, she admits to feeling "tired all the time" and hates taking meds. We align on the goal of trying neurofeedback to "give her more energy" and, possibly, to reduce her meds.

Test results

Elizabeth's TOVA is normal, but, notably, the variability score is low-average. Possibly, this TOVA is better than it would be without meds. In any case, attention (as in the ability to focus on demand) does not seem the predominant issue, although the lower variability score is suspect. In this case, the TOVA is not as instructive as we might hope. Her complicated history suggests that Elizabeth is suffering from nervous system instability coupled with a syndrome of emotionality and behavior typically diagnosed as a mood disorder.

Elizabeth performs normally on both Trail Making A and Trail Making B (Halstead-Reitan Neuropsychological Battery), although she starts exclaiming frustration as she does Trail Making B. This raises the hypothesis that, when she has to change mental set or become flexible, it strains and taxes her. Ambivalence and ambiguity may be vulnerabilities that push her over the edge.

Modified Rorschach assessment shows that ambiguity and reality-testing are problems for Elizabeth. She has trouble interpreting the messages from others and their intents. Given this problem and her predisposition to instability, it is no wonder that she overreacts. Medications seem to apply a temporary damper.

Her memory and modality scores (visual and auditory processing) are average. Her neuropsychological screening measures are normal. She seems to warm up slightly during the one-to-one assessment, though she offers comments meant to provoke reaction ("I think most teachers and parents are sick!")

EEG baseline

Elizabeth's EEG is unremarkable. Though our EEG baseline is not a medical clinical study, we know better than to expect a "signature" in the EEG for diagnosing specific disorders. The amplitudes of her EEG are somewhat low; this could just be a characteristic of her neurophysiology.

She is taking some heavy-duty medications. It is unclear whether they are changing her brainwaves. Regardless, we will be able to use the EEG neurofeedback to modify her functioning through operantly training her EEG.

Her symptomatology and history strongly suggest that she get a medical EEG study. We are going to recommend a Quantitative EEG (QEEG) to rule out seizure activity and to assist with developing and testing hypotheses about how best to help Elizabeth.

EEG Neurofeedback protocols

We prescribe a training regimen of 30 minutes of inter-hemispheric training at 9-12 Hz at sites T3 minus T4. This protocol is often helpful in stabilizing the brain, and can be instrumental in relieving mood instabilities and emotional lability. Elizabeth's profile of mood swings, acting out, emotional impropriety, and normal cognitive processing suggest that her problem is more a disregulation of emotion than one of executive function (the ability of the brain to pay attention and maintain focus and vigilance). Elizabeth is disregulated and displays many of the classic ADD symptoms, but her brain stability and balance calls for a slightly different approach.

We expect a person with Elizabeth's particulars to respond very rapidly to neurofeedback. We will probably see some improvement in her mood and attitude within one to three sessions. If not, we will adjust the protocol. People like Elizabeth are typically quite sensitive; this usually reflects in rapid response to neurofeedback.

We have to be aware that medication effects may obscure neurofeedback effects. Therefore, we remind her parents to keep us apprised of medication dosages and changes. We will monitor Elizabeth, and advise her parents to let her physician know about the neurofeedback treatment. We encourage the communication with her physician, and are hopeful that less medication may be imminent.

The QEEG study will help confirm or reject hypotheses about the causes and correlates of Elizabeth's rages. One of our hypotheses is that she may have temporal lobe or cingulate gyrus disturbance. These can result in episodic rages.

We consider an alternate or follow-up protocol of training at 8-11 Hz at site FZ on the fronto-central cortex. This protocol tends to reduce anger in people with Elizabeth's profile.

JOHN

This adolescent was referred because of intractable surliness and "attitude" problems. He has been diagnosed with ADD/ADHD, took Ritalin previously, is a discipline problem at school and at home, and is barely on speaking terms with his father.

History and presentation

John will be 16 years old in two months. He has been suspended from school for the second time this year. He has a history of conduct problems and "pranks" showing questionable judgment. He is described as "often mean and uncaring." His father described John as having "a heart that wants gold" — he only looks at life for what's in it for John. Ritalin was tried for 2 years in elementary school — no significant differences except it was easier for John to do homework. His parents stopped Ritalin after John complained and the dosages were continually climbing.

The parents are concerned about John's choices of friends and activities. He was tested and found to be very bright (IQ of 122) with no learning handicaps. He's often been accused of taking the shortcut approach to life. He likes aggressive and violent movies. He's not interested in sports. He likes girls, but puts them down. (Parents think he's sensitive to rejection.) John will not back down from his father. Threats and discipline make him worse; he collects grudges.

John has a serious case of "righteous indignation" — he thinks the world is unfair to him. Many injustices are perpetrated against him.

People are truly sick of his crafty manipulations and stories, which always portray him as the innocent, hapless victim. John displays guile in equal proportion to his intellect, which is substantial. If he has empathy, it is hidden where no one can find it.

John gets headaches several times a week. This was more of a problem when he was younger. Now, he minimizes the headaches, preferring to appear tough and independent. He challenges the examiner, and he appears to be showing off. John will not admit to having problems. He claims to be at the neurotherapy office only to appease his "uptight" father. John's manner is disdainful. He appears to move with occasional jerkiness. He sleeps fitfully, often thrashing around in his sleep. He complains about the noise in the house when he is trying to sleep. He is sloppy, and seems unaware of how he steps on other people's toes. He complains about the slovenly, disgusting habits of family members. This leaves his family aghast at his obliviousness.

John had night terrors when he was younger. He also wet his bed until age six.

Test results

John's TOVA shows classic overarousal: Normal Omissions (inattention) score, very fast Response Time, moderate Variability, and a terrible Commissions score (elevated impulsivity).

Additionally, subtests from the Wechsler Intelligence Scale for Children-III confirmed John's high intelligence. His scores ranged from the 91 to the 98 percentiles. Though his Trail Making A and Trail Making B (Halstead-Reitan Neuropsychological Battery) performances were normal, John did reveal something striking on the Halstead-Reitan Finger-Tapping Test and Grip Strength Test: John's right-handed finger-tapping exceeded his left-handed tapping by 63 percent. His right-handed grip strength exceeded his left-handed strength by 14 kg.

The hemispheres are contra-laterally wired to the motor systems of the left and right sides of the body; thus, the left hemisphere controls the right side of the body and vice-versa. John's significantly worse performance with his left hand indicates a weak right hemisphere. The magnitude of the right-left differences highlights a deficit in right cerebral functioning.

These results are consistent with John's impulsive, fast TOVA, his nighttime restlessness, and his lack of empathy, and his stark defensiveness. These are hallmarks of an overaroused nervous system and right hemispheric impairment.

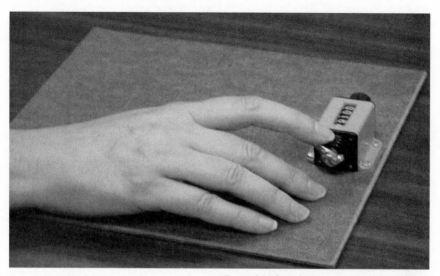

Fig. 5.4 Halstead-Reitan Finger-Tapping Test

John's "ADD" qualities would be seen in his restless motor activity, his thrill-seeking and tendency toward disruptiveness, and his lack of awareness and sensitivity to the needs of others. John is at serious risk for substance abuse, violations of societal and legal standards, and further antisocial infringements. His type of disregulation is likely to manifest in the absence of affection (or warped transformations of it, such as domination or stalking). Because of his nervous system vulnerabilities, he is prone to vengeful and spiteful retaliations that would undoubtedly impair his relationships and his work.

EEG baseline

John's EEG shows inconsistency in the right hemisphere. There are spindle bursts of mid-range activity alternating with drops in amplitude over the same region. We observe subtle occasional slowing, particularly on the right side.

EEG Neurofeedback protocols

This profile calls for right side training at lower frequencies in order to calm down an overactivated right hemisphere. There is an irritated quality to John's nervous system and EEG (as well as his personality) which tends to respond well to neurofeedback training of the right hemisphere.

We set a training protocol of 30 minutes of 10-13 Hz at site C4 over the right central cortex.

John is the type of client who reluctantly goes along with the training either from a self-aggrandizing generosity in which he "humors" his parents in this misguided attempt to rid him of problems he's sure he does not have, or because of some restriction contingent upon his compliance.

We will look carefully to observe any "softening" in his manner, any lessening in his brittle blaming and self-justification, any changes in his headaches or sleep patterns, and changes in his TOVA performance after about 20 neurofeedback sessions. (We would expect better Impulsivity and reduced Response Time scores.)

Along the way, we will talk with his parents and gather data by obtaining, tabulating, and evaluating rating scales completed at each session by his parents. After about 20 EEG training sessions, we will re-administer the TOVA and gather any other pertinent information for a review consultation with the parents.

Here is one example of a rating scale we use formatively to monitor progress:

STATUS LOG

Name:_____Date:_____

Behaviors rated by: _____

Rate each item as it has seemed in the last 24 hours on a scale from 1 through 10:

    1 = No problem; not an issue or not needing improvement

    10 = Very poor or having great difficulties

CONCENTRATION			TENSION / ANXIETY	
ENERGY LEVEL			PHYSICAL COMPLAINTS	
MOOD			IRRITABILITY	
GENERAL PERFORMANCE			SELF-ESTEEM	
ATTENTION-SEEKING			DIET	
FRUSTRATION TOLERANCE			DIGESTION / STOMACH	
ORGANIZATION			RESTLESSNESS	
MEMORY			COMPULSIVE HABITS	
WITHDRAWAL / AVOIDANCE			COOPERATIVENESS	
GENERAL ATTITUDE			WORRIES / FEARS	
SOCIABILITY			ANGER / TEMPER	
SATISFACTION			HEADACHES	
INAPPROPRIATE BEHAVIORS			SLEEP	
DISTRACTIBILITY			NEGATIVE REACTIONS	
MENTAL PREOCCUPATIONS			PROCRASTINATION	
COMMUNICATIONS			SENSITIVITY	
EXPRESSIVENESS			TASK ACCOMPLISHMENT	

SUMMARY OF NEUROFEEDBACK ASSESSMENT

We outlined a prototypical EEG neurofeedback assessment, and gave three case examples of how the assessment translates into prescriptive training protocols for neurofeedback treatment. Naturally, the clinical acumen of the therapist and experience administering neurofeedback play significant roles in the determination and evaluation of treatment.

Hopefully, this glimpse into the assessment process and the manner in which it incorporates our model of brain regulation helps to understand how your child can get better. To summarize, the following ingredients combine for happy outcomes a high percentage of the time.

1. Competent analysis of the client's presenting situation, including history and symptoms, observations, direct assessment of brain function through performance and EEG measures, notation of medical status, significant experiences, and responses to other interventions.
2. Selection of training protocols based on the factors listed above, clinical experience, and reference to the disregulation model of brain function and a decision-tree methodology.
3. Adequate practice through EEG brain-training on a regular schedule.
4. Monitoring and follow-up by the therapist to track client progress, incorporate new information, and make adjustments to the training regimen, as necessary.

Bear in mind: Twenty hours of training isn't a solution to all of life's problems, but it brings most ADD/ADHD under control. Twenty hours is about the amount of time most children spend in three days at school. As a colleague wryly quipped:

"A mind is a terrible thing to waste, but a wonderful thing to (EEG) paste."

Although we can accomplish meaningful assessment for neurofeedback in a brief amount of time, there are a number of purposes for assessment and a number of levels of assessment, both in theory and in practice. A brief review of these may help you further understand the benefits for you and your child.

LEVELS OF ASSESSMENT

It is understandable that tests are intimidating to many people. Perhaps our culture and our professional community have erred in the interpretation and meaning often assigned to tests, as well as the agendas they have served. Regrettably, tests are sometimes used to exclude people or to weed out some from opportunities for which they are deemed unfit.

When used appropriately and diagnostically, tests can save time, pinpoint areas of need, and greatly guide diagnosis, description, and meaningful interventions and recommendations. One of us authors (Dr. Steinberg) has used tests strategically and invaluably for 28 years in providing assistance to children and adults.

However, most of the public and much of the professional community misunderstands or misjudges fundamental elements and principles of testing and assessment.[13] Unfortunately, the competitive applications of testing have obscured the broader scientific bases for the measurement of individual differences.

Most testing (and the general perception of testing) is based on an expectation and familiarity with a mode known as *level of performance*. Though level of performance is only one facet of assessment, it is the aspect most people recognize. Let's review the larger picture:

1. Level of Performance

Level of performance testing encompasses how well the subject (examinee) does. This is measured either in reference to a similar population (group of children the same age, for example) or to a criterion standard (e.g., number of words spelled correctly). The vast majority of tests yield information only in the level of performance domain. Norm-referenced, criterion-referenced, and mastery-referenced scoring systems all compare performance levels, though how they compare them varies. This information is basic and useful because it assesses competencies and shows them in reference to known or assumed standards.

Intelligence tests, academic tests, and personality tests reveal information about how a person performs relative to the performance of others. You can think of level of performance as measuring the height, for instance, of all fourth-graders, or measuring how many push-ups each child does, or reading levels of all the students. One could then rank order the scores and judge a particular child's demonstrated competency or position within the group.

What this information does not reveal is whether the performance shows abnormalities or anomalies with respect to the individual's own self. For this, we need to use other neuropsychological techniques.

2. Occurrence of Specific Deficits (Pathognomonic Signs)

Pathognomonic sign testing is concerned with errors and performance deviations that occur almost exclusively among certain populations. For

---

13 Tests, also known as instruments, refer to specific scales, challenge tasks, or measures. Assessment is the overall process of gathering information, interpreting data, and reaching conclusions and judgments.

example, as a medical analog, consider tuberculosis or AIDS. Although the blood and skin of people differ, positive markers for AIDS or tuberculosis would only be expected to occur in people carrying these diseases. In a population comprising people with and without these diseases, we could gather lots of measurements across which people with and without the diseases would differ. However, specific signs would distinguish the people with tuberculosis or AIDS because these signs do not occur in others.

Pregnancy is another example. Though it is not a pathological condition, pregnancy is a good example of the principle of pathognomonic sign testing. You (women only, please) can be a little or a lot pregnant, but as far as pregnancy testing goes, the main consideration is whether you are or are not pregnant. Only pregnant women have certain blood and urine characteristics.

Let's take this a step further with regard to behavior. Would you ever expect to drive into your neighbor's driveway, thinking it's your own? Or put your key into your neighbor's door lock, mistaking it for your own apartment? Or confuse a sink with a toilet? Hardly. These silly examples give a sense of the breach represented by specific deficits. In neuropsychological testing, the breach occurrences are subtler, but they are highly significant.

3. Patterns and Relationships Among Test Scores

As Mark Twain once said, "There are liars, damn liars, and statisticians."

Test scores alone can be misinterpreted. A scientific guard against this is the clinical and mathematical analysis of combinations of scores and patterns and relationships among the sores and performances. The old saw — *where there's smoke, there's fire* — must be subjected to the rigorous scrutiny of comparing performance variability with known profiles of deviations in brain function.

Does the subject show striking variability in scores on different tests that fits a pattern with regard to the known functions of the two cerebral hemispheres or areas within the cerebral hemispheres?

An example: Two children the same age can have Full Scale IQ scores of 98. These are average IQ scores. However, our two children may be far from the same or even similar. Child A might have a Verbal IQ of 98 and a Performance (nonverbal) IQ of 99. His "scatter" or variability among the subtest scores could be minimal — no conspicuous weaknesses, strengths in moderation and balance. Child B could have a Verbal IQ of 78 and a Performance (nonverbal) IQ of 123 with variability ranging between the fifth and the 98th percentiles. Child B would probably have significant language learning and academic problems along with superior abilities at nonverbal learning. Such a child would undoubtedly excel at spatial and mechanical tasks, but would struggle with the codes of language that suffuse reading, spelling, writing, and listening. Neurofeedback for this child would likely include a lot of high-frequency left hemisphere training.

All composite IQs are not the same. Patterns and relationships among scores are critical in properly assessing brain function.

4. Differences in the Adequacy of Motor and Sensory-Perceptual Functions on Two Sides of the Body

Neurotherapists and/or neuropsychologists are very interested in the integrity of and relationship between the two hemispheres. Are they different in the way they function? Do they work together to enhance performance? Are there specific deficits in either hemisphere that are correlated with compromised performance?

In neuropsychology, such findings are known as *lateralization* — disparities between left and right sides of the brain that go beyond expected limits for subjects with normal brain functions.

When administered properly, even brief screenings contribute valuable information about your child's neuropsychological makeup that can guide neurotherapy, indicate deficits needing further attention, and provide predictive information on treatment length and outcomes. The process is complex, however. As wonderful and malleable as the brain is, we need to give it adequate information. Part of the sequence is to gather relevant information in a methodical and translatable manner. That is the essence of assessment.

INTEGRATING ASSESSMENT APPROACHES

We recapitulate by stating that assessment has purposes beyond labeling and diagnosing. Comprehensive assessment uses a scientific methodology that compares thousands of data points to "rule out" competing hypotheses that would account for the same sets of data. The job of the examiner is to guide you and your child through this process and unravel information that can alert you to difficulties and help you achieve defined goals.

The mental fitness model we have defined uses assessment to individually tailor powerful tools like neurotherapy. Assessment can guide, supplant, or support a variety of decisions and interventions besides neurofeedback.

The neuropsychological model draws upon theory and methodology of testing and interpreting brain function. In-depth understanding requires going beyond a simple level of performance assessment. But, what about practical applications? We need some "outside the skull" guidelines.

What Should a Competent Comprehensive Assessment Include?

Have the assessment done by someone appropriately trained and licensed (preferably with a doctoral degree). Assessment is a clinical process, and should investigate all areas of development relevant to your child's functioning or suspected difficulties. Tests, observations, records, and interviews are tools — but there is no substitute for experienced clinical judgment. When a child manifests symptoms of significant under-achievement or maladjustment, a differential diagnosis is necessary to pinpoint the source of the problem. Proper assessment (just like medical diagnosis) uses scientific techniques to "rule out" different disorders or conditions that present similar symptoms.

The comprehensive assessment process (one that goes beyond the neurofeedback intake assessment) should include a consultation with you, a written report of the results, and specific recommendations for implementation in your child's learning and home environments. Don't settle for some test scores you don't understand plus a statement about whether or not your child qualifies for special services. Look for the following information in your child's assessment:

- Intellectual capacity for school.

- An equating of school achievement with intellectual potentials.

- An alert to reading, spelling, arithmetic, listening, language, memory, or writing problems.

- Measurement of perceptual-motor capacity.

- Discovery of dominant learning modality — auditory, visual-spatial, kinesthetic, mixed.

- Determination of developmental grade level and discrepancies in standard score terms.

- Insight into cognitive style — convergent and divergent.

- Assessment of factors affecting development, family/peer adjust ment, and school performance — self-esteem, motivation, anxiety, depression, anger, and other emotional indicators.

- An alert to developing attitude problems and contribution of stressors.

- Identification of temperament, interpersonal strengths and weaknesses, and influences on learning.

This kind of comprehensive assessment takes longer than a neurofeedback intake assessment. It usually requires between five and ten hours. Besides the individual testing, this time includes scoring and interpreting, interviews and observations, reviewing records and history, and time spent consulting with you at the beginning and after the testing. It may or may not include writing reports, which can be time-consuming and add cost. Expect to pay for all aspects of the assessment process at the professional's hourly rate.

After the assessment is completed, you may want to apprise your child's educators of the results and how they influence your child's learning, development, and achievement. Getting school staff to implement the results and recommendations can be tricky, but advocating for your child is a major role you can play in modeling responsibility and ensuring a suitable environment for growth.

GENERAL ASSESSMENT MODEL

The following assessment model encapsulates an overview of assessment, and may assist you in appreciating its value:

ASSESSMENT MODEL

The following notations describe the components of comprehensive assessment from the perspectives of diagnostic methodology and categorical information yielded as an outcome of assessment:

- Levels of performance
  - compares and quantifies
  - *inter-individual* — compares performances with those of others
  - measures functioning in relation to others at same age or grade level

- Clinical / descriptive
  - identifies preferred styles of learning, behaving, perceiving
  - *intra-individual* — compares strengths and weaknesses shown by examinee
  - identifies indicators of distress and potential or manifest disturbance

- Achievement / mastery
  - specifies what the person knows or can do (knowledge, skills, performance)
  - assesses achievement of developmental milestones and readiness for learning
  - criterion-related (relative to task mastery rather than relative to performances of others)

- Differential diagnostic
  - process of *ruling out* possible disorders
  - uses scientific methodology of hypothesis testing
  - tests for presence of specific deficits which differentiate conditions
  - identifies factors which sustain or hinder performance
  - interprets why some performances are elevated and others reduced

- Predictive / prescriptive
  - prescribes recommendations, interventions, treatments
  - offers prognoses, expectations
  - predicts probable outcomes with or without interventions

ASSESSMENT MATRIX

	1	2	3
Abilities	1	2	3
Strengths	4	5	6
Weaknesses	7	8	9
Styles	10	11	12
	Coping/Inhibiting	*Applicative/Stunted*	*Adaptive/Maladaptive*

1. Do the identified abilities integrate in the person's coping mechanisms or do they interfere?

2. Is the person able to apply his abilities to everyday demands and real tasks?

3. Are the abilities used toward adaptive or maladaptive results?

4. Are the strengths properly channeled or overextended?

5. Are the strengths advantageous in accomplishing practical tasks at levels commensurate with abilities?

6. Do the strengths attain adaptive purposes or do they result in manipulation and self-sabotage?

7. To what extend do the weaknesses predominate? Do they exert balancing or humbling effects?

8. Does the person try to use skills beyond what he has in those areas?

9. Are the weaknesses and vulnerabilities controlled and compensated?

10. Do the problem-solving styles provide advantage or do they get in the way?

11. Are the styles efficient and well-matched to the challenges, or are they ill-suited?

12. Do the habits, talents, idiosyncrasies, and processing mechanisms facilitate adaptive functioning?

QUANTITATIVE EEG ASSESSMENT

One other dimension we can add to the assessment picture involves a medical study of the brain's electrical physiological patterns. This is called a Quantitative EEG (QEEG), also known as a "Q" or a "brain map."

QEEG studies typically include a conventional waking EEG (like the EEGs administered by some neurologists or at hospitals) and a quantitative EEG. The same data are used for both analyses. The painless procedure takes under an hour, and some neurotherapists do these procedures themselves. Others refer out or have a technician run the test and then send the data to a lab, where they are read and interpreted by a neurologist, a neuropsychologist, and other EEG specialists.

The output from a QEEG is typically a report of the conventional EEG reading, the QEEG reading, colorful graphics displaying the electrical distributions within the areas of the brain (thus, the "map") tabular data highlighting significant correlations, and a narrative interpretation.

The conventional EEG is helpful in ruling out or determining the presence of disease processes (pathology). Seizure activity (epilepsy, convulsions), brain lesions, tumors, hemorrhages, or cerebral irritability can be detected this way. The conventional EEG is read by the trained eyes of professionals who study the morphology (shape) of raw EEG waveforms that are either normal or consistent with pathology.

However, many professionals believe that the EEG reveals much more useful information than merely that which confirms disease. In order to make sense of this information (much of which involves multiple simultaneous comparisons which cannot be done with the naked eye), computers analyze the data — thus, the Quantitative EEG. The advantage of this technique is that the brain's electrical activity and patterns can be analyzed even between and among areas where the 19 scalp electrodes are not connected. Quantitative analysis helps uncover subtle patterns of brainwave distribution where there are no easy visual correlates.

QEEGs can be very helpful in the following ways:

1. Comparing intra-hemispheric and inter-hemispheric electrical patterns and differences.

2. Providing information about the brain's organization, particularly with regard to rigidity (under-utilization) or chaotic disorganization.

3. Documenting medical evidence of impairment.[14]

---

14   One of the authors, Dr. Steinberg, has provided expert witness testimony in litigations where the QEEG was used to document head injury.

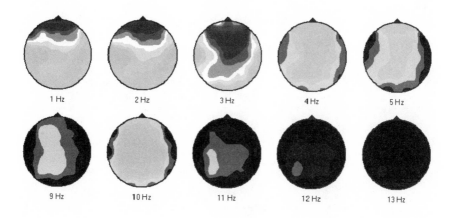

Fig. 5.5 Section of a Quantitative EEG (QEEG) brain map display

4. Identifying brainwave patterns that typify certain ADD/ADHD syndromes and may predict successful responses to particular medications and/or neurofeedback protocols.[15]

5. Generating hypotheses about neurofeedback protocols that could be effective with particular EEG profiles.

Some practitioners rely extensively on QEEGs. Some even use the QEEG as the exclusive basis for directing EEG neurofeedback — a practice which we cannot endorse.

While the QEEG can provide valuable documentation, help to provide insight in decision-making, and serve as a grounding or reality check on the neurotherapist's impressions, it cannot replace the global decision-making based on clinical acumen, history, neuropsychological assessment, and the patient's responses in the real world.

The QEEG is a snapshot in time of the brain's electrophysiological functioning. It is usually a very good one. However, once again, perspective is important. It would be hard to tailor a suit for someone based on only a snapshot of that person. You might need multiple fittings and adjustments. In the final analysis, it might technically "fit," but still be apparel that simply didn't feel or appear good to wear.

---

15   See the article by Suffin and Emory — Suffin, S.C., & Emory, W. Hamlin. (1995). "Neurometric Subgroups in Attentional and Affective Disorders and the Association with Pharmacologic Outcome." *Clinical Encephalography*, 26, 76-83.

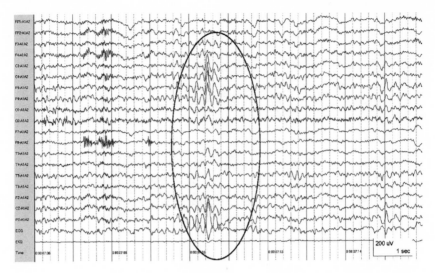

Figure 5.6 Quantitative EEG (QEEG) multichannel tracings

Accessing Resources and Making It Happen

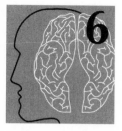

FINDING AND SELECTING A NEUROTHERAPIST

For many people, finding the right health care professional can be a difficult endeavor, shadowed by self-doubt about making the right decision, fraught with anxiety about the unknown, or complicated by a lack of understanding and information (or, sometimes, by too much information). Some parents may be determined to pursue EEG training, only to face long distances between their homes and the nearest suitable provider. Others may live in a metropolitan area with numerous providers. For many parents, the decision is simplified by a referral or recommendation from someone they trust — a doctor or therapist, teacher, or a parent whose child improved greatly through the treatment.

Recommendations from satisfied parents are excellent and confidence-inspiring leads to successful neurotherapy. Besides the natural kinship and identification with those who have "walked in your shoes," parents who have tried neurofeedback can give you tips about their journey and the beneficial decisions and mistakes they have made. Veteran parents are likely to have waded through the doubts and misgivings of those opinionated professionals who cast doubt on neurotherapy (despite their conspicuous dearth of knowledge about it!).

As the practice and benefits of neurotherapy become widely known and accepted, more and more medical professionals are considering and recommending it. Grass roots word-of-mouth, however, remains a valuable inroad to finding and selecting a neurotherapist for your child.

In writing this book, we are, of course, dedicated toward that end. We have compiled a list of neurofeedback professionals throughout the United States and internationally (see Appendix C). Those listed in this book have successfully completed training offered by EEG Spectrum International or EEG Institute. Many of these professionals have trained with both organizations.[16] Many (but not all) of those who trained enlist with one or both of these organizations as affiliates, participating in ongoing training and internet professional list group discussions and consultations to improve upon individual and collective professional experience.

---

16 Dr. Siegfried Othmer founded EEG Spectrum and taught their courses for many years. He then founded EEG Institute, through which he now offers training.

By the time you are reading this book, the number of trained professionals offering neurotherapy will have multiplied. You can augment the resources listed here by visiting the websites of:

EEG Institute (www.eeginstitute.com),

EEG Spectrum International (www.eegspectrum.com), and

EEG Directory[17] (www.eegdirectory.com).

Once you've found one or several potential neurotherapists, you may want to consider the variables most important to you in entrusting your child to such a professional. (After all, we are talking about working with your child's brain!) We suggest you review the discussion in Chapter 4 about procedures, expectations, and questions you may want to ask a prospective therapist. In addition, the material in Chapter 5 on assessment and monitoring may be valuable in guiding the selection of an appropriate professional, depending upon the individual needs of children and their parents.

We wish to emphasize the dual components that make neurotherapy so inviting and so powerful:

A. Neurofeedback is reliable and robust enough that people from many backgrounds (parents, too!) can successfully administer it to the benefit of children (and adults). Its effects have been well established and replicated many thousands of times; therefore, to a great extent, successful neurotherapy is a *likely* outcome, even with wide variation in experience and technique.

B. As you might expect — and, as happens in so many fields — technique, training, and experience do matter; in some cases, they make all the difference. Though the actual effects of neurofeedback grow from the natural abilities of your child's brain to learn and to regulate itself when given appropriate information, there are important variables that can influence your decisions, your confidence, follow-through, and the overall efficacy and thoroughness of the treatment. The matters of comfort, confidence, respect, and communication between the therapist and you and your child can determine how much you and your child derive from neurotherapy.

Your search and selection for a neurotherapist may depend on particular criteria important to you — perhaps credentials, experience with a particular condition, insurance coverage, etc. We wish to facilitate your success and satisfaction by providing a list of resources (Appendix C) and guidelines for making a choice you will savor.

---

17   Kurt Othmer, son of Siegfried and Sue Othmer and brother of Brian Othmer, featured in Chapter 9, wrote the epilogue to this book. Kurt founded and operates EEG Directory.

As you seek a provider, bear in mind the three salient factors we anticipate will determine whether the neurofeedback experience is likely to be a good one for you and your child:

1. Training and experience in neurotherapy — where has the therapist trained, how long has he/she practiced neurotherapy, and how does he/she keep up with developments and advances in the field?

2. Therapist training and experience overall — what are the credentials and training of the therapist besides the field of neurotherapy? Education, kinds and amounts of experience, and what types of clients and problems the therapist has worked with all count toward the likelihood of a good outcome. Some therapists specialize in certain disorders, while others treat a wider variety of problems. The important factor is whether the therapist has been successful with people, using the modes and methodologies he/she has employed.

3. Your comfort level with the therapist — the personality, office location, ambience, and décor, and the manner of the therapist will not determine the effectiveness of neurofeedback for your child. However, these factors may determine your willingness to openly share, confront, and continue with the therapist and the process. After all, the therapist is working with your child's brain, and your commitment will be to follow through for multiple visits.

You are likely to find a wide variation in credentials, disciplines, and experience among neurotherapists. We believe this to be fortuitous, and we are not convinced that any particular specialty makes for a more effective therapist. Skilled counselors, nurses, or teachers are often great neurotherapists, even though they are lower on the professional pecking order than medical doctors (and, there are an increasing number of medical doctors including neurotherapy in their practices, too.) By asserting this, we are neither patronizing particular specialties, nor minimizing the value of specialized training, schooling, and expertise. We simply see that the effectiveness of neurofeedback stands on its own merits as a robust and replicable treatment. All of the other rules about professional care and competent and appropriate relationships between therapist and clients still apply.

Some of the key elements of an effective therapeutic relationship to facilitate neurofeedback have been outlined in Chapter 4, along with questions you might ask of the prospective therapist.

We will summarize this section by suggesting steps for finding a suitable neurotherapist for your situation.

1. Review the material in this chapter and in Chapter 4. Use what you deem relevant in guiding your search and decision process.

2. Locate one or more neurotherapists within driving distance from your home or office. Remember that you will be making the trek at least two times per week; that is part of your commitment, but be realistic.

3. Ask about office hours. Most neurotherapists have evening hours. Some work on weekends.

4. Decide how important credentials are to you, and factor that in with other variables ahead of time. Credentials often make a difference in third-party (insurance) reimbursement.

5. When you speak with your physician, ask what he/she *knows* about neurofeedback, not what he/she *thinks*. You can ask your physician for a recommendation or referral, but be prepared to come up empty. You might even get a lecture trying to deter you from trying EEG biofeedback. If this happens, have sympathy for your doctor, but stand your ground. Tell the physician that you are determined to follow through, even without his/her support, which you would like. Ask the physician if he/she would be willing to work with your neurofeedback provider (especially where medication is already prescribed), and whether he/she would be interested in the results of your experience with neurotherapy. Depending upon the physician's response, you will either forge a better relationship and increase your doctor's breadth of understanding — or you may find another physician.

6. Get recommendations from people whose children have experienced neurofeedback. Ask at school, ask at parent groups, ask at church or synagogue.

7. If your child (or other family member) visits a psychotherapist or speech therapist or educational therapist, these may be good resources to locate a neurotherapist.

8. Visit the following websites:

   www.eeginstitute.com
   (EEG Institute and the Brian Othmer Foundation)

www.eegspectrum.com
(EEG Spectrum International)

www.eegdirectory.com
(EEG Directory)

www.aapb.org
(Association for Applied Psychophysiology and Biofeedback)

www.futurehealth.org
(FutureHealth)

www.snr-jnt.org
(International Society for Neuronal Regulation)

ARRANGING A SUITABLE TRAINING PROGRAM
AND SCHEDULE

The "20-hour solution" does not necessarily mean exactly 20 hours, nor does it imply that you won't see very pleasing benefits in two hours. It takes about 40 half-hour sessions (hence, 20 hours) to equip most ADD children with the self-generating mechanisms they need to function much, much better, minimize and control the deleterious aspects of ADD, and orient themselves on a significantly improved course of development.

As with antibiotics, this treatment will work regardless of your beliefs and attitudes — but, you have to follow through with the treatment. Consider the antibiotic analogy: The usual recommendation is to take the medicine every day in the prescribed dosages for two weeks. You will probably start feeling better in a few days, but it's important to take the medicine for the prescribed course. This holds true for neurofeedback. Some children will show improvement almost immediately. Some will take many sessions.

Stay the course for the long haul. Most neurotherapists will echo our guidelines. Many therapists have 40-session programs. It's not a prevalent requirement that you sign up for 40 sessions. Most therapists charge by the session (usually offering discounts for pre-payment of groups of sessions), and are willing to work with you session by session. However, the keys to success are commitment and consistency. Toward this end, you should establish a training schedule anticipating at least 20 — but probably 40 — sessions on at least a semiweekly (twice per week) basis.

A common question is: "Does it matter how many times per week?" In our collective experience,[18] the answer is that a minimum of two times

---

18 Over 300,000 sessions.

per week is sufficient. This appears to be more critical at the beginning of training. Think of it this way: If you were to embark on a physical exercise program from a sedentary baseline, how might your body respond to one day a month at the gym? Hardly enough to get the momentum going, wouldn't you agree? It's the same with exercising the brain. The brain needs consistency and practice. Two 30-minute sessions per week is enough, even for relatively inefficient brains at the outset.

Here's a most interesting (and fortunate) observation, gleaned from the results of hundreds of practitioners treating thousands of patients: The overall benefits for each individual child share a collective commonality — the number of sessions overrides the frequency of sessions as a principal factor determining outcomes.[19] This finding is astounding for two reasons:

1. It attests to the robustness of the EEG training. The treatment works under a variety of conditions and across a range of symptoms and severity.

2. From a practical standpoint, this allows for greater flexibility in planning and pacing treatment.

Though it's probably not efficient to start with two sessions, go on vacation for three weeks, and then resume training (better to start with regularity of at least twice per week), the evidence is that successful treatment accrues from a wide variety of training schedules, the key component being a minimum of twice-per-week training, especially for the first 20 sessions.

We have found that, for the vast majority of children, training at the rate of four sessions per week produces about the same results as training at the rate of two sessions per week — but four sessions per week brings the results in half the calendar time!

Due to expediency or necessity, some families engage in a training regimen known as massed practice. This is where the family travels to the provider's location and the client trains every day (up to three sessions per day) for several weeks. Obviously, this requires a significant commitment, if only for a relatively short period of time. For some families, however, this is the most practical (or only) way to obtain neurofeedback.[20]

The brain's capacity to accommodate this type of schedule — to store up, in essence, the subroutines of learning and operate them systematically as new functional cerebral and behavioral patterns independently —

---

19 This presumes appropriate training protocols and monitoring with results commensurate with individual differences, degrees of impairment, and baseline functioning.

20 Dr. Steinberg has trained quite a few international clients, notably from South America, Korea, Singapore, and the Philippines. The Othmers have trained many out-of-towners from around the US and from Europe and Australia. Both Dr. Steinberg and Sue Othmer supervise remote clients who began their training locally and have rented or purchased home units.

is a scientific discovery of immense impact. It is also a pragmatic bonanza, for it allows great flexibility and accessibility of the training.

MAKING TIME DURING THE DAY TO ACCOMMODATE TRAINING

Whether you travel to engage in an intensive massed practice regimen or you participate in the more typical twice-or-more weekly neurofeedback schedule, you must allow time for the training and give your child the chance to learn under the most optimal conditions available.

Although this seems obvious, the pressures and demands of daily life intrude on even the most responsible and well-meaning parents. Neurofeedback is not a simple as popping pills, but it is far safer and more effective in the long run. However, you have to pay its dues; this includes, especially, time in your busy week.

Here are some tips (both practical and philosophical) to make the accommodations easier:

1. **Plan your commitment** — For most families, two or three times a week for several months will be the most likely and practical venue. Although each session typically involves only 30 minutes on the instrument, travel time (depending upon your situation) can make each session a several-hour imposition. Long distances in rural areas require determination and persistence, but so do grueling commutes on crowded urban roadways. Your child may have to temporarily sacrifice some extracurricular activities in order to make time for neurofeedback. This is temporary, but may be necessary in order not to over-schedule.

2. **Anticipate stressors and work around them** — Long commutes, hungry children, homework, housework, dinner, maddening traffic, delays, anxiety about tardiness — these are all routine visitors, leaving footprints of stress in their wake. It's not that we can avoid them entirely; but expecting some intrusions and setbacks and planning responses to them will minimize their impact. Anticipating these events and rehearsing your responses to them can minimize frustration and help you carry out intentions even in the face of unforeseen obstacles. Make sure your child is fed, so that forays to neurotherapy do not become starvation trips. Allow enough time to arrive early for your appointment. Bring activities for yourself and/or your other children to do during the session while you wait. Arrange dinner ahead of time, and make it easier on yourself those nights when neurotherapy sessions will

bring you home late, with less time and energy in your evening. This is old advice, but it bears repeating with a special emphasis: This is not only a sacrifice for your child, but a special commitment to create space in his/her life to learn to relax and offset stress. Help by being a good model. Show your respect and esteem for the treatment (and for your child) by reserving time and energy so that you and your family will not be at the end of your ropes.

3. **Keep your child well-rested** — It is scientifically proven that people learn better when they are less fatigued. Indeed, on a micro level, the whole neurotherapy process is about conditioning the brain to rest regularly and integrally in its ongoing and momentary activities. On a macro level, you can institute conditions that will favor this process. The fact is that children go to school and parents work during the day; so, most neurofeedback occurs in the late afternoon or early evening, even though these are not optimal times for learning. Still, it is possible to learn effectively under less than ideal conditions. Witness the plethora of late-hour homework and the mounds of evidence that neurofeedback — done in the real-world, later-in-the-day, can't-wait-to-get-home mode — works! But, it helps to have your child as rested and unburdened as possible.

4. **Inquire about medications** — As a general rule, neurotherapy works well with or without medications. You should discuss medications with your neurotherapist and with your child's physician. Remember that medications are very common (whether or not you favor them) and that neurotherapists are accustomed to treating children on and off meds. The issue here is whether medication effects — particularly the short-acting ones, like some stimulants — affect neurofeedback training. Since neurofeedback involves learning of a reasonably active nature, children learn better when they are not tired, irritable, cranky, or sick. At the end of a long and trying day, your child's medication may be wearing off. This is not the best circumstance under which to do neurofeedback (or homework, for that matter). Perhaps it is unavoidable, but it is worthwhile to discuss this with the therapist and physician. Alterations in the time of day medications are administered (or introducing sustained release medications) could make the neurofeedback sessions more profitable and efficient.

5. **Establish a schedule** — Neurotherapists who treat children usually keep evening hours. Some offer weekend hours. As you would expect, the busiest times are after school. Work out a schedule so your child will have a reserved and consistent place for treatment. Consider the schedule like music lessons: Established times during the week when you are expected to be there. These appointments need not be rigidly fixed, but most people find that regularly scheduled appointments work best for child, parents, and therapist. Incidentally, it is okay to schedule sessions on consecutive days or with several days in-between. As mentioned, the brain's flexibility seems to accommodate variability in the administration of EEG sessions.

6. **Allow for recovery** — Neurofeedback typically carries no side effects, a term we use in the medical sense. However, the process of training the brain involves *challenging* it, which (we hope) will necessarily induce some reactive effects. Just like a physical workout or rigorous sport will tire your child, neurofeedback exercises your child's brain, and this will often induce transient fatigue. Sometimes (as with physical exercise), the training will incur appetite increase right after the session (this is usually temporary, and occurs much more frequently in children than adults). These are transient effects, as the body reacts and eventually rebounds toward normalization. Your child may be tired after the session, and then "wake up" as the hours progress. Or, he/she may go to sleep surprisingly early. Some children become ravenous after the first few sessions, and some become noticeably quieter or more talkative. Your child may show any or none of these reactions; they are most often temporary, as your child's system accommodates to the challenges of brain adaptation. You should be prepared for them, discuss them with your therapist, and allow your child the time and environmental accommodations during this transition.

WHO PAYS FOR EEG NEUROFEEDBACK?

The cost of neurofeedback will vary according to several factors: geographic location, therapist experience and training, market conditions, and commitment (financial and otherwise) on the part of the client.

Many therapists give substantial discounts for package programs that are pre-paid. Financial matters aside, neurotherapists are very interested in clients' commitment. Neurotherapy involves repetition and practice; it is not a quick fix (usually). Pre-payment and other forms of commitment demonstrate clients' integrity and priority for taking brain improvement seriously. As such, it provides incentive for both client and therapist, and should be duly rewarded.

Individual EEG biofeedback sessions (30 minutes) generally cost between $50.00 and $150.00. Alpha-theta sessions are often longer in length, more intensively therapist-supervised, and usually higher in cost than "eyes-open SMR/Beta" sessions. Typically, the cost is at the rate of the therapist's hourly fee.

The initial evaluation costs anywhere from $150.00 to $500.00 or more. When you are quoted a price for evaluation, inquire about what the evaluation includes. As covered in the Chapter 5, assessments vary greatly, according to purpose, experience, and intended outcomes. Neurofeedback intake evaluations need not be exorbitant, but make sure a low price does not exclude the requisite attention needed to properly train your child.

If the therapist provides services in addition to neurofeedback, ask questions to clarify what services are included in the neurofeedback costs and what services are separate. Most therapists charge by the hour and/or by the neurofeedback session. This is considered appropriate standard-of-practice. Don't expect other services to be included, unless they are stated as such. Don't expect free consultations, unless specifically offered by the therapist. Ask about the policies on refunds and missed appointments or late cancellations.

Talk to the therapist. These are professionals who have extensive experience and training in human relations. They have additional preparation in the fine art and science of training brains with computers. If there are misunderstandings or gross uncertainties, endeavor to clear them up quickly. Neurotherapists are professionals with added expertise. At minimum, they should be skilled at and interested in helping you cope, not making life more difficult.

Doing the math on costs is not difficult. At an average price of $100.00 per session, 40 sessions will cost $4000.00. The initial assessment and follow-up consultations and assessments will cost between $300.00 and $1000.00 additionally. A pre-paid arrangement will reduce the cost significantly, perhaps up to 40%.

Expect to pay $2500.00 to $5000.00 for the 20-hour solution to ADD/ADHD.[21]

---

21   This is a fraction of the cost of medication and doctor visits over a prolonged period of years.

THE CHALLENGE OF FUNDING NEUROFEEDBACK TRAINING

If you think the cost of health is expensive, imagine the cost of suffering. We are not being facetious. As interested as we are in providing this wonderful treatment and spreading the word about its efficacy, we are also interested in promoting a culture where brain function is valued.[22] Though the health care industry (and particularly managed care) is in a sorry state, people still make choices. Free will applies to finances and priorities, including attitudes about other people's money.

If you have health care coverage that will pay for EEG biofeedback, consider yourself fortunate. Some policies will, and some won't. It is tragic and unfair that insurance companies will pay for invasive treatments like medications that go on indefinitely, but that they often exclude non-invasive, time-limited effective treatments like EEG biofeedback.

The battles over health care reimbursement for neurofeedback continue in the larger context of the tenuous relationships between the health care industry and consumers. We expect that, as the irrefutable evidence for neurofeedback's efficacy continues to mount, insurance companies will discover that neurofeedback saves them money.

Whether insurance coverage plays a role or not, the choice to spend money on this treatment involves more than belief in the data on effectiveness.

For some families, financing neurofeedback training will not involve major sacrifices. For other families, finding the money can be very problematic, especially if their medical insurance does not cover the fees. In this era where so many of us are overextended financially, just being able to pay the monthly bills can be a major challenge. Adding the expense of neurofeedback can loom as the straw that breaks the camel's back.

What it comes down to in the final analysis is priorities. ADD/ADHD children who cannot learn to regulate their impulsiveness, who cannot learn to filter out distractions, and who cannot stay on task are at a severe disadvantage in school and in life. Unless there is meaningful intervention, these children are likely to be on the receiving end of a continual stream of negative feedback from their teachers, peers, and parents. This disapproval can irreparably damage their self-esteem. As these youngsters become increasingly discouraged and demoralized, they are likely to lower their expectations and aspirations. Despite average to superior intelligence, many dysfunctional ADD/ADHD children choose the path of least resistance: They shut down in school, accede to

---

22   One of our colleagues tells the story of being contacted by a potential patient who inquired about EEG biofeedback to treat the furrows in her brow caused by repeated tension headaches. When told that the treatment would require at least 15 sessions and quoted a price, the woman replied, "Gee, I don't know if I want to spend that much money on my head."

inferior scholastic performance, and fatalistically acquiesce to social rejection. Unless they are fortunate enough to stumble onto a career that capitalizes on their natural talents, they are likely to continue to perform marginally and, in the process, become prototypic "underachievers."

Recently, an Hispanic family was featured in an article appearing in the Los Angeles Times. The parents supported themselves by collecting cans and other recycleables. Every morning at 3:00 AM, they would each get on their respective bicycles and visit the disposal bins of the restaurants in their community. As they were known and liked by the restaurant personnel, the chefs and waiters would intentionally set aside their recycleables for them to collect. Despite working ten hours a day, seven days a week, they lived in a tiny two-room apartment. As they were growing older, the travails of climbing into the bins and then carrying the sacks of cans had begun to exact a mounting physical toll, but they never felt sorry for themselves. It was the only life they knew.

Why would the LA Times feature this family when other immigrants work equally long hours to eke out a subsistence? Well, in this case, these two parents had not only put their son through college, they had also financed his education at MIT, where he was about to graduate at the top of his class with a Master's degree in electrical engineering. None of their son's professors knew that the parents of this talented young man were scavengers. His education now having been financed, the parents had been saving every cent they could so that they could fly to Boston and watch their son graduate.

It is a question of priorities. Responsible parents want to do whatever they can to help their child prevail in a world that can be harsh and unforgiving of those who cannot regiment their minds and function efficiently. Resourceful parents who conclude that neurofeedback will level the playing field for their child and allow their child to compete successfully will somehow figure out how to fund this vital training. The solution may be a bank loan or forgoing the purchase of a new car or a new flat screen TV. These parents are wise enough to recognize that the payoffs for getting their child on-track will more than offset any sacrifices they must make.

TALKING WITH DOCTORS, THERAPISTS, AND TEACHERS

There are several reasons why talking about neurofeedback to professionals in your child's world is important. Firstly, it is a natural impulse to find out what other people think as a means of determining whether you are on the right track and what the pitfalls are that you wish to avoid. In life, we are constantly negotiating the lines between benefiting from the experiences, advice, and admonitions of others and clinging in dependency upon what people think. Neurofeedback folds into this mix, no different in that you will be interested in what others have to say, yet different in that people who have little to no knowledge of it will express a confident opinion (which you should take with a grain of salt, considering the lack of factual basis or first-hand experience). It is amazing what little data spawns the certainty of people's opinions on this subject. It is almost as if anybody with an internet connection feels entitled to be a pundit. We are not denigrating free speech or independent initiative; we simply believe that internet search engines are only one form of research (and unscientific at that). So, be discerning in your communications, and recognize the motivational power and emotional inhibition that comes from the opinions of others.

Secondly, you should consult the medical community. Your child's health is paramount and, even if you decide to eschew a physician's advice on neurofeedback, you need your child's doctor for other reasons. Your child may be on medication for ADD or other conditions. If he/she is taking ADD medications, the doctor should know what you are doing. Often, the motivation for obtaining neurofeedback is to reduce or quit meds. Your doctor needs to know if you are reducing medications or changing dosages (this is called titrating) and about other efforts to treat problems because:

a) Some medications have withdrawal effects and should be reduced gradually.

b) As neurofeedback begins to take effect, your child will probably need less medication.

c) It is to your child's benefit that the doctor has documentation of interventions and medication schedules.

d) If you don't keep your doctor informed, should you eventually seek advice or treatment, he/she will not have continual up-to-date information.

e) Lack of communication will send a message to the doctor that you don't value his/her opinion and input.

f) Your physician may conclude that you are noncompliant or negligent. (It's funny how easy it is to conclude that people are wrong or have character flaws because they disagree with us.)

g) You have a privilege and obligation to participate actively in your child's health care. This requires that you engage your doctor in discourse and decision-making, even if you ultimately disregard his/her advice.

Thirdly, you should talk to professionals in your child's world because you need feedback — not necessarily their opinions about neurofeedback, but — about your child's performance and any changes in it. If your child sees a therapist or tutor, be sure to give as much information as you can. We are not suggesting this to advertise, and we are well aware of the influence of demand characteristics (power of suggestion or "hands-on" effect). Rather, we know from experience how powerful EEG training is in changing children's behavior and learning capabilities. Therefore, we (and you) can fully expect significant, and sometimes sudden, improvement. Other professionals will be delighted with these improvements, but, frankly, are not accustomed to such rapid change with their own interventions. They will likely congratulate themselves on their own skills and the success of their treatments. Of course, it is diplomatic to allow them their credit (and, after all, you do want what they are working toward with your child); however, it is very important that you see the effects of neurofeedback in your child's functioning in the real world. Telling about the intervention, soliciting feedback, and structuring methods of measuring progress are ways you can determine your child's progress and benefit. A wonderful and natural feature of neurofeedback is that it catalyzes the effects of other interventions — psychotherapy, speech therapy, tutoring, etc.[23]

Last but not least in the entourage of reasons to communicate about neurofeedback is the moral and ethical obligation to spread the word and to put something back into your community. You are the most credible and realistic source of information to other parents, as your own experience will verify. If misfortune befell your child, you would want to save other parents and children from suffering. If you find a blessing, you will want to share it with others. Besides being fortunate to come upon neurofeedback, you are potentially in a leadership position. Teachers, parents, therapists, doctors all need to know about tools that will help children and make their professional reach exert more positive influence.

In addition to improving cognitive function, attention, and self-regulation, the EEG training will probably boost your child's empathy. Since this is a gift you already have, share it with others.

EEG TRAINING AT HOME: REMOTE NEUROFEEDBACK

Many people will finish their 40 sessions in the therapist's office and be significantly better for their 20-hour brain investment in EEG biofeedback. Some will want or need to go further.

EEG biofeedback can continue at home, and should be done under the auspices and supervision of a neurotherapist.

---

23   A common and joyous gratification — experienced regularly by the authors and many neurotherapists — is receiving reports and phone calls inquiring about this wonderful neurofeedback treatment that is causing such leaps and bounds of improvement in their clients and students.

We emphatically caution against independently purchasing any of the variety of amateur biofeedback machines available on the market for as low as several hundred dollars. These are difficult to use, and generally do not deliver feedback with the precision, timing, and accuracy of the higher-end professional models. However, only professionals can purchase the professional models, and there are good reasons for this.

You need training and supervision to administer neurofeedback at home. You need reliable instrumentation and a professional to show you how to use it and ensure that it keeps working properly. You also need to be accountable to a professional for your child's (or your own) training. Otherwise, you could end up "training" room noise. Or cluttering the room with an expensive, underused "exercycle." Or worse. You could hurt your child.

EEG biofeedback is a safe, effective, natural treatment — when used properly and judiciously. Like anything else, it can be abused or misused. This is a technique that profoundly influences brain function!

Fortunately, with modest amounts of instruction and practice, a little humility and perseverance, and a baseline of EEG training sessions at the therapist's office, most parents and adults can train their children and/or themselves at home.[24]

For families living great distance from a neurotherapist, or, for those who need continued training (e.g., children with autism, pervasive developmental disorders, seizures, or significant learning disabilities), home training is an economical and practical solution.

Some neurotherapists include home training and supervision in their practices, and some do not. It is a big responsibility for the therapist, as well as for the parent. However, it is both manageable and rewarding. Home training also allows parents to become intimately involved in their children's improvement, and it encourages responsibility, freedom, and independence. We want people to be in charge of their own brains, and we want to encourage the professional therapeutic relationship to develop as a partnership, not as a leash.

Neurotherapists who engage in remote use home supervision generally lease the equipment to the home user for several months. Some therapists will sell equipment to clients, or will arrange for the clients to purchase new or used equipment of a suitable quality. Most therapists will not facilitate the sale of equipment until the client has demonstrated over some period of time (usually a few months) a competency and responsibility with home training. This is for the client's protection.

Clients demonstrate competency and responsibility by communicating with the therapist regularly, by completing and returning

---

24　We have many families where parent and child train together for mental fitness. This models wonderfully for the child as it benefits both parent and child. It also makes the cost of training more economical.

forms or computer disks, and by arriving for office visits at regular (albeit progressively less frequent) intervals, so the therapist can check up on the client(s) and on the progress of training.

What You Can Do: A Parent's Guide

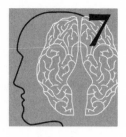

HELPING YOUR CHILD FEEL SUCCESSFUL

Every parent's desire is to see his/her child attain success, make the most of abilities, treat others with respect, fairness, and compassion, and stay out of harm's way. By providing your child with the means to vastly improve brain fitness, self-regulation, and functionality, you are creating opportunities for him/her to experience success *routinely*, instead of success surfacing as the occasional and unfamiliar respite that so typically characterizes ADD. Watching your child improve and participating in these positive changes will also make you more successful, more confident about your child's future, and probably more recognized, appreciated, and esteemed in your child's eyes.

Let's use some of the principles by which neurofeedback works to equip you to help your child feel and *be* more successful all the way around. We will explain in practical terms how you can integrate the scientific principles of operant conditioning — the very mechanism by which EEG neurofeedback trains the brain — into your child's daily life to heal, reform, and reprogram those five ADD characteristics (review Chapters 1 and 3) to make your child more adaptive and your interactions with him/her more productive.

Remember the two organizing principles of mental fitness:

1. Learning adaptive responses.

2. Eliminating maladaptive responses.

Earlier (Chapter 5), we defined mental fitness as a blending of learned skills, effortless self-regulation, and both automatic and conscious adaptation to the flow of changing conditions. It involves goal-oriented, purposeful, and organized behavior unimpeded by disruptions in the emotional, nervous, or energy system of the mind and body.

We have cited behavior and habit changes as functions of acquiring or relinquishing responses. In the EEG training, we encourage the brain to acquire new habits (collections of similar and connected responses) by nudging it toward and rewarding those responses. We facilitate relinquishing undesired responses by ignoring such activity. This process happens a little bit at a time, and it is known in psychology as *shaping*. Neurofeedback equipment can shape at the rate of 4000 reinforcements per hour — but you can shape, too. And, here's a terrific and practical secret: Though you may not be able to reinforce your child neurologically at a rate as fast as computers, you can:

- Plan and direct your reinforcements in the natural environment toward those behaviors that your child needs to adapt and function better.

- Alter the *timing, outcomes,* and *schedules* of your child's behaviors in ways that will teach his brain to recognize and meet challenges at increasingly higher levels of performance and adaptation.

Little by little, you will nudge your child almost imperceptibly into patterns of more adaptive responses; after awhile, the pattern of favored responses forms an *ingrained expectation* of success, and the nasty cycle of attention-to-negative-behaviors-causing-more-negative-behaviors-requiring-more-disapproving-attention-further-strengthening-negative-behaviors is finally broken!

EEG training focuses on brain timing mechanisms that help survival and adaptive functioning. It routinely encourages those brainwaves, and it generally disregards errant, nonproductive or maladaptive activity. After awhile, the brain forms this habit, thinks such activity is normal, and carries it on independently. The brain expects itself to do so. This is the essence of self-regulation, and you can induce such habits into your child's daily life and outlook, using the same principles that run the world as we know it.

The following sections will help you put this into practice.

HEIGHTENING AWARENESS AND REINFORCING
GOAL-ORIENTED BEHAVIORS

There is a saying that "behavior serves a purpose." In the arena of behavior modification, professionals interpret even seemingly senseless or self-defeating behaviors as serving some end, conscious or not, that has been strengthened, or reinforced, either intentionally or inadvertently. The problem is that:

- The purposes that particular behaviors serve may not coincide with your purposes.

- Your ADD child most likely has not developed sufficient skills of self-monitoring to accurately observe, evaluate, correct, and re-direct his/her behaviors.

Although your child's behaviors may serve a purpose (in the behavior modification sense of reinforcement theory), his/her *self-regulation* and *perceptual focus* difficulties may occlude awareness of how effective certain behaviors are and toward what ends.

This is where you can enter the picture with some positive influences. First, consider the baseline (what happens before intervention): If you are like most parents, you probably often react with censure to your child's misdeeds. When you try to inhibit yourself, it is likely that you refrain for awhile, until you are stressed, caught unawares, or your child accelerates his/her negative behavior, and then you react again. This vicious cycle (known as *variable ratio intermittent reinforcement*) is the most powerful strengthener of behaviors, whether or not you desire or are conscious of the particular behaviors to which the reinforcers (in this case, negative attention) are applied.

Instead, let's substitute a more effective intervention. In EEG training, we know that errant brainwaves will occur, so we prepare to disregard them (by setting the computers to not reward them). This process is practical only when we have some preferred brainwaves to focus upon and a *plan to reinforce* them *whenever* they occur. (Reinforcement means presenting a consequence in close association with a response so that it increases the occurrence of that response in the future.) You need a plan to substitute effective responses (consequences that will produce child behaviors you want subsequently) for the more predictable and destructive censure and negativity your child may invite. Here are some suggestions:

1. **Make lists of things your child does appropriately** — you will be surprised by how many these are. It's just hard to notice them when the misbehaviors are so much louder. (See *Positive Behaviors to Look for in Your Child, Page 117.*) Point them out, and comment on how they effectively lead to results she/he wants. Look for very simple behaviors. "I notice you go to the bathroom when you have to, and you flush the toilet each time. That shows you know how to take care of yourself." "How nice that you put on your shoes when you go outside!" "Mommy watched you sleep lying down — your body knows what it needs!" Although this may seem silly, it really does serve a purpose: Setting up a new tenor of positive interaction with your child and conditioning him/her to become more aware of behaviors that are automatic, functional and self-regulatory.

2. **Gradually transition your comments to reframe observations into goal-oriented behaviors** — "I see you run down the stairs

when you have someplace to go. You must know where you're going and be in a hurry." Such observations will stimulate your child to observe and think about how others see him/her (in a non-threatening way).

3. **Reframe undesirable behaviors into questions that will impel your child to examine his own behaviors in light of their results** — "Do you think that hitting your brother will really keep him away from your things and make you seem grown up to Dad?"

4. **Instead of scolding or criticizing, describe the behavior just observed and ask if and how it fits with what he wants to accomplish** — "You said you really wanted to get better grades on this next report card, right? How will watching TV when you haven't finished your homework help the result of better grades you want?"

5. **Compare your child's activities to the challenges of EEG neurofeedback to get him/her back on-track** — "You know how, during biofeedback sessions when you find your mind drifting or getting bored, you have to call yourself back to focus on making the game go and getting points? Well, it's the same way when you need to remind yourself to complete your chores and ask Mom for feedback about when you've finished satisfactorily."

These types of positive re-directions will not only re-structure the emotional valence of your interactions with your child (to a more pleasant attraction), they will help your child overcome the *poor integration with environmental demands* and *compromised flexibility* that keep him/her stuck or fixated in one gear. By suggesting very simple alternative perceptions and approaches and then following up with reframing and reward, you will help and reinforce your child's abilities to "drive at the appropriate speed for the circumstances."

Does this sound familiar? Of course! By reinforcing in the natural environment what your child is learning in the neurofeedback sessions, you help smooth the transition and generalize the learning more quickly to the real world what his/her brain and nervous system are now more ready to accomplish.

Be patient, persistent, and supportive. The 20-hour solution for ADD relies on machinery that is a lot more efficient and operates without the emotions and fatigue that we experience! You've spent much more than 20 hours trying to change your child. Hang in there, and

Positive Behaviors to Look for in Your Child

- Asks a relevant question
- Helps someone
- Accepts correction or suggestion
- Interacts effectively with a peer, sibling, or pet
- Answers a question
- Enters the room in an orderly manner
- Enters/leaves on time
- Ignores a distraction or provocation
- Smiles genuinely
- Uses creativity
- Volunteers information
- Remains quiet
- Displays attentiveness to adults
- Expresses emotions
- Shows honesty
- Greets or acknowledges others
- Completes a task
- Works or plays cooperatively
- Defers to authority
- Appears clean and groomed

become allies with EEG neurofeedback by heightening your child's awareness of his/her behaviors and re-directing them in purposeful, organized, and desired directions.

EXPERIENCING THE BENEFITS OF MENTAL FITNESS CO-TRAINING
(Parent and Child Train Together with EEG Neurofeedback)

Consider the saying: "You don't have to be sick to get better." This applies to training the brain, as well. Just as in physical health, where people exercise to attain better levels of fitness — even in the absence of disease — mental fitness can improve by many methods. Few are as fast or efficient as training with EEG neurofeedback.

Many parents embark upon training programs in concert with their children. The benefits are both obvious and subtle. Undertaking the training yourself communicates a clear and unambiguous message to your child that you think this is worth doing. It also allows you to experience directly the nature of the treatment and, to a large extent, what your child is experiencing. Your personal involvement will likely eradicate any objections or excuses your child may have. It will also forge a new and unique bond between you, based upon shared and advanced positive experience. EEG training is an unusual domain in which the boundaries between parent and child can be healthfully subsumed in the interest of commonality and personal growth. In a way, by co-training, parent and child embark upon a neural family tree, exploring and improving the less-than-perfect genetic influences that affect behavior, health, and self-regulation. After all, where else can you and your child participate in discipline and correction without censure, bad feelings, punishment, or sacrifice of your authority? (And, as a shared activity, it's easier on the ankles than skateboarding!)

Co-training will motivate your child, earn his/her respect, model appropriate behavior, increase your credibility (compared with "Do what I say, not what I do"), and help you to work better, sleep better, play better, and feel better.

Many neurotherapists treat parents and children together, and some even offer discount packages for multiple family members.

GETTING MORE FROM YOUR NEUROTHERAPIST

We have made reference throughout this book to the neurotherapist as the administrator of EEG neurofeedback training sessions, as the person who assesses and monitors your child's condition and progress, and as the professional who has special training in helping people self-regulate as a way of life.

At this point, we wish to highlight some similarities and differences that distinguish neurotherapists from other professionals and uniquely qualify them to assist you with your child in many ways.

Professionals who undertake neurofeedback come from a variety of disciplines: Medical doctors, psychologists, marriage and family counselors, chiropractors, educators, nurses, social workers, and other disciplines as well. Though each discipline brings its own set of beliefs and conventions, professionals seek and practice neurotherapy because it works and because it adds dimensions of improvement to the lives of patients beyond what they would have without it.

Some providers practice neurofeedack exclusively, and others offer it in complement to a variety of professional services. The scope of a professional's practice does not reflect upon his/her competence within that scope, nor does the breadth of services predict skills in performing neurofeedback or guiding your child to the desired improvement. The sheer power and efficacy of brain training is impressive enough that hundreds upon hundreds of professionals have incorporated this technique into their practices.

This uniformity of positive results (along with some standardization of training and practices by those listed in this book) should inspire confidence in families seeking neurofeedback. Additionally, the diversity among professionals offering neurofeedback benefits the patient community in that a wide variety of orientations and services accompany neurofeedback and validate its efficacy which, in the eyes of some professionals, is perhaps enhanced by combination with other modalities.

For example, if your child is on medication, or you believe that medication is helpful, it may be preferable for you to seek treatment with a medical doctor who offers or oversees neurotherapy. (Such practitioners do exist, and it is likely that their numbers will increase.) Many neurotherapists have years of experience in counseling psychotherapy, and can offer services to support your child's developmental needs and/or pertinent family issues.

Some neurotherapists have educational backgrounds and may offer educational services, behavior modification training, or nutritional counseling.

Over the years, certain neurotherapists acquire particular experience, expertise, and interest in specialty areas or conditions. If your child suffers with Tourette's, epilepsy, Bipolar Disorder, learning disabilities, autism, or any of a plethora of maladies or developmental irregularities, you may find a fountain of helpful resources in or through your neurotherapist.

Here are some explicit suggestions for deriving the most from your neurotherapist's expertise:

1. **Ask about auxiliary services.** Inquire whether your neurotherapist provides them or recommends them. If your therapist recommends or endorses such services, get a referral and ask for a personal recommendation.

2. **Discuss medications.** This is a big issue and still a controversial one. You and the neurotherapist are both wondering where the other one stands on medication. Whether you have uncertainties, or medication is simply not a part of the picture, bringing this variable into the discussion of treatment and of ADD in general will help you align with the therapist and may avoid potential miscommunications or treatment detours.

3. **Ask about educational and/or behavioral matters.** These may arise as a matter or course during your intake or consultations with the neurotherapist. If not, be sure to access the therapist's knowledge base. You may discover a wealth of information and expertise. People who practice neurofeedback usually have a master's degree or higher in some relevant discipline.

4. **Decide what is important to you in understanding the process.** When a field of endeavor is new or unfamiliar, so many questions can arise. Curiosity is important, but it, too, can distract from the tasks at hand. You are entitled to information and explanations about how neurofeedback works and about the particular treatment plan for your child. Remember that training brainwaves is not a linear logical procedure (like so much of the way we have learned to navigate the world), so there are limits to how much can be explained (and, the best way to understand it is to try it yourself). Remember also that your therapist has invested huge amounts of time and money into acquiring expertise. It is unreasonable to expect that such a vastly complicated science can be summarized for you in a short consultation. The neurotherapist will give you lots of time, but be prepared to pay for it. This is an area of professional expertise; like other specialties, it should rightly be compensated.

5. **Ask your neurotherapist to leverage connections.** As we have indicated, there is an international network of neurotherapists who share similar training and consultation lists and forums. If you have specific or technical questions, perhaps your therapist can pose these questions to the affiliate community, and both of you (and others) can benefit from the expertise and experience of a

Fig. 7.1 Dr. Steinberg working with a youngster

practitioner in another part of the world. Another way you can leverage connections is to ask your therapist for a practitioner and recommendation in another geographic region. If you have a relative in a different state, chances are your therapist knows a good neurotherapist practicing in that area.

6. **Discuss personally relevant information.** Your therapist may not have ADD, but chances are he/she was drawn to neurotherapy for particular reasons and has experienced the benefit of the training him/herself. Your professional relationship with the therapist does not preclude you from asking about or sharing personal issues, such as children, relationships, medical or therapeutic experiences, medications, life-changing events, beliefs about how people get worse and get better, and your own list of obstacles and aspirations. Opening the communication and inquiring and volunteering information will enhance your connection with the therapist and foster an environment of maximal benefit for your child. Your neurotherapist is a pioneer, willing to brave adversity and seek success, even working with a difficult population. This person is an ally who understands "you don't have to be sick to get better."

DEALING WITH MEDICATIONS

In confronting the issues surrounding medications, it is helpful to recall our discussion about self-regulation and the consistent management of a balance between arousal and relaxation, two basic functions of the nervous system. Regulating one's internal responsiveness to ever-changing conditions involves a management of internal state. This concept of state includes attention, awareness, mood, impulses, and physiological factors influenced by the "state" of arousal of the brain and nervous system. Medications biochemically alter state, and neurofeedback alters state by using operant conditioning (learning) to create the changes through new neural pathways. Leaving aside the technical aspects of how this happens, let's deal with the practical issues of medications by bearing in mind that the ADD child has great difficulty in adapting and maintaining proper self-regulatory states for changing conditions.

Most medications for ADD are aimed at controlling state through changing the speed and consistency with which nerve cells transmit messages among themselves. Some drugs do a very good job at this, but the problem is that they don't work exactly the same for everybody. Also, they tend to have side effects and (obviously) they need to be replenished regularly, usually on a daily basis. Very often, the brain accommodates to them, and, either they don't work as well as they once did, or you have to increase the dosage to get the desired effect (which increases or induces undesirable side effects).

The ability of the brain to accommodate is what we are most interested in, both for behavior improvement and for making medication decisions. Neurofeedback maximizes the brain's capacity to accommodate and to induce state changes and adaptations to them. It is a relatively active process that manifests itself in brain *flexibility*. Medications that alter state change brain chemistry in what is (for the brain) a relatively passive process that manifests itself in dependency. In both cases, the brain changes state and responds as though the changed state is the reality (e.g., in going from very excited to calm, the brain assumes a reality that calmness is preferred, more comfortable, and that there is nothing to get overly excited about).

Both medications and neurofeedback are attempts to regulate the brain's accommodation and adaptation — so your child can sit when that behavior is called for, turn his/her attention to schoolwork, notice important signals like a call to cease one activity and begin another, not overreact to internal moods or provocations by others, etc. When the behaviors improve, we say that the child is stabilized — that is, the interventions or changes introduced are balancing his/her state consistently.

Using neurofeedback, this process takes a number of sessions, and it is usually not well-established until about 40 sessions (on average). With medications, it sometimes happens very quickly, but it often takes many dosage adjustments, changes in medications or combinations, physician consults, and even many months. Ironically, the nuisance of side effects often exceeds any positive changes.

The point of all this is that self-regulation doesn't come in a pill, and it doesn't come in an electrode. You must monitor the child, and allow his brain to adapt and accommodate to a more functional management of state. With regard to medication, this has some implications.

1. The brain is plastic enough to use medications, neurofeedback, other interventions, or combinations thereof to achieve its own balance of regulation. Neurofeedback works with or without medications.

2. Since neurofeedback teaches and conditions the brain to self-regulate and change state on its own, as the brain does this more and more independently, less medication will be needed. It is our collective experience that people become more sensitive to medications (and even coffee and alcohol) after they practice neurofeedback.[25] Thus, some reduction in dosage is usually expected and appropriate. We strongly recommend that you discuss this with your neurotherapist and physician. If possible, encourage communication between the physician and the neurotherapist. Here's an important tip: Acknowledge (particularly with the neurotherapist) in an off-hand manner that you understand the discomfort that professionals of different disciplines sometimes have among themselves, and that you sincerely appreciate (your therapist's) willingness to put that aside in the interest of your child, and to collaborate with others. In our experience, physicians are usually so incredibly busy, that they don't often take the initiative to call therapists. However, they do respond to calls, and many of them are deeply appreciative of the overtures by other professionals to communicate with and include them.

3. Talk to your neurotherapist about signs and symptoms of overdosage reactions and interactive effects between medications and neurofeedback. Fatigue and hyper-excitability are two of the most common problems, and these can be relieved through adjustments in medications and/or neurofeedback protocols.

---

25   One of our European colleagues tells the story of a patient who complained that neurofeedback had entirely ruined his ability to enjoy heroin! Its use in treating addictions notwithstanding, this improved sensitivity augurs well for reducing ADD medications.

4. Shorter acting medications (such as stimulants) often cause rebound effects, leaving the child irritable, tired, or distractible as the medication wears off. Dragging a child off to an appointment in this "state" can be a hellish experience for you and the child. Adjustments in time schedules and dosages can make life saner and treatment more efficient. You are obligated to cope with your child at his/her worst, but you are also entitled to see him/her at his best.

5. If your child has a serious medical condition (such as a seizure disorder) or is taking anticonvulsants or medications for Bipolar Disorder, do not attempt to discontinue these medications without medical supervision. While we (the authors) are of the opinion that reduction or elimination of medication is a desirable and achievable condition for the vast majority of people with ADD, we are aware that, for some individuals, medication withdrawal can be dangerous.

6. Develop a relationship with your physician that is open enough to include your reports, complaints, and considerations. Moreover, cultivate your own expectation that such a relationship is both possible and appropriate. You may have to work a little harder at the relationship or the communication, you may have to weather some anxiety, or you may even have to go through a few doctors to find one who will listen and honor (not necessarily agree with) your opinion. If you feel put upon or embarrassed, remember you are not alone. There are many parents like you with children like yours who are the customers of doctors. Be polite and diplomatic, but make yourself heard.

EDUCATIONAL SERVICES AND COOPERATION

The ADD child is uniquely disadvantaged in most contemporary American educational settings. This is because the very nature of ADD symptoms comes into conflict with the requirements of standard curriculae: Sit quietly, pay attention, listen and follow directions, organize your work, follow through, hand in your work, don't forget, write neatly, and so forth.

Many parents will shudder in identification with the plight of Matthew and his mother, the characters in Chapter 2. School is simply anathema to the ADD child, even those with high intelligence or exceptional talents. As if the attendant symptoms and deficiencies weren't enough, many educators unfortunately worsen the situation for ADD students by poor educational practices, ignorance of the condition and the child's needs, and attitudes, beliefs, and resentments (often subconscious) that subvert the efforts of the child and his family to adapt and accede to the set standards.

When parents or professionals endeavor to inform teachers and their cohorts about the obstacles and impairments faced by such youngsters, inevitably they are met with a variety of objections, defenses, and blockages to these communications. Though the responses may vary in tone from flat rejection and dismissal to passive stonewalling or deflective questioning, usually the objections and resistance to understanding and assisting ADD students fall into a few categories. These categories may be voiced outright, or they may be exemplified as themes, expressed to the astute listener through subtle, though recognizable statements:

- "There's nothing really the matter with him."

- "Your expectations are unrealistic." (This means more work and greater exposure with less reward for me [the teacher].)

- "There is a problem, but I can't help him because..."

- "If he gets special assistance, what would the other kids (administrators, colleagues, people who will hold me accountable) say?"

- "Nobody made accommodations or excuses for me (or someone significant in my life) and I/we/they survived. Why, therefore, should you get special treatment?"

- "If you would only get him treated (medicated), we could do our job teaching!" (It's your resistance to medication that's the problem.)

Though treatment for ADD happens mostly outside the school environment (and neurofeedback is often sufficient to change behavioral patterns so as to afford children new beginnings), let's face it: Children spend upwards of six hours per day at school, and, for some children, this time is a series of exercises in embarrassment, humiliation, failure, and reinforcement of problem behaviors. If your child is impacted by such negativity and trauma, you need to get involved. Pills do not make better teachers, nor do medications or errant behaviors absolve the educational system from its responsibilities to provide appropriate and nurturing environments for all children.

Unfortunately, you are not likely to change the educational system singlehandedly. You can, however, improve conditions for your child, ease his/her transition from *stressed brain syndrome* to better adaptation, introduce accommodations reasonable for the child's limitations, and implement an atmosphere conducive to recognition of the child's gains.

You can accomplish this whether or not your child is receiving special educational assistance or has been recognized by the school district as "eligible for services as a handicapped learner."

The following guidelines should prove valuable:

1. **Educate yourself on state and federal laws regarding handicapping conditions, including civil and educational rights.** There is potent legislation protecting the rights of children with disabilities. Acquaint yourself with these laws; they are readily available through your school district (by law, actually) through parent organizations (such as CHADD – Children and Adults with Attention Deficit Disorder), on the internet, and through educational advocates and attorneys. Some neurotherapists[26] have extensive experience in advocacy, educational negotiations, IEPs (Individual Educational Programs) and even litigation.

2. **Consult an expert source outside the school.** Market economics operate in education, too. Be cautious of educational recommendations that are made by people paid by your child's school. Such recommendations may be sound, and the people who run your child's education should be paid. But, get a second opinion, one that is free from the economic influence and pressures of your child's school. Independent advocates, educational psychologists, and educational attorneys are good sources. Your child's educational options and self-concept are more than worth your investment of a consultation fee.

3. **Recognize the controversy about ADD, and become informed.** In many states, ADD is considered a learning disability and, therefore, deserving of legal educational entitlements. In other states, it is not. Become familiar with Public Law 94-142, the federal law governing education for the handicapped. You need not become or hire a lawyer to get smart on what this law means for the ADD child. For example, if your child has been diagnosed as ADD by a reputable professional, he/she may qualify as a special needs learner under the category of "other health impaired," regardless of test scores. This does not necessitate or even imply special education — but it can give you leverage and bargaining power in attaining modifications at your child's school.

4. **Educate the educators.** It is amazing how few of them know about neurofeedback, much less the essentials and ramifications of ADD.

---

26   Dr. Steinberg, for example.

Most of the educators will be interested, particularly if they sense that your child's behavior and learning will improve. They do care, and they are sensible enough to consider interventions that show promise to make their jobs easier.

5. **Request participation from the educational institution.** Schools are constantly asking for money, holding fundraisers, lobbying legislators and the community, and asking for parent participation, both in money and involvement. As the saying goes, "What's good for the goose is good for the gander." Ask the educators to participate in your child's treatment (after all, it is for his/her education). Ask for homework modification (without penalty) on those days when your child has neurofeedback sessions. Explain the time commitment involved and the likelihood your child will be temporarily fatigued from the brain exercises, at least initially. Ask the teacher to read up on neurofeedback and, perhaps, visit the neurotherapist's office to watch your child train. This qualifies at least as a field trip and probably as continuing education for the teacher. Consider asking for partial reimbursement for neurotherapy from the school. This is not as far-fetched as it may at first seem. In public education, many states reimburse school districts and nonpublic agencies for "necessary and appropriate" educational services for which public schools contract with private vendors. This happens with transportation, behavior management services, occupational therapy — why not neurofeedback? There are pilot programs offered by public and private schools.[27] If your child is in private school, talk to the directors about instituting a school-based or school-affiliated neurotherapy program run or supervised by your neurotherapist. (We suspect that many neurotherapists would be interested in this challenge.) The school may become more motivated if you outline a plan that raises money for the school.

6. **Schedule lectures and opportunities for education.** Most neurotherapists would be delighted to speak at your child's school, to confer with teachers and administrators, and to provide in-service opportunities for the community to learn more about ADD and neurofeedback.

These kinds of initiatives will not only create a healthier environment and more positive attention for your child — they may very well accelerate his/her stature as a positive role model and leader.

---

27 Two notable programs were those offered in Yonkers, NY and by the Dallas, TX Public Schools.

The Cult of the Neurotransmitter: A Philosophy of Self-Control and Responsibility for Behavior

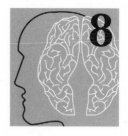

IS HE RESPONSIBLE FOR WHAT HE DOES?

So many parents agonize over what should be their responses to their children's misbehavior. The principal concern is very often represented in the following question:

"Is my child responsible for what he does, is it deliberate, or can he not help it?"

Is the ADD responsible? Ought we to excuse unacceptable behavior and violations of social norms on the basis of an imputed medical condition or biochemical imbalance? If so, to what extent, and where do we draw the line?

Of course, these are difficult questions, and they are hotly debated and answered by varied legal, medical, educational, and parental approaches.

We believe that an intelligent, moral, and practical approach to the question of behavioral responsibility should include an understanding of brain function and its responses to modification in social and historical contexts. In keeping with this idea and with empathy for parents who struggle with a range of emotions and moral imperatives in their discretion, we offer this discussion on keenly relevant aspects of responsibility for behavior.

Following this discussion (in Chapter 9) is the very personal story that led to the vanguard of EEG neurofeedback and the birth of this book.

WILL OR ILL?

What ever happened to free will?

Once the province of philosophical and religious inquiry, this question enjoys a resurgence in popularity among the denizens afflicted or affected by dysfunction and maladaptive behavior. The issue of free will and personal responsibility has surfaced with tenacious significance in step with the explosive growth of neuroscience and the increasing understanding within the scientific community about how the brain functions and how it can be modified. Ironically, the mounting discoveries about brain complexity have had a troubling side effect:

Behavior is increasingly seen as a function of biochemistry, which can be targeted by designer pharmaceuticals. As personality and behavior are reduced to products of neurotransmitter efficiency, people find it easier to disown responsibility for their actions, often attributing reckless or harmful acts (with the sanction of advocates or the applied biochemistry industry) to biochemical imbalances.

While wrestling with the causes of problems considered as emotional, behavioral, or "mental," consider the stakes:

People function and dysfunction. Millions muddle through their four score and ten years unhappy, stressed, fearful, depressed, frustrated, and insecure. They are run by powerful negative emotions that jade their perceptions and undermine their mental and physical health. Nonetheless, the majority of these quietly suffering people are somehow able to get through the day. They grow up, get through school, go to work, have relationships, raise children, and more or less go about their business. They may appear functional to outsiders, but they know that they are desperately struggling to hold on. The powerful negative feelings that drive so many people through years of silent suffering often skulk as carefully guarded individual and collective secrets.

The data describing the status of mental health in the United States are startling. A recent report prepared by the Surgeon General of the United States contains some astounding statistics:

1. One in every five Americans (including children) experiences a mental disorder in any given year.

2. Half of all Americans have mental disorders at some time during their lives.

3. Fifteen percent of all Americans between the ages of eighteen and fifty-four have anxiety disorders.

4. Eight to fifteen percent of the elderly manifest symptoms of depression.

5. After heart disease, mental illness is the second leading cause of disability in the United States.

Americans spent a staggering $69 *billion* for treating mental disorders in 1996. We spent another $12 *billion* on direct treatment of drug and alcohol abuse. Despite these astronomical outlays, nearly two-thirds of all people with mental disorders do not seek treatment. Ironically, the probability of satisfaction and success for those who do seek treatment is marginal.

THE HIDDEN COST OF HELP

In desperation and with seemingly no other recourse, dysfunctional people often turn to mental health providers for help. The objective of most of these interventions is to free the patient of negative emotions by means of comprehensive self-examination, methodical retraining (operant conditioning) of counterproductive response patterns, or drug therapy.

Once the reluctance to seek help is assuaged, patients face wrenching conflicts between their inner relief from depending upon all-knowing professionals and their opposing yearning for independence and self-direction. Besides the intended alleviation of symptoms, the benefits of dependence include being cared for, feeling understood, yielding to passivity and reduced effort, and the absolution of (at least partial) responsibility for one's circumstances and actions. The downside is that one bargains away portions of self-sufficiency, autonomy, personal beliefs, and control in submitting to treatment. A price for ascribing dysfunction to being ill is the erosion of one's free will.

These dynamics apply to a range of mental/behavioral health and medical conditions and cogently to the inscrutable ADD/ADHD.

As the controversies over ADD/ADHD intensify, concerns about who and what is ultimately responsible for its detriments claim center stage. Where should we focus? Parenting? Moral laxity and cultural evils? Family decline? Educational deficits? Genetics? Biochemistry? Diet? In a maddeningly vicious cycle, the cause continues to elude the chase for fitting solutions. All the while, the recriminations and frustrations continue: *Why me? Why this? What next?*

Our first chapter elucidated a working model of ADD/ADHD characteristics and the effects of disregulation. Chapter 2 highlighted this issue through eyes of Matthew and his parents as they each wrestled with their torments. In Chapter 9, we visit the very personal struggle of the Othmers in ascertaining the "volitional" versus "neurological" determinants of Brian's troubling behaviors.

Here we confront the issue of personal responsibility, cause, and responses to ADD/ADHD in the current social and medical context.

THE TRUE IMBALANCE

Our era has seen a proliferation of technological marvels. These have extended into the biological domain to reach sophisticated achievements, such as cloning and genetic engineering. Medical science has brought us "designer" drugs that increasingly pinpoint neurotransmitter functions in the effort to tailor somatic and emotional reactions.

Modern imaging techniques allow us to see how the brain responds to stressors, tasks, and substances, as well as the physiological and structural effects of these things over time. It is said that, after the internet, the explosive growth of the neurosciences will be the most influential scientific frontier in the coming decade. This is heady stuff!

What, then, about personal responsibility, free will, and choice? We suggest that any conceptual framework (scientific or otherwise) that wrests control and responsibility from the intention of individuals is seriously misguided and flawed. The wonders of technology (including brain-training technology) must be balanced against the risks of medical "reductionism" so that we don't excuse or condone bad behavior on the basis of technical explanations for justifying who people are and what they do.

We are not denying the systematic and meticulous discoveries about biochemical and genetic influences. In most cases, we have developed parallel explanations of behavior — parallel in that, for EEG neurofeedback, we use models of neurotransmitter functioning similar to the medical models, only that we propound changing these neurotransmitter patterns through brain training rather than solely through psychoactive drugs. Indeed, we go so far as to suggest that learning is so basic to brain function that the brain actually learns to respond to psychoactive drugs).

We caution, however, against relying upon these "medical" explanations as the entire determinants of behavior and the implications and effects of such views upon treatment, self identity, human relations, legal jurisdiction, and social behavior. Certainly, people are propelled by biochemical realities. Yet, this is no rationale for the flippant and pervasive "biochemical imbalance" explanation given by doctors and patients alike to settle concerns about untoward behavior. The true "imbalance" would be that of worshipping with the cult of the neurotransmitter: Accepting facile technical explanations as a substitute for combining the wealth of developing knowledge about the brain as a control system with new methods of modifying it and the historical cultural treasures we have cherished about human free will and responsibility.

ON BIOCHEMICAL IMBALANCE

It seems that theories of biochemical imbalance are both fashionable and scientific. Like other universal truths (e.g., gravity and reinforcement effects upon behavior) biochemical imbalances exist and exert their influences whether or not we believe in them. The practical challenge is to gain enough understanding and control over them so as to predict and modify their desired outcomes.

The real issue, from our perspective, is that biochemical imbalances exist in normal, and even optimal, functioning. To ascribe ADD/ADHD, depression, etc. to a biochemical imbalance is to miss the point — which is the appropriate and functional management of biochemical imbalances on a homeostatic, automatic, internal basis.

Life is a series of imbalances. Hunger, fatigue, ambition, sexual desire, cell reparation — these are all cyclical imbalances that require adjustments and corrections constantly. This is, part and parcel, the fabric of living. The body and mind detect, respond to, assess, and evaluate challenges regularly. These challenges involve routine biochemical functions (even maintaining body temperature), as well as perceptions of, accommodations to, and integrations with the environment. The distinct and persisting difficulties that many people have in regulating these imbalances comprise *vulnerabilities*, not necessarily diseases.

There are markers, of course, for disease that are not merely categorical. Certainly, disease processes impinge upon and deteriorate our systems' abilities to regulate internal balances. But the tendencies toward and prevalence of disregulation (lack of consistent and effective management of the shift of balances) far exceeds the occurrence of disease.

We emphasize that the traditional medical model frequently errs in the understanding and treatment of these mismanaged balance shifts by "over-pathologizing" states of disregulation into bona fide diseases (or, as they are known, *disorders*). The effort to objectify, distance, and render dispassionate those behaviors and symptoms that stir emotional controversy too often results in a diagnosis that legitimizes an unquestioned and distinctly culpable "biochemical imbalance" whose existence would seem to require the latest pharmaceutical key to lock and unlock its gatekeeping.

We caution against such a simplistic and narrow view of neurotransmitter isolation and supremacy. Consider the analogy of regulating vehicle propulsion: Though we may program and accurately target rockets and cruise missiles, the human motor vehicle driver still must constantly adjust to ever-changing conditions on the road. For this, he needs a flexible brain, one that works and adjusts on a dose-independent basis, 24 hours a day, seven days a week, as necessary.

THE NEUROLOGICALLY "DIFFERENT"

Many children and adults with ADD/ADHD or other conditions do have systemic functions (and sometimes biological structures) that are distinctly different from what is considered normal. Genetic contributions and predispositions to behavioral and emotional styles are increasingly accepted and assumed.

We have no dispute that some people function neurologically "differently" than others, probably for a variety of reasons. We assert however, that these individuals cannot adequately be typecast into formulae for neurotransmitter designer modification, either by drugs or other intrusions. Despite the convenience of labeling and diagnosing people and the mass production of chemicals that do modify brain function, symptomatic individuals have whole brains that respond interactively. Some are more flexible than others, and some have more limiting genetic vulnerabilities. Yet, all are capable of changing for better function through learning and of retaining those improvements.

Alas, it seems that the neurologically "different" are often cast as the sport objects for contests between the proponents of self-directed will and the acolytes of the medical "ill" model — this thankless social role in addition to their personal struggles. When the question arises regarding who or what is in charge of personal responsibility and/or dysfunction, political movements and individual constituents can become passionate indeed.

THE ATTITUDINALLY AND LINGUISTICALLY "DIFFERENT"

The "ill versus will" or "neurological versus volitional" arguments have played out along different societal cadres and belief systems. In one sense, it is an archetypal philosophical dilemma about the nature of man. In another sense, it has very real, present-day impact upon the self-images and courses of action of the thousands of families who struggle with ADD/ADHD and/or neurological differences.

We see that today, perhaps in reaction to past moralistic excesses and recent scientific discoveries, technology is frequently used to objectify, distance, and render dispassionate the very personal experiences and attitudes that are — let's face it — passionate and emotional. This trend does not get around the problem; it merely evolves into another movement. The cult of the neurotransmitter has recast the dilemma into nouveau science.

Though they espouse different attitudes and language, the medical establishment and traditional psychology have viewed dysfunction from the "ill" perspective, relegating the patient to limitations (or even incapacitation) due to suffocating influences beyond his control. Physicians use the language of neurophysiology, speaking in neurotransmitter lingo that describes the "lack of access" to brain capacities. Psychologists articulate the problems as the "inaccessibility of coping resources" due to a variety of factors ranging from childhood experiences to poor modeling to inadequate development of cognitive or emotional skills.

The bottom line messages decoded from the commonalities between mainstream medicine and psychology have traditionally been:

1. The brain cannot recover from lost function or damage inflicted.

2. Biochemical imbalances and learning are each state-dependent, virtually static entities that are independent of each other.

3. Personality and behavior change (to the extent that these can change beyond the "damaged" condition) require years of therapy devoted to understanding, reprocessing, and rescripting faulty childhood patterns.

4. Patients are the recipients of the designated treatment, playing a passive (compliant), rather than active role.

Fortunately, these dogma have begun to yield to new scientific discoveries about brain function and structure, progressive psychological treatments, and advances in pharmacology.

We are no longer bound by rigid classification or the adherence to a cultish party line about the limitations of brain function or the role of the brain's owner.

INSIDIOUS "BRACKET CREEP"

Ironically, the cult of the neurotransmitter has brought about some startling discoveries and changes in practice across numerous disciplines dealing with mental health issues.

Important amongst these is a phenomenon described by psychiatrist Peter Kramer in his landmark book, *Listening to Prozac*. The phenomenon is known as bracket creep. (No, it is neither a mold nor bacteria!) This seemingly unsanitary term refers to the cross-migration among symptoms and diagnoses of mental conditions — the "creeping" of one category of mental disorder across the boundaries of others; that is, across once-rigid brackets of diagnostic classification.

After the introduction of SSRI antidepressants, doctors noticed that drugs approved and prescribed for one condition were often very effective for others. Prozac, the vanguard SSRI, was ancestral in this process.

Soon, the cross-migration and cross-prescription of drugs became commonplace, evolving into the current ubiquitous "polypharmacy (multi-drug) management" of dysfunction. Physicians often try to manage symptoms by prescribing "off-label" (this means prescribing drugs for conditions other than for which they were FDA-approved). Thus, antidepressants and anxiolytics (anxiety-reducing drugs) are often prescribed for ADD/ADHD. Psychostimulants are used to treat depression. And, anticonvulsants (used to treat epilepsy) are prescribed to subdue the behavioral disinhibitions often seen in conjunction with ADD/ADHD. A surprising but common practice is the prescription of hypertension (high blood pressure) medication or antihistamines to induce sleepiness in youngsters wired by either their hyperactive nervous systems, the effects of stimulants prescribed for ADD/ADHD, or both.

Regardless of the serious practical concerns and long-term effects of such polypharmacy management, the implications of these results are striking: Bracket creep evidence shatters older rigid notions about the sanctity, boundaries, and even the classification legitimacy of diagnoses held as indisputable.

All of a sudden, the game has changed! The relief that accompanies diagnosis must be tempered by the lack of substance in the diagnosis. Imagine the refrain:

"Thank God, someone finally figured out I have ADD/depression/OCD/anxiety disorder/cerebral irritability/central nervous system disorder/temporal lobe syndrome…"

Here is the good news: Despite the uncertainty of traditional diagnoses, bracket creep evidence is quite consistent with robust and pragmatic models of brain functioning. DSM-IV (the psychiatric classification manual) has more concern for the brain than the brain has for DSM-IV; the brain simply does not follow its rigid rules! The overlap in pharmaceutical off-label efficacy for different conditions parallels our own findings with regard to people's responses to EEG neurofeedback.

When the brain becomes organized and self-regulated, symptoms from disparate conditions ameliorate. The ADD child sheds depression, the migraine patient loses her PMS, the epileptic becomes less obsessive and more evenly focused!

What a marvelous testimony to the innate flexibility and plasticity of the human brain! A death knell, indeed, to the narrow-minded cult of the neurotransmitter.

At first blush, bracket creep sounds like something to be cleansed. Actually, its reality cleanses our clouded preconceived notions about how the brain works.

Speaking of which, a funny epithet to this discussion comes from a reluctant boy who didn't want us to tamper with his brain. He resisted Dr. Steinberg's attempts to attach the electrodes with the objection:

"But, isn't this brainwashing?"

"No, it's actually a training so that your brain can get in touch with and demonstrate your intelligence on a regular basis."

"Okay."

"Then again, maybe your brain does need washing."

THE IDEOLOGICALLY "DIFFERENT"

On the issue of personal responsibility and causative origins for behavior, it seems we have come full circle. The traditional and Victorian view of will as the governor of action and compass of discretion had yielded to the rebellion of recent ages that promoted extradition of cause from people in the name of illness. If one's ship were listing or even sinking, it was duly because of biological imbalances in the captain. Indeed, the pursuit of rescue in this domain led to the conclusion that so many captains were laid low (or missing) due to circumstances beyond their control that the vessels could not independently navigate, and had to be towed by scientific and administrative guard.

We have something different to offer — different in the sense of resolving the issue of division between "ill or will," "neurological versus volitional." We propose the self-regulation model.

In this model, the natural plasticity of the brain is the vehicle for reaching the resolution of symptoms. Treatment is the catalyst for healing, rather than the indispensable additive.

Brain-training through EEG biofeedback is a natural vehicle for brains of all varieties to exercise their opportunities. We have provided a well-tuned instrument (computer electronics), but the brain is the musician. The notes are the neurotransmitters of communication, of melody and background, harmonics and dissonance, rhythm and solo, text and context. Neurotransmitters, like musical notes or alphabet letters, are merely building blocks — characters in a production that must be synthesized, developed, executed, and appreciated by the individual.

We believe that self-regulation fuses the compatible aspects of neurobiology with personal responsibility and self-control. Self-regulation is not a new invention, but rather a rubric for explaining what is already at work and determinative in brain function and behavior. Like other natural forces in the universe, self-regulation is a given, always there, always exerting its influence, always lending its leverage to those who follow its rules. Just as we can find ways to defy or cooperate with gravity (which, incidentally, always has its way), we can use a variety of tools to promote self-regulation.

Thus, our model is, in fundamental ways, consistent with many medical, psychological, and environmental approaches.

1. **Medical** – the self-regulation model emphasizes neurophysiological modification. We are "neurotransmitter-friendly," though we purport to use operant learning to create the changes through new neural pathways.

2. **Psychological** – the self-regulation model emphasizes integration of thought and affect, the cognitive and emotional components of brain function and behavioral stabilization. Our method accomplishes this integration by training, balancing, practicing, stabilizing, and regulating the bio-electrical communication and neurotransmission of the cerebral hemispheres. The end result is a functional and comfortable integration of thoughts and feelings — this is the bedrock of psychological health and the goal of most psychotherapies.

3. **Environmental** – as with other behavior modifying methods, the interaction between organism and environment is pivotal. This interaction is continuous, mutually modifying, and depends upon adequate feedback to make effective adjustments. To encapsulate the efficiency of neurophysiological modification by brain-training, we may describe EEG biofeedback as the "token economy of the subconscious."

This new ideology draws upon some poignant parallels. Here is an example: In *Listening to Prozac*, Dr. Kramer recounts the story of a patient with years of psychotherapy to reconstruct her faulty personality. Ostensibly, this was necessary to correct what was psychologically determined to be damage caused by early childhood experiences. However, Prozac quickly intercepted this incomplete, lengthy, and arduous process. It made the patient well *despite* the history. With immediate evidence too stunning to ignore, Prozac obviated the patient's history as an inevitable determinant of illness and of a supposedly necessary treatment method.

Neurotransmitter changes? Certainly. But let's not ignore the transformation. By such experiences, our philosophy and our openness to the realities that science only insinuates should widen. We should be aware that causes and effects are not the delineated province of double-blind studies funded by the pharmaceutical industry.

The parallel? The patient who comes in for his EEG biofeedback session, and beams,

"Hook me up, Doc, and let's rewrite my history."

PILL OR DRILL FOR WILL OR ILL

In the search for answers to the travails of ADD/ADHD and other disregulation disorders, we run into dichotomies. One side says we are ill, that we can't help it. It wrests control from us as individuals and conscripts us into the cult of the neurotransmitter, swallowing the sacraments, and worshipping technology and science we can barely fathom. The treatment is an impersonal neurophysiological modification of biochemical imbalance.

The other side blames us for wanton lack of discipline, possible moral turpitude, and certain selfishness and self-absorption. It accuses us of suffering from the "Me generation" dressed up as medical diagnosis. Its treatment is spiritual transformation.

The very process of diagnosis and classification presupposes and manufactures a kind of "Panama Canal" disorder with man-made locks and levels and artificial controls. All in the name of regulation, safety, and commerce. Then "bracket creep" floods us in a continuous flow, and the force of reality carries us downstream with the feeling we are drowning.

What to do? Assert our will… or take a pill? Be passively ill… or engage in active drill to rectify the problem?

We insist that disregulation is the problem, and that correcting disregulation solves these paradoxes.

Patients engage in EEG biofeedback training to relieve symptoms. They enter treatment in distress, and leave in transformation. People are not reducible to chemical formulae, response times, or neurosynaptic uptake. They are whole individuals. In the process of becoming again whole, they undergo transformations in entirety, integration, aliveness, and personal responsibility. We may change electrical settings to encourage their brains to learn more effectively, but they are active participants who are very much "in charge."

Whether they hide behind "ill" or "will" in the service of dysfunctionality obscures the real issue: A disregulated brain cannot be as "response-able" as it wants to be; and the disregulated state depletes the brain of its natural wants. When given the right information — its own functional information — the brain wants to want, on its own. That is the essence of will, and it is the best way, where possible, to heal ill.

Taming the Tempest:
The Othmers' Story

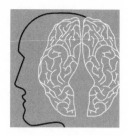

Traditional psychology teaches that our childhood significantly shapes who we become as adults. Real life often carries ironic reversals, as when your children determine much of your adult character, your choices, and your important decisions. The Othmers' story exemplifies the power of children to significantly change their parents' lives, and to reverberate for subsequent years with impact on the lives of many other children and adults. This story recounts the real events of one family (of author Siegfried Othmer) whose tribulations and legacy launched a movement of vast influence and whose experience recapitulates the familiar quandary faced by millions of families every day: Who is responsible for my child's behavior, and what can be done about it?

BRIAN'S ARRIVAL

Brian entered this world with colorful surprise. Though he arrived unexpectedly, he was wanted and welcomed. He joined a student marriage, where Sue and I were both graduate students at Cornell, our focus very much on academics, and with only the usual stipends to sustain us. Starting a family was not our priority at that time. It was fall, 1968, in Ithaca, New York. Against the autumnal brilliance, Brian was born blue. Sue remarked about it at the time, but was told there was no problem. The obstetrician had to contend with two deliveries concurrently, and Sue was asked to "wait." (In retrospect, we have reason to believe that the anoxia Brian suffered at birth contributed to his later difficulties.)

At first, Brian developed favorably. He grew ambulatory on schedule. Despite some early signs of verbal ability, he later seemed a little slow to develop his language skills — nothing serious enough to raise concerns. Our only recollection of any questions about his development was from a friend taking child development classes. She asked if Brian was habitually a headbanger, as she watched him bang his head against the floor. We did not know this was a syndrome that deserved a name. Did he bang his head on the floor more than other children? How would we know? We thought no more about it.

FURTHER DEVELOPMENTS

After moving out to Los Angeles in the fall of 1970, Brian became more of a challenge. We quickly found a home in the Santa Monica Mountains where, fortunately, Brian had room to roam. And roam he did. He would often leave home on his own to parts unknown. At one point, neighbors called the fire department to rescue Brian from a cliff from which he was hanging. He was not in trouble at all, but it looked ominous to the neighbors. At the time of the call, I was searching the hills for Brian myself. We feared he would find the rescue by the firemen so exciting that he would orchestrate a re-enactment; fortunately he spared us that encore.

By this point, he was also falling more significantly behind in verbal skills and in their translation to following directions. The pre-school staff told us that, when the class did "hop, skip, and jump," the other children were on "jump," while Brian was still on "hop." Of course, one could identify attention problems, impulsivity, distractibility, and hyperactivity. But this wasn't ordinary ADD. For a long time, Brian mystified us all.

When first grade loomed, we thought to hold him back because of his immaturity, but the school encouraged going forward with first grade. Not quite six years old, Brian failed to perform with first-grade skills. His teacher, who had a positive approach, would either say something nice about a child in her class or she preferred to say nothing at all. At first, we did not know that Brian was sitting in the back of the class and not participating. This in itself did not concern school personnel, but, by second grade, behavior problems intruded. We always heard his side of the story — for example, the trauma of other students stuffing our poor son into trashcans. Naturally, we never heard the other side of the story. However, we assumed that Brian was partly responsible, since other children weren't getting stuffed into trashcans. Sadly, Brian was becoming a rather sullen and unhappy child.

As reports of his bad behavior continued, we became increasingly concerned.

"Just what do we have to do, Brian? This behavior has to stop!" we would remonstrate. During one such heated exchange, Brian said disarmingly and with resignation: "I am just an evil person. I'm going to go to prison when I grow up." We were astonished and horrified! Such depressing fatalism from the mouth of an eight-year-old! We wanted to rewind and start the conversation all over again.

"No, Brian, you are not an 'evil' person. It's just that some of your behavior is unacceptable. You will simply have to learn to control your behavior."

Brian was way ahead of us. He was aware that he was not in control of his behavior. It was not a matter of willpower.

"Mom, I don't understand. If prison is not for people like me, who is it for?"

What could we say? His logic rang ominously true. People with Brian's behaviors do fill the prisons. He was not saying this to get us off his case. He genuinely struggled to understand himself and the world that so strongly disapproved of him. Brian frequently considered suicide. After yet another argument about his behavior, he announced in resignation, "I'm just going to kill myself." This was clearly not a fresh thought. He had ruminated this way many times before. Again, he was not saying this to back us away. Rather, he was saying, 'You're right. I'm so awful that I can't claim any right to live." On another occasion, he declared that he was a "warlock." When our verbally inhibited child delivered this bombshell, we were stunned. From where did he grasp such strange ideas, such uncommon words? Perhaps, for Brian, the concept of warlock seemed a rational framework in which some of his behavior made sense.

IT COULDN'T GET WORSE (OR COULD IT?)

Brian made one Sierra Club picnic in Malibu Creek State Park a memorable event. Out of nowhere, Brian was beating up a little girl in her best Sunday clothes. I rushed over to restrain him, and peripherally saw the girl's father approaching with flaring nostrils, vengeance stamped on his face. I demonstratively gave Brian a spanking to forestall the man's personal intervention. It was also to vent my own frustration, and compensate for my sense of helplessness. Utterly shaken and embarrassed, we left the picnic. Brian offered no explanation for what had happened.

Shortly thereafter, Sue took Brian to the shoe store. A child sat next to him, also waiting for service. Before long, Brian started to punch the child mercilessly. Sue quickly restrained him. Again, no subsequent explanation for that behavior. Imagine our frustration and humiliation!

At the local Sherman Oaks Park, Brian played T-ball. People admired his batting, but sportsmanship was not his strength. Two incidents stand out with shuddering incongruity. During one gathering for a team photo, I glanced away from the group for a moment, only to look back and see tears rolling down the face of the kid standing beside Brian. He tried not to show his pain. Brian had undoubtedly "rabbit-punched" him the instant I had taken my eyes off the group. Brian stood there appearing angry, but reluctant to give himself away.

On another occasion, when he was seven, Sue and I watched Brian's team play. As it came time to leave, we got into one of the increasingly frequent arguments with Brian. He did not want to leave just yet. His oppositional behavior escalated to the point where he fell down on the ground and made strange noises. We were mortified. Mercifully, the rest of the crowd carried on as if nothing unusual were happening. We lifted Brian off the ground and hustled him into the car. This episode did not seem to represent voluntary behavior on Brian's part; yet, its persistence and continuity were unnerving. At a younger age, this behavior would have been dismissed as an ordinary tantrum. Throwing himself on the ground at his age, however, certainly seemed odd. We wondered: Just what was going on?

School officials called, asking for a conference. We had heard nothing from the school for some time, so we did not know what to expect. We met with a whole committee of school officials, solemnly facing the two of us. One by one, they unleashed a litany of complaints about Brian. He was getting into fights at school. A girl's face had been scratched. He was uttering obscenities in class, and insulting the teachers. The tenor of this barrage made clear that our parenting skills were suspect, and that we were ultimately at fault. *Just what did we have to say for ourselves?* The educators suggested a medical exam, and they said they would give Brian one more chance. Munificently, they would assign a special teacher who would give him the love, affection, and attention he needed, and which was apparently lacking at home. Their approach seemed excerpted from the Bruno Bettelheim school of parenting: Brian was, no doubt, stuck with a "refrigerator mother."

MEDICAL MANAGEMENT: MARVELS AND MYSTERIES

We related all this to the pediatrician, who suspected that epilepsy might be responsible for the behavior. Temporal lobe epilepsy, we were told, often involves adverse behaviors as well as seizure activity. I told the pediatrician that sometimes Brian walked around the house in his sleep. We could not awaken him during these episodes. At other times, he had night terrors. He would jerk violently in his bed, even sit up and bark strangely — again impervious to awakening. When I heard Brian begin his thrashing behavior, I would simply sit with him so that he could not hurt himself by hitting the edge of the bed or the wall. Sometimes, this transpired several times during the night.

Had these peculiarities occurred with dramatic onset, we probably would have become alarmed and done something sooner. The nighttime behaviors, however, had been going on for years, beginning innocuously and only gradually getting worse. We had heard of sleepwalking, of course, and night terrors, too. Perhaps these were things to endure, like bedwetting.

As we surveyed the whole picture together, though, it all began to make some sense. What we thought were night terrors were more likely nighttime seizures, and the daytime behaviors were also seizure-like in character (we later learned that this is called sub-clinical seizure activity). Brian was neither fully in control, nor fully unaware — just what he had been telling us!

The physician prescribed Dilantin, an anticonvulsant medication. The nighttime seizure activity stopped almost immediately. We allowed ourselves a sigh of relief. Perhaps we were on to something. The daytime behaviors, however, continued as before. We were referred to a neurologist for an EEG. When Sue took Brian there, he decided to lock himself in the men's room. It was a while before they could get him out. More bizarre behavior! Our threshold of surprise was rising.

We tried other medications. None of them were effective in quelling this problem. Phenobarbital made everything worse. Brian left home in the afternoon, and we had no idea where he had gone. Hours later, we received a call from his friend's house, several miles away in Encino. He had simply walked there, a greater distance than he had ever gone before. He was truly wired. Panicked, we returned to our doctor, pleading for either a change in meds or a prescription for a ball and chain. The doc seemed unsurprised at our report.

He really wanted Brian on Tegretol. However, that was an experimental medication at the time, and he was required to first attempt all the authorized alternatives before prescribing Tegretol. Thus, we tried the list, one by one. Simultaneously, the school counselor earnestly tried her best to mollify Brian. It made no difference in his behavior. Alas, when he eventually hurled obscenities at her as well, she gave up and rejected him. She relinquished her manipulative coaxing and cosmetic display of affection. It must have been hard for her to keep an act like that going. The next time we met, she glared at us icily. Sue and I sensed that the counselor held us responsible for sabotaging her efforts. If Brian was unable to respond to her kind ministrations, then his emotional resources had clearly atrophied — and we were probably at fault. *Monsters!*

It became gradually apparent that our son was suffering from neuro-logically driven, or brain-driven, dysfunction. His brain had a seizure focus at the left temporal lobe, which was disturbing the normal electrical function of the brain. This activity would ripple through the emotional part of his brain, causing him to act weird at some times, violent at others. It also sponsored paranoia and odd somatic sensations. Sometimes, one side of his body felt warmer than the other.

Despite these erratic phenomena, other things held consistent. He was bound to a routine in many ways, and could tolerate no sudden change in plans. He seemed perpetually depressed. He could not read facial expressions, take jokes, or carry on conversations. He had no real friends. Yet, he was bright in many ways, and had an incredible spatial sense. He figured out the various sizes of Rubik's cube (2x2, 3x3, and 4x4), and could manipulate them through permutations faster than the untrained eye could follow. In a certain way, he was quite the cognitive magician!

Brian fit so many diagnostic criteria. ADHD? Surely. Depression? Yes. Asperger's Syndrome? Probably. Tourette Syndrome? Mild, but yes. Nowadays, he would be called Bipolar. And, then, there were the seizures…

Subsequently, our understanding of neurofeedback would allow us to see all these conditions as aspects of one reality, rather than existing as five distinct disorders. For the moment, however, we were utterly dependent on what the medical field had to offer. The medications had brought the seizure-like activity under control, but at significant cost: Brian was more subdued. His eyes showed that he wasn't really home. He could no longer hit the ball in T-ball like he did before. Yet, we really had no choice about the medication. It was a lifesaver for him.

"DON'T COMPLAIN — IT'S JUST MY BRAIN!"

Ironically, Brian was partially relieved by the diagnosis of his condition. He told schoolmates with great reassurance, "Hey guys, it's not me. It's my brain." It helped him to depersonalize the issues and discuss them objectively. This moral escape hatch can be abused; but, in this case, it had only a positive effect.

Brian received some special schooling for a couple of years before he entered Waldorf School, in sixth grade, where he flourished to the extent he was able. The school was maximally accommodating of his particular talents and shortcomings. Most important, the teachers accepted him. This acceptance allowed him to progress with "soul work," and Brian needed that more than anything else. No one was more troubled about Brian's situation than Brian himself. The school allowed him to build on that good core self that he knew he possessed, instead of the prickly and disagreeable persona that others might encounter. He prematurely acquired that profound tenet of Eastern philosophical wisdom: *I am not my personality.*

Brian was in the eleventh grade when we found out about EEG biofeedback. Nature made him taller and stronger than either of us, and he would still behave unpredictably at times. After high school, he would hardly be able to just hang around the house. He would need an institutional setting with appropriate supervision. Time was taunting us.

Brian undertook the EEG training with relish. Here, at last, was something that he could do competently for himself. He had a love-hate relationship with his meds. He knew that he needed them, but he also knew that they interfered with his mental abilities, cognitive functioning, and manual dexterity. Additionally, they exacerbated his depression. EEG biofeedback training opened a world to him in which he could actively pose questions about his brain and get useful answers in return.

In the first month of his training, at the rate of two sessions per week, Brian's mood became more even. He started smiling. He fought less with his younger brother, Kurt. Instead of disappearing into the local hillside chaparral (where he had his various forts), he started coming into the kitchen for conversations after school. His mother looked forward to what she affectionately called his "daily conversation fix." He was beginning to make friends. Indeed, for the first time in Brian's life, relating to other people brought positive experiences for him, and he craved human interaction. Brian's life was burgeoning. His academics improved significantly in his erstwhile weak areas, especially language, literature and the arts, which were the mainstay of the Waldorf curriculum.

Once Brian discovered that he had some measure of control over his own brain, he took charge with vigorous determination. He managed his sleep better, as well as his diet and his exercise. Everything revolved around conditioning his brain toward greater stability and better function. The more his efforts were rewarded, the higher and more dogged was his reach. He understood his sleep patterns to a degree that defied comprehension. He became intimate with his own brainwave patterns to the point where he could predict his electrical activity in upcoming sessions. He knew what each of those patterns felt like.

In the early days of his EEG training, Brian had minimal awareness of how he was changing. His only impression was that Kurt was being nicer to him. He could not see that he was, in fact, being a lot nicer to Kurt. Eventually, he commented that, whereas before the biofeedback he would always concentrate on the bad things in his life, he was now thinking about the good things. Later still, he volunteered that he was starting to forget just how bad it was in the days before biofeedback.

LEAPS AND BOUNDARIES

The same year he started biofeedback, Brian enrolled in college. He attended Cal Lutheran, in Thousand Oaks, a small liberal arts school not very far from our home. He was within reach of his brain-training sessions in Beverly Hills. He wanted to study computer science, a different path from the strengths of Cal Lutheran's liberal arts curriculum. By his junior year, he transferred to Cal Poly in San Luis Obispo.

At Cal Poly, he earned acceptance into the Math Honorary in his senior year, despite the fact that he was not even a math major. His math professor proclaimed him as his best student, even though he also had math graduate students in the class. Brian continued to experiment with his medications. He had been off the Dilantin since his first year with EEG biofeedback, and the Tegretol was down to a miniscule 125mg per day, which he divvied out in 25mg chunks throughout the day.

During the summer of 1990, he was staying with us at our home in Los Angeles, writing new software for the biofeedback instrument we were developing, and learning how to drive a car in the Sepulveda Basin. After celebrating my birthday with a commercial birthday cake, a carrot cake, Brian sustained a grand mal seizure the following night. His bed linen lay knotted up on the bed in the morning. After some more birthday cake the next day, another seizure occurred at night. Sue suspected an offending dietary ingredient, and found it in the cake: It had been baked with Allspice. We were aware of Brian's sensitivities to various spices. After all, spices are intended to stimulate the nervous system — chocolate, nutmeg, paprika, MSG, etc. In a nervous system that is already hyper-excitable, spices can push the brain over the edge into instability. We had learned to be vigilant. So had Brian, but this birthday cake accident was portentous.

Brian had the strong intention to become medication-free, because it was still impacting on his cognitive function. But he was walking a knife-edge of instability. By managing his own state carefully, he was able to keep the medications at low dosage and still remain seizure-free. He had to be exceedingly careful to avoid offending dietary toxins — especially, paprika, Allspice, and chocolate. These could easily provoke a grand mal seizure. Without all the meds to buffer him, he needed to take even great care with his diet.

No doubt, this explains the seizure Brian had the following March back at college. In the middle of the night, his seizure awakened his roommates. But there was nothing they knew to do, so they simply returned to sleep. The following afternoon, Brian was still in his bed.

When his roommate went to awaken him, his body was cold. The seizure disrupted either his breathing or his heart function. Though rare occurrences, these devastating seizures can happen. It was March 6, 1991. Brian had lived six years with neurofeedback. It had given him a life that medications alone could not offer.

BRIAN'S LEGACY

In our minds as parents, Brian had already died a thousand deaths over the years, while tree climbing, mountain climbing, and bicycle racing. He had been told not to go above 6,000 feet; yet he had climbed Mt. Langley in the Sierras at 14,000 feet. He had hiked with the Sierra Club peak baggers. For Brian, all of these activities were riskier than for most people. But, this is the life that Brian had chosen for himself. He was not imprudent or heedless. He did not even view himself as a risk-taker. On the contrary, he considered himself risk-averse. Because in his young life he frequently confronted the issue of death, he was perhaps more mature in some ways than other college students, while remaining naïve in other significant ways. Though his life was cut short in time, it was long and rich in courage, discovery, and motivation.

During his college years, Brian had written the software that we used in the first neurofeedback instrumentation we developed. His software is still used today. Over time, we came to understand more and more the condition from which Brian suffered, and we did so from the perspective of neurofeedback. It is necessary to understand how the brain organizes itself and regulates its own activities in order to understand this new technique of neurofeedback. In that sense, Brian's condition vividly presented the stark, black-and-white brain-driven behavioral determinants that compelled us. Certainly, ADD/ADHD comprises similarly brain-driven behavior, but, with ADD/ADHD, the boundaries blur and confound between the neurological and the volitional. In Brian's case, the behavior was unequivocally brain-driven. Hence, if we develop a technique that can rescue the brain from the instability of seizures, it should certainly resolve the more minor disregulation of impulsivity, distractibility, hyperactivity, temper tantrums, and rages.

From the vantage point that neurofeedback affords, all the diagnostic categories that could pigeon-hole Brian are not separate realities, but aspects of one reality: The vulnerability of the brain to its own disregulation. Scientists maintain a core belief that nature is ultimately simple — at least when it comes to its basic organizing principles. When we reflect upon Brian's profound response to a single, simple brain-training technique, we conclude that the problems addressed through this training must also be clear-cut and amenable to basic organizing principles of biology that extend also to larger realms of nature's operations. In other words, the intervention's efficacy leads us to understand and define the origin and nature of the problem.

PARENTS' CHALLENGE

Why did a couple of struggling scientist/parents take on the monumental problem of brain malfunctioning? Perhaps, in part, because mainstream science was barking up the wrong tree. The answer, quite simply, was not to be found in changing brain chemistry with the new medications. We have to understand how the brain operates in the bio-electrical domain, how it interacts with itself and regulates its own functions from moment-to-moment. Neurochemistry alone cannot answer the fundamental questions about how the brain gets off-track and how to best help it regain its proper track. And neurochemistry cannot singularly account for the "self" that must integrate biological drives with free will and social conscience.

These challenges notwithstanding, playing the scientist role with respect to your own child has obvious limitations. Our roles had to be those of parents, first and foremost. In that regard, we share experiences with so many parents of ADD/ADHD children. The world may disapprove of our child, but we must be among the steadying influences that hold the child's world together. We always have to navigate the art of the possible. Understanding disorder or dysfunction does not mean that we can rectify it at will or in the moment. Our children need us; from the depth and persistence of those needs, we take our cues. We learn, we grow, and we contribute.

RESPONSIBILITY, UNDERSTANDING, FORGIVENESS, COMPROMISE

As suggested at the beginning of this chapter, the child also raises the parents he needs for his own survival, protection, and care. In fact, even very imperfect children manage to exquisitely detect imperfect parenting. Any shortcoming is immediately thrust back in your face. Somehow, it seems unfair; perhaps, this allows us to glimpse the unfairness the child experiences. One particular anecdote from Brian's youth illustrates the lessons we had to learn over the years regarding what we could genuinely hold him responsible for, and what was beyond his control. Often, the distinction was hardly apparent. Acts that appeared to be volitional were, in reality, neurologically driven.

This dawned on me in an episode I am embarrassed to recall. Brian had a bad case of runny nose, and he was far from either a handkerchief or a Kleenex. He did what came naturally, which was to suck up air through his nose and retain the mucus in perpetual suspension. This frequent and increasing "snurfing" progressively got on my nerves.

"Blow your nose, Brian!"

Snurf.

"Blow your nose, Brian!"

Snurf.

"BLOW YOUR NOSE, BRIAN!"

SNURF.

"Get a Kleenex and blow your nose, Brian."

Snurf.

I brought him a Kleenex.

Snurf.

I held it under his nose.

Snurf.

"Blow out, not in, Brian."

Snurf.

"OUT, Brian. Not in."

Snurf.

The legacy of my Prussian genetic heritage was taking over. I was going to have my way with this obstreperous child if it took me all evening. Surely, he could understand such a simple instruction, and this was merely a case of intolerable stubbornness. I had not chosen the time or the battleground, but, if this was the time, and this the place, then so be it.

The back-and-forth continued. I gave him time to comply. I reasoned with him. I thundered. I cajoled. I threatened. I promised. We reduced the issue to its simplest essence: *Out, not in!* By this time, Brian was a whimpering lump, sitting on the floor in the hallway, saying nothing, but occasionally snurfing. I finally managed to rise above the situation and realize that this was not a child engaging in a battle of wills with his father. This was a child whose brain was caught in a kind of loop from which he could not voluntarily escape — much like a software subroutine that, when finished, returns to the beginning and starts over again. In the case of the computer, you can press "Ctrl-Alt-Del." In Brian's case, he would have to get out of the loop on his own. I was only making it worse. *I was the command that simply re-initialized the subroutine.*

It was a difficult lesson to learn. Brian was conscious; he was processing what we were saying. But, he could not voluntarily act as he would wish! This was so similar to what transpired with his violent episodes. Some part of his brain took command, and he did things over which he had no control at the time and which he later regretted. For his own self-preservation, he had to learn to distinguish between his "self" and the "non-self" that did things he did not wish to do. We also had to make that distinction, so that we did not blame him for things that were not under his control. Since there was often a seamless transition from controlled to uncontrolled behavior, this was something we could only learn over time. At least we now had a framework for understanding our son.

To understand your son is also to forgive him. As we learned that we could not blame him for the quirkiness and instability of his brain any more than we could hold him responsible for his genes and for what fate dealt him, we also realized that the same thing applied to us as parents. Whereas Brian demanded that we be perfect parents, we learned to accept that we weren't going to be perfect, and that doing our best was going to have to suffice. The positive effects of biofeedback training on Brian confirmed for Brian, Sue, and me that we were dealing with neurologically-based phenomena. We learned to talk matter-of-factly about our observations of each other, as well as about our subjective experiences. This objectification of problem situations was enormously helpful in dissipating the emotional baggage associated with such discussions. We replaced blame with a mutuality of concern and interest; it was then no longer an issue of us-versus-Brian.

THE LARGER PICTURE

Though the pressure of emotionality and maladaptive behavior may make circumstances seem like "us-versus-them" issues, these struggles are really reflections of learning to survive — the brain exerting itself to balance and to integrate as best it can with the surrounding world.

As the brain recapitulates nature's organizing principles in its microcosm of self-regulation, so the brain imposes its order upon the larger external world, reflecting in task accomplishment, environmental maintenance, and social interconnectedness.

The challenges of ADD/ADHD lead us to a higher order of adaptation in this neurocybernetic loop that fuses biology, genetics, chemistry, physics, and the mathematical probabilities of behavior.

Fortunately, with ADD/ADHD (more so than with seizure disorders), "normal" function is within the capacity of most children. We have not found a pervasive organic flaw underlying ADD/ADHD (most likely because one does not exist). ADD/ADHD is a disorder of disregulation, and like most disregulation problems, it is, in general, resolvable.

Such resolution is exemplified through trials and successes of our son, Kurt.

THE STORY OF KURT

Brian's younger brother, Kurt, was a more classic case of Attention deficit hyperactivity disorder, and he benefited immensely from EEG biofeedback. His story bears witness, as well, to the power of neurofeedback in enhancing the quality and direction of development. Early in Kurt's life, as in that of most ADD/ADHD children, no one would have imagined any story to tell. Kurt was rambunctious and energetic. He was lovable, highly verbal, and very engaging. Sitting on the lap of a visiting adult in his pre-school years, he could hold forth at length, eyeball-to-eyeball, interspersing his conversations with long words that made you wonder. He could converse like a miniature adult. Kurt seemed perpetually happy and up-beat. What else could a parent ask for? This kind of child made parenting a joy.

HOW SWEET IT IS

One Halloween, when Kurt was four years old, he wore a spiffy little policeman's uniform, his face graced with a black moustache, primed for an evening of trick-or-treating with his friends. He returned home from this sortie absolutely "wired." He was like little space cadet, motoring around the house, eyes ablaze. It took a long time to get him calmed down enough to go to bed. Kurt had discovered that food could do more than satisfy hunger: He'd discovered the powerful effects of *sugar*! Just nibbling on a few candies was enough to send his behavior out of control. This was not totally surprising. Sue was severely hypoglycemic, so we were running a strict low-sugar household. Kurt really had no occasion to sample this delectable temptation in concentrated form.

From that point forward, Kurt sought sugar. We knew the nature of this craving, and, fortunately, it was not difficult to control the diet of a four-year-old. He learned once again to live life without sugar. There were other lessons. When Kurt took medicine with codeine, he became extremely hyperactive. The "wired" reaction also ensued when he was very fatigued. This typically happened at parties at our house, where Kurt would feel duty-bound to serve as Master of Ceremonies. He would escalate more and more into hyperactivity, eventually collapsing into slumber, exhausted from his domestic duties.

THE "GOOD" CHILD

During this period, teachers at his Presbyterian pre-school mentioned to Sue that Kurt could really benefit from Ritalin. Sue responded, perplexed: "You've got to be kidding. You don't understand. This is my *good* child!" Seasoned by the rigors of Brian, we were too inured to complain about Kurt. Over time, their suggestions grew more insistent. We resisted the pressure, figuring that Kurt's natural development would soften the rough spots. We weren't ready to start a four-year-old on a potential lifetime of stimulant drugs.

Kurt had the chance to attend a Waldorf School, too. The Waldorf method is extraordinarily tolerant of the individualities of the little persons that greet them in Kindergarten and first grade. They tolerated Kurt's excesses, and the temptation to resort to medication simply was not there. Rather than constricting or chemically inhibiting his extraordinary energy, a thoroughly calming, engaging, and supportive environment channeled Kurt into a semblance of order.

TRAINING KURT

Nevertheless, we were happy to offer nine-year-old Kurt EEG biofeedback, too. Kurt was still wetting his bed occasionally, so that was reason enough to try the training. Besides, there was the sugar sensitivity, which also might be assuaged. Additionally, there was the propensity toward hyperactivity when Kurt was either fatigued or sick. Though we didn't realize it at the time, Kurt was one disregulated young fellow.

The bedwetting essentially stopped after the very first session of biofeedback. There may have been an accident or two or three in the succeeding weeks, but basically the matter was resolved from that time forward. Over time, Kurt also lost his craving for sugar. Also, the obvious hyperactivity subsided. We were quite impressed. The training allowed Kurt to be more himself. His own experience of this was probably no more than that life had become a little easier. Academically, he moved to near the top of his class — though it was a small class, and, during the elementary grade levels, there was no grading in the Waldorf School. Kurt did well throughout school, graduating successfully from college. He now runs his own business.

The EEG biofeedback we encountered in 1985 had helped both of our children significantly. But, it did not stop there. Since the training was helpful with Kurt's sugar sensitivity, Sue tried the training for her own hypoglycemia, which she was managing with diet. The training made an enormous difference by giving her more energy and by promoting more flexibility in her body's accommodation of dietary variations.

I, too, benefited from the training for a minor whiplash injury that I acquired on a school class outing to Yosemite. I suffered from episodes of dizziness after that injury, and from a lowered threshold of anger. The training effectively handled both symptoms — in my case, in a mere six sessions of training. EEG biofeedback had now scored four out of four successes with the Othmer family. While we were taking Brian in for his many sessions, we observed the changes gradually taking place in others, as we noticed them, week after week, routinely awaiting their sessions.

EEG biofeedback had changed each of our lives for the better. It not only improved attention — it deserved our full attention.

Epilogue

by Kurt Othmer

When my parents discovered EEG neurofeedback for our family, it made perfect sense to them as a way to help my brother Brian with his ADD/ADHD and epilepsy. Everything they knew from their physics and neurophysiology backgrounds indicated that this treatment made sense. They knew that exercising the brain should naturally lead to some improvements. They hadn't anticipated that those improvements would be so tremendous. As they witnessed Brian's great strides forward through neurofeedback, their joy was mitigated by the regret that they had not come upon neurofeedback sooner.

I'm glad my parents had the foresight and courage to investigate and try what seemed right to them. Because they saw developmental and mental health in broader terms than tampering with my chemical soup through drugs, I, too, was afforded the opportunity to find myself naturally and fully, and to develop my brain with the skills I need and use daily. I am indeed more fortunate than many of my peers who are dependent upon drugs, both prescribed and otherwise.

My parents, Siegfried and Susan Othmer, and I have created the Brian Othmer Foundation, an organization devoted to raising awareness of EEG neurofeedback. The three paths of the foundation are: Research, Education, and Clinical Services. The research will encourage broader acceptance of the field; education will develop public awareness; clinical services reach people in need, and, thereby, increase understanding. (Visit www.BrianOthmerFoundation.org) I have created another company to support professionals already practicing neurotherapy, and to develop both awareness and standards of technical competence. This company, EEG Support, has a website at www.EEGinfo.com that is devoted to giving information about the field: www.EEGinfo.com is a website for novices seeking information and for experienced neurotherapists. Material on the site provides information about various equipment manufacturers, training courses offered by different companies, and — most importantly — the EEGinfo site includes a listing of neurofeedback practitioners throughout the world. In this book, you will find that very same EEG directory list from EEGinfo.com.

My family has come a long way, personally and professionally. We have all benefited immensely from EEG neurofeedback. It has changed our lives, and I speak from first-hand experience.

If you have a child with ADD/ADHD, or a child like Brian, or know someone who does, you now have access to an invaluable tool for making these children's lives more successful. This book sheds light on the availability of neurofeedback, what it has done, and what it can do for people in need.

Don't wait or hedge in indecision. Look at the information and take action. We only wish that we had known about neurofeedback sooner. It is our fervent desire to help families avoid suffering and get their children on the right track.

Kurt Othmer

Appendix A
Case Histories

A NOTE FROM DR. STEINBERG

My confidence and gratefulness regarding the ability of neurofeedback to change lives has grown over the years. I have grown as a mental health professional and as a person. Through the powerful alliance of technology and the marvelous human brain's capacities, I have been privileged to participate in a movement that improves lives naturally and with endurance.

The following cases are examples of children and families whose lives took flexible and "correct" turns at the critical intersection of their children's ADD/ADHD and a world unforgiving of accidents.

JAKE

One of my memorable cases was Jake. He is a colorful example of the right road taken to divert disaster. In terms of the effectiveness of treatment modalities, Jake's history illustrates the efficacy of EEG biofeedback at resolving ADD/ADHD in patients who had responded unsatisfactorily or marginally to other interventions.

Jake had received a lot of treatment, including medications, counseling, and special education. Nothing had done much good. Using traditional psychological approaches (counseling, behavior modification, environmental supports, altered expectations), I wasn't doing much good with him either. We had a rapport based upon our mutual failure with each other.

Jake came to me just as I was incorporating neurofeedback into my practice. I suggested neurofeedback to his parents, who were willing to give it a try.

In a comparison of EEG biofeedback with other forms of treatment, Jake would be an ideal test case. We didn't think of him as such, however; he was a series of failures looking for a tube to go down. Most of his family had given up on him, as he lived from one scrape to the next. Jake was as ADD as someone gets. To boot, he had several manifestations of learning disability, and a mood disorder. Medications did not seem to modify Jake according to society's wishes. He was oppositionally defiant with a twist. I had never seen a student who inspired such active contempt from teachers. I had worked with Jake and his family across several grades and schools. No fewer than five public schools tried to get rid of him. Teachers who disliked each other would unite to get Jake out of their classes. This boy was not mean, by the way. He just had raw talent for getting people's goats, coupled with a nervous system that couldn't adjust to the demands of school. He had a sordid educational history, punctuated by academic failure and a rap sheet of memorable pranks. He was not simply a class clown; he was genuinely funny. Like many impaired people, however, Jake had the misfortune to become the victim of his own humor. His talent, his frustration, and his coping mechanisms lit fuses that led back to him.

The baseball cap incident was an example of Jake's notorious career in the principal's office. At his middle school, Jake was repeatedly reminded that school rules forbade the wearing of hats in class. Jake persisted in wearing his favorite baseball cap. (Defiance notwithstanding, many adults remain unaware or insensitive regarding the habits and needs of certain ADD individuals: Difficulty with change, attachment to security objects, tactile sensitivity.) When administrative pressure escalated, Jake rose to the challenge. He clung to his cap, claiming he had head lice. Briefly, this backed people away. The authorities tried to regain control by insisting that Jake wear his cap with the bill forward. Jake insisted on turning it around (catcher-style) with the bill behind his head. This was viewed as impudent, and a contest ensued. Imagine the charade of Jake pitted against a school faculty turning his cap 180 degrees numerous times daily. After several days of this, Jake accumulated a record number of "referrals" and was basically enduring a curriculum of Dean's Office. In some comic relief, Jake took it to another level. I got a call from his father saying that Jake had (once again) been suspended. The offense? After many rounds of teachers turning his cap around to face the bill forward, Jake simply cut off the bill, quietly and victoriously smirking beneath his "beanie" at an exasperated array of teachers.

Therapy with Jake had been arduous for both of us. He was distractible, and felt uncomfortable with talk. I knew Jake liked me and understood that I was on his side. (It became apparent that loyalty was a prime motivator for him.) He really did not want to sit with me developing "insight." He could barely sustain a conversation, unless he stimulated himself by infusing wisecracks indiscriminately. Jake was funny but inappropriate. He simply could not sit still. He hated to write, and he was terrible at it. Math was a losing battle. Jake was excellent working with his hands, and he was a gifted athlete. Indeed, he played high school football until he was disqualified by poor grades. He had tried stimulants and antidepressants, but they did little for his performance, and he did not like to take them.

Jake trained with neurofeedback for many months. Nothing seemed to happen for a long while. Though I didn't know it at the time, Jake was among the small percentage of people who do respond well to neurofeedback only after many sessions. We kept it up because his parents trusted me and because no one knew what else to do. At times, I felt that discontinuing biofeedback would signify giving up, rather than reflect an appraisal of his progress. Then, something unexpected happened. As if to spite everybody (a superbly developed skill of his), Jake became observably better. In the middle of our wishing and hoping that he would respond positively to the treatment, Jake surprised us. He began to calm down. The daily screaming tirades that were a part of his repertoire for years suddenly diminished. He cooperated with household tasks, sometimes volunteering. He was on time much more often, and he was findable when he needed to go somewhere with his parents. Jake's mother fell in love with him all over again. His father, a former policeman, took great pride in the development of his son, whom he had lavished with copious amounts of time and patience. He thanked me for diverting Jake from what he dreaded as an almost certain clash with the justice system.

Jake graduated high school and is gainfully employed. He is outstandingly sober, and free of medication. He helps his extended family with child care. He is still very funny and quite a bit absent-minded. He is the kind of wise guy you can trust. After about 60 biofeedback sessions, Jake was able to discuss his relationship problems and satisfactions with me. We did some brief counseling therapy directed at helping him make some practical career choices, grieving over the loss of a dear relative, and disentangling himself from some unsatisfying relationships. Jake and I had developed an understanding of what we could and could not do. It was enlightening for both of us. He learned about his limitations, even as he broke new ground in accomplishment and in self-control. I discovered a productive alternative to hitting my professional head against a wall in therapy (this was not the first time!). Biofeedback made a huge difference for Jake. It was a seminal experience for me in discovering how this fantastic technique could empower people who were stifling in their own disarray. The gradual learning of internal control, improved management of biological "housekeeping," and the ability of the brain (even one with quirks) to regulate itself more efficiently would lead many people to plateaus of functioning and happiness well beyond what I could induce through coaching, behavior management, and insight.

ANDREA

She was only five years old — but what a handful of tragedy, pathos, charm, and need! From beneath the thick and lustrous hair swaddled by her pink helmet, Andrea fired her smiles like sudden darts. Her mercurial expressions led me on a rollercoaster of beguilement and emergency.

Though I had treated many epileptics and patients with seizures and ADD/ADHD, Andrea was a special challenge: Her parents had called me as a last resort before capitulating to the neurologist's recommendation to schedule brain surgery. Andrea had intractable seizures — hundreds of them every day — and these could not be controlled or managed medically with drugs. Despite years of intense and varied chemotherapy, Andrea's brain was still an earthquake factory, generating disruptive patterns from deep within that shook her feet out from under her.

She could rarely walk across a room without falling down. She looked to her parents for support, as they literally had to hold her hands and body, lest she stumble, seize, and fall. This child with the bubbly eyes hobbled with more dependence than if she were blind, her zestful glow quickly replaced with panic and then vacancy. She startled so easily, and any sudden noise or movement launched her into an epileptic emergency. Her waking hours required that she wear a helmet, and so this little charmer fashioned her movements under the aegis of pink plastic — a hard pink band-aid across a head that lived in slow motion and was headed rapidly for destruction. What limited life she led was threatened internally by electrical revolt every few moments.

Her parents were desperate. Family life revolved around her fragile condition. Both parents worked, and they had another small child. Still, their lives revolved around Andrea's constant needs, guiding her steps, keeping vials of medicine in each car and location, and making frequent crisis visits to the hospital emergency unit.

We pulled out all the stops: EEG neurofeedback, parent counseling, communications with the neurologists, a QEEG, neuropsychological testing, behavior modification, anxiety-reducing techniques. This family was in grave trouble. Seizures can be life-threatening, and Andrea was stumbling against time. The medical recommendation was to cut the corpus callosum, the structure connecting the left and right cortices of the brain. Such a surgery might save her life, but would undoubtedly have severe repercussions, likely causing significant brain damage. Despite her medical fragility, Andrea was precious, and her parents did not want to sacrifice her personality and abilities. This was a girl who sparkled and who demonstrated normal intelligence and verve.

As if they didn't have enough burdens, the parents were fighting, even considering divorce. The stresses were becoming intolerable. Their medical insurance would not cover EEG biofeedback (or any medical service outside the restricted plan), but the parents shouldered the cost, and we began Andrea's training.

I contacted the new neurologist. This was a doctor the parents considered receptive. For years, they had been lambasted, pushed around, and ultimately ignored. They became increasingly suspicious that the medications were making their daughter's seizures worse and more frequent. The sharing of these thoughts made them unpopular with the doctors. Whenever they inquired or challenged the medical recommendations, the result was that the physician referred them away. One physician even went so far as to threaten them with calling Child and Family Protective Services if they deviated one bit from his prescriptive care plan.

The new neurologist was courteous to me, but she seemed indifferent to the neurofeedback intervention. She told me, "I think your counseling will do way more good for all concerned than any biofeedback." This prediction would prove quite errant.

Training Andrea was difficult. She was so unstable that slight variations threw her into seizures. I had trouble finding protocols that her sensitive brain could tolerate. Often she would slump off the chair, and occasionally she delved into paroxysmal grand mal seizures. Once, the paramedics headed for my office. Her brainwaves were so erratic that I wondered how my computer screen could contain the spikes. Setting her thresholds and containing the brainwaves on the screen required a continual manipulation of instrument controls.

Andrea, however, learned to control her brain! After her 24th session, her parents reported the following:

1. She had had no seizures at all for over three weeks.

2. She was walking on her own, without fear.

3. She was eating at the table willingly. (This was a major family problem for the past two years.)

4. For the past month, she slept in her own bed (a behavior unseen previously).

5. She was apparently well-adjusted to Kindergarten, and enjoying it.

As of this writing, Andrea has been seizure-free for nine months! She is thriving at school. She no longer wears a helmet, and this has facilitated her participation in activities and her development of social friendships.

Andrea's parents are getting along much better. They are living together as a family unit. Though the parents have engaged in smatterings of other interventions (such as a few sessions of counseling), they attribute their newfound harmony, relief, and relative contentment to their daughter's amazing progress. They are extremely grateful.

I have kept the current neurologist apprised of the treatment and of Andrea's progress. During one phone conversation, I mentioned how thrilled I was about Andrea's lengthy tenure of seizure absence (nine months), especially in light of her several-year history of virtually continuous and accelerating seizure activity. The neurologist never mentioned neurofeedback, nor the miracle of Andrea's progress. She never expressed thanks or acknowledged my work, nor did she even ask any questions. She merely said, "It's a strange phenomenon. It doesn't make sense. Something is clearly out of whack."

Appendix B

Commentary on the Psychiatric Classification of ADD/ADHD

Attention deficit disorder (ADD) and Attention deficit hyperactivity disorder (ADHD) are conditions listed as developmental disorders in the classification manual for psychiatric, psychological, and mental disorders (DSM-IV, or Diagnostic and Statistical Manual, Fourth Edition). The DSM-IV is a categorization of mental disorders listed by types, symptomatology, and diagnostic criteria. It is a "common language" agreed upon by experts to classify, interpret, and communicate about psychiatric and psychological illnesses and disorders.

Standard psychiatric practice[28] (as reflected in the DSM-IV) uses a multiaxial approach to describing mental disorders. There are five axes upon which different components of a disorder are listed (coded):

Axis I   Clinical syndromes (e.g., depression, anxiety, etc.)

Axis II   Developmental disorders and personality disorders (e.g., ADD/ADHD)

Axis III   Physical disorders (where they exist)

Axis IV   Psychosocial stressors

Axis V   Current level of patient functioning

ADD/ADHD is coded on Axis II and is listed as a developmental disorder. These are defined as conditions that emerge during the developmental period (birth to 18 years). Axis II disorders, which include but are not limited to developmental disorders, are thought to be generally lifelong conditions.

Interestingly, the DSM-IV describes ADD/ADHD diagnostically as having its "onset before seven years of age." Although current trends indicate earlier diagnosing of ADD/ADHD (with increasing medication of pre-school-age children), most ADD/ADHD is diagnosed after age 7. Indeed, there are many people who stumble into this diagnosis as adults (and there are emerging specialties of professional practice treating adult ADD). Nonetheless, a key diagnostic criterion is that the onset of the symptoms occurs prior to age 7. The idea is that the symptoms are present in early childhood, irrespective of the notice taken or diagnosis

---

28   The conventions set by standard psychiatric terminology and the DSM IV are used by psychologists, counselors, social workers, and other health professionals.

rendered. As you are probably well aware, notice is increasingly taken of the ADD/ADHD symptoms (diagnostic criteria) listed in the DSM-IV[29]:

A. Either 1 or 2

(1) Six (or more) of the following symptoms of *inattention* have persisted for at least 6 months to a degree that is maladaptive and inconsistent with developmental level:

Inattention

   (a) often fails to give close attention to details or makes careless mistakes in schoolwork, work, or other activities

   (b) often has difficulty sustaining attention in tasks or play activities

   (c) often does not seem to listen when spoken to directly

   (d) often does not follow through on instructions and fails to finish schoolwork, chores, or duties in the workplace (not due to oppositional behavior or failure to understand instructions)

   (e) often has difficulty organizing tasks and activities

   (f) often avoids, dislikes, or is reluctant to engage in tasks that require sustained mental effort (such as schoolwork or homework)

   (g) often loses things necessary for tasks or activities (e.g., toys, school assignments, pencils, books, or tools)

   (h) is often easily distracted by extraneous stimuli

   (i) is often forgetful in daily activities

(2) Six (or more) of the following symptoms of *hyperactivity-impulsivity* have persisted for at least 6 months to a degree that is maladaptive and inconsistent with developmental level:

Hyperactivity

   (a) often fidgets with hands or feet or squirms in seat

   (b) often leaves seat in classroom or in other situations in which remaining seated is expected

   (c) often runs about or climbs excessively in situations in which it is inappropriate (in adolescents or adults, may be limited to subjective feelings of restlessness)

---

29   Verbatim from *Diagnostic and Statistical Manual of Mental Disorders, Fourth Edition (DSM-IV)*, Washington, DC: American Psychiatric Association, 1994.

(d) often has difficulty playing or engaging in leisure activities quietly

(e) is often "on the go" or often acts as if "driven by a motor"

(f) often talks excessively

Impulsivity

(a) often blurts out answers before questions have been completed

(b) often has difficulty awaiting turn

(c) often interrupts or intrudes on others (e.g., butts into conversations or games)

B. Some hyperactive-impulsive or inattentive symptoms that caused impairment were present before age 7 years.

C. Some impairment from the symptoms is present in two or more settings (e.g., at school [or work] and at home).

D. There must be clear evidence of clinically significant impairment in social, academic, or occupational functioning

E. The symptoms do not occur exclusively during the course of a Pervasive Developmental Disorder, Schizophrenia, or other Psychotic Disorder and are not better accounted for by another mental disorder (e.g., Mood Disorder, anxiety Disorder, Dissociative Disorder, or a Personality Disorder).

According to the DSM-IV, the presence of six or more of these symptoms is sufficient to warrant a diagnosis of ADD or ADHD. (ADHD is the presence of the condition with the hyperactive component.)

The reaction of many people who read the DSM-IV list of defining criteria is, "Aha, that's my child!" However, another common reaction is to notice how general the symptoms are — there are relatively few people who do not display at least some of those symptoms. Yes, there is a lot of ADD out there in the world. However, when the diagnostic net is broad enough to include most people (who, at certain times, exhibit the symptoms), one has to question either the identifying characteristics, the disorder itself, or both. Furthermore, the traditional methodology in medicine has been differential diagnosis — that is the systematic ruling out of disorders with similar symptoms. If the symptoms and criteria for identifying ADD are so general, then not only are we diagnosing a disproportionate number of people with ADD, but perhaps we are lumping into the category of ADD a more varied and subtly differentiated spectrum of mental disorders. Notice the caveat in the DSM diagnostic criteria stating that the symptoms "are not better accounted for by another mental disorder" (ibid). One gets the idea that some diagnosis is assumed, and the important distinction is not to confuse one diagnosis with a more fitting one. This diagnostic methodology reflects modern psychiatric convention much more than it does brain function.

CAN YOU CATCH-22 ADD/ADHD?

This leaves the family with a maladapted or disruptive child in a circular dilemma: If you want to intervene (conventionally), you need a diagnosis. The diagnosis itself legitimizes and constrains both the condition and the indicated treatment (medication), relieving both patient and environment, ultimately, of control.

It's a potential Catch-22: You can overlook ADD by attributing errant actions to normal childish behavior, or you can pathologize the spectrum of normal variations into a one-size-fits-all dysfunctional label.

In this black-and-white paradigm, the "normalization" view sees ADD/ADHD behavior as the result of poor discipline and questionable environmental influences, such as permissive parenting, education, and the cultural media. It is an outlook that enshrines the power of modeling. As the brother of one patient ventured, "I stay away from my brother because I don't want to catch his ADD."

The "medicalization" view regards ADD/ADHD behavior as the visible evidence of a biochemical imbalance (see Chapter 8) requiring, for effective solution, proper and consistent medication.

A significant flaw in this black-and-white view of ADD underscores the discomfort that many people feel with either of these extremes: The flaw derives from the assumption that human behavior and brain function — with all their subtleties, overlaps, and variables — can be neatly categorized into a disease model. The medical model imposes this assumption upon the symptomatology and patterns it calls ADD/ADHD. While the medical model diagnostic nosology[30] finds much utility for diseases, we are hard-pressed to include ADD/ADHD as a disease, or even as the traditionally construed developmental disorder.

When faced with the stringent conceptual choices of "normal childhood mischief" or "chemical imbalance dysfunctional disorder," most people agonize over the precipice of a veritable control issue. To what extent are these maladaptive characteristics evidence of the trials

---

30   Nosology refers to classification and categorization according to etiology (origin), symptoms, and course of the disorder.

and pains of growing and socialization or of a medical disorder that is best relegated to classification and treatment by physicians?

In the absence of any hard and conclusive scientific evidence that ADD/ADHD is a specific disease, it is more realistic and practical to encounter and resolve ADD/ADHD problems with the following in mind:

(1) People differ in degree along a spectrum of self-control and self-management functions.

(2) Problems of self-control and self-management reflect vulnerabilities originating in genetic predispositions and manifesting according to a litany of environmental variables.

The key point is that, rather than using arbitrary cut-offs to declare that someone has a "condition," behavioral and neurological variables can be productively modified to lessen the negative influences of symptoms that accrue as diagnostic indicators of a disorder. Thus, the important issue is not whether a person meets the DSM IV criteria for ADD/ADHD, but rather how much that person needs better, more consistent, and more flexible control of the internal mechanisms which extrude into maladaptive behaviors.

Nevertheless, many people feel the need for a rubric, category, or cohesive description that combines a collection of difficult symptoms into a recognizable "condition" with its own fitting prescription. Additionally, such a description should be consonant with what we observe about how the brain works and what we know about modifying its functioning.

Appendix C
NEUROFEEDBACK PRACTITIONER LISTING
(for post-publication updates, consult www.eegdirectory.com)

UNITED STATES

ALASKA
Wasilla

Lori R. Gorsch, BA
Brainworks
830 Lanark Drive
Wasilla, AK 99654
(907) 373-2073
flgorsch@gci.net

ARIZONA
Mesa

Alberto Texidor, Ph.D., P.C.
East Valley Neurofeedback Center
1855 W. Baseline Road, Suite 170
Mesa, AZ 85202
(480) 899-0238 (602) 432-4962
texidor@doitnow.com

Paradise Valley

Sanford Silverman, Ph.D., BCIA
Center for Attention Deficit/
  Learning Disorders
10505 N. 69th Street, Suite 1100B
Paradise Valley, AZ 85253
(480) 314-4299 (480) 609-1798

Scottsdale

Nancy Wigton, MA, LPC, BCIA-EEG
Arizona NeuroDynamics
7117 E. Mercer Lane
Scottsdale, AZ 85260
(602) 828-0423
nwig@cox.net

Parker

Sharon L. Hansen, Ed.S.
Indian Health Services
12033 Agency Road
Parker, AZ 85344
(928) 669-3256
sghansen@redrivernet.com

Peoria

Bud Leikvoll, MA, CPC, CSAC
Arizona Counseling Services
10559 N. 99th Avenue
Peoria, AZ 85345
(623) 974-0357
info@arizona-counseling.com
www.arizona-counseling.com

ARKANSAS
Fayetteville

Rick Kirkpatrick, LCSW
Healthsouth Rehabilitation Hospital
153 East Monte Painter Drive
Fayetteville, AR 72703-4002
(479) 444-2270 (479) 444-2376
rickk@nwark.com

Springdale

Elise Burt, MSW
Advanced Therapies
20859 Lakeshore Drive
Springdale, AR 72764
(479) 409-6038
ekburt@aol.com

CALIFORNIA

Beverly Hills

Orli J. Peter, Ph.D., DABPS
280 S. Beverly Drive, Suite 407
Beverly Hills, CA 90212
(310) 228-3627
orlipeter@cal.berkeley.edu

Burbank

Joy Ann Lunt, RN, BCIA
Jack Johnstone, Ph.D.
Q-Metrx, Inc.
2701 W. Alameda, Suite 304
Burbank, CA 91505
(818) 563-5409 (310) 418-6743
info@q-metrx.com

Calabasas

Stephen A. Kibrick, Ph.D.
4766 Park Granada, #208
Calabasas, CA 91302-3339
(818) 222-2024

Camarillo

Sherrie Hardy, MA
Hardy Braintraining
697 Mobil
Camarillo, CA 93010
(805) 389-8144
hardybraintraining@yahoo.com

Cameron Park

Lynda King
Cameron Park Medical Group
3581 Palmer Drive, Suite 401
Cameron Park, CA 95682
(530) 676-9970
peaceclimber@hotmail.com

Canyon Lake

Christine Diane Kraus, Ph.D.
Clinical Neuropsychologist
31532 Railroad Canyon Road
Canyon Lake, CA 92587
(909) 246-1020
krauscd@aol.com

Cardiff By The Sea

Carole Menefee
1235 Windsor Road
Cardiff By The Sea, CA 92007
(760) 635-0113
nfblimited@cox.net

Cerritos

Diana Elliott, Ph.D.
18000 Studebaker Road, #700
Cerritos, CA 90703
(562) 467-8967

Chico

David Graham, MA
Brislain Learning Center
1550 Humbolt Road, Suite 3
Chico, CA 95928
(530) 894-6651

Citrus Heights

Sarah DeCesar, M.Ed.
Center for Learning and
  Achievement
Post Office Box 3711
Citrus Heights, CA 95611
(916) 863-1395 (916) 524-5114
oreps37@aol.com

Costa Mesa

Lisa S. Enneis, MA
The Neurotherapy Center
2900 Bristol Street
Building D, Suite 104
Costa Mesa, CA 92626
(714) 545-9401
lisaenn@aol.com

Culver City

Jan Aura
4230 Overland Avenue
Culver City, CA 90230-3736
(310) 559-0200 (626) 584-7139

Cupertino

John Doonan, MFCC
20430 Town Center Lane, Suite 5B
Cupertino, CA 95014
(408) 314-2618

Dana Point

Catherine Osborne Becker MA,
    CCC, ACE/SLP
Catherine Becker and Associates
24612 D Harbor View Drive
Dana Point, CA 92629
(949) 842-9456
cathco@cox.net

Diamond Bar

Karen Kiefer, MS, DO
S.M.A.R.T. Medical
1111 S. Grand Avenue, Suite J
Diamond Bar, CA 91765
(909) 861-2291
smartmed2@aol.com

Encinitas

Jaime Castano, Ph.D.
A+ Attention Center
355 Chapalita Drive
Encinitas, CA 92024
(760) 632-5423
drcastano@cox.net

Fresno

Sydney J. Farr, MS
Neurotherapy Associates
2890 E. Huntington Blvd., #120
Fresno, CA 93721
(559) 907-6309
sydneycgc@cvip.net

Glendale

Sharon Rae Deacon, Ph.D.
3245 Verdugo Road
Glendale, CA 91208
(818) 957-5166 (626) 446-6626

Half Moon Bay

Jane Kingston, Psy.D.
625 Miramontes, #105
Half Moon Bay, CA 94019
650-726-6774
jane@igc.org

Huntington Beach

Veronika Tracy-Smith, Ph.D.
16052 Beach Boulevard, Suite 228
Huntington Beach, CA 92647
(714) 841-3465 (714) 308-5759

Irvine

Jeffrey Wilson, Ph.D.
The Hope Intstitute
20 Corporate Park, Suite 125

Irvine, CA 92606
(949) 955-0565
Patrick L. Healey, Ph.D., MFT
4010 Barranca Parkway, Suite 253
Irvine, CA 92604
(949) 733-1441
plhealey@cox.net

La Jolla

Dan Galant, Ph.D.
Addiction Hypnotherapy
and Neurofeedback
8950 Villa La Jolla Drive, #B112
La Jolla, CA 92037
(858) 546-9257
drgalant@yahoo.com
www.practicalrecovery.com

Ain Roost, Ph.D.
4180 La Jolla Village Drive,
  Suite 250
La Jolla, CA 92037
(858) 552-0501
ainroost@aol.com

Laguna Beach

Catherine Osborne Becker MA,
  CCC, ACE/SLP
Catherine Becker and Associates
24612 D Harbor View Drive
Laguna Beach, CA 92629
(949) 842-9456

Larkspur

Jan Davis, Ph.D.
Davis & Thronson Associates
3 Hillcrest Avenue
Larkspur, CA 94939
(415) 458-1995 (408) 244-6792
davisandthronson@earthlink.net

Livermore

Deb Lefort, MFT
1080 Concannon Blvd., Suite 160
Livermore, CA 94550
(925) 245-0666
debaney2000@yahoo.com

Long Beach

Noemi Bancod-McInnes, Psy.D.
4195 Viking Way, #270
Long Beach, CA 90806
(562) 421-6196
nbmcinnes@aol.com

Penny P. Irwin, Ph.D., MFT
4265 E. Ocean Boulevard
Long Beach, CA 90803
(562) 987-4804
pirwin@charter.net

Los Angeles

Kathy J. Forti, Ph.D.
12401 Wilshire Boulevard,
Suite 300
Los Angeles, CA 90025
(310) 709-7221
kjforti@aol.com

Caroline P. Grierson, RN, BSN,
  CBT
Train Your Brain
941 Westwood Boulevard, #206
Los Angeles, CA 90024
(310) 478-1961
griereegbf@aol.com

Elizabeth J. Kim, Ph.D.
Brain Fitness Center
2727 W. Olympic Boulevard, #208
Los Angeles, CA 90006

(213) 384-8700
ekimphd@wcis.com

Gislene Mariette, Ph.D.
4929 Wilshire Boulevard, Suite 710
Los Angeles, CA 90010
(310) 677-1247
mariettephd@earthlink.net

Evelyn J. Shapero, MA
12401 Wilshire Boulevard,
    Suite 306
Los Angeles, CA 90025
(310) 207-2995
shapero317@aol.com
www.brainfitnesscentre.com

Los Gatos

Mark Steinberg, Ph.D., M.Ed.
14601 S. Bascom Avenue,
    Suite 250
Los Gatos, CA 95032
(408) 356-1002
mark@marksteinberg.com
www.marksteinberg.com

Malibu

Susan J. Stiffelman, MA, MFT
Learning How to Learn®
P.O. Box 4246
Malibu, CA 90265
(310) 589-7020
sjs902@hotmail.com

Manhattan Beach

Margaret Tolleth Wright
2100 N. Sepulveda, Suite 33
Manhattan Beach, CA 90266
(310) 545-6610 (800) 228-1286
Marina Del Rey

Allen Darbonne, Ph.D.
EEG Spectrum Peak Performance
    & Relaxation
4676 Admiralty Way, Suite 409
Marina Del Rey, CA 90292
(310) 578-6400

Menlo Park

Lilian Marcus, Ph.D.
Biofeedback Associates
825 Oak Grove Avenue,
    Suite C-502
Menlo Park, CA 94025
(650) 328-5581
lilianmarcus@earthlink.net
www.brainwavetherapy.com

Merced

Karen Carlquist-Hernandez,
Ed.D. & Assoc.
3319 North M Street
Merced, CA 95348-2714
(209) 385-3585

Mission Viejo

Stephanie Jona Buehler, Psy.D.
27281 Las Ramblas, Suite 200
Mission Viejo CA 92691
(949) 367-4595
neurotherapy@cox.net

Orange

Pilar Bossenmeyer,
BA/Sports Medicine
Mindwalktraining
1402 E Madison Avenue
Orange, CA 92867
(714) 404-1965
pilichang@lycos.com

Paul Sullivan, Psy.D.
Center for Individual & Family
  Therapy
840 Town & Country
Orange, CA 92868
(714) 558-9266 x960
drsullivan@cift-usa.com
www.cift-usa.com

Jay Gattis
1028 Town and Country Road
Orange, CA 92868
(714) 541-7100 (714) 214-3730

Palmdale

Barbara A. Linde, Ph.D.
3031 East Avenue R-12
Palmdale, CA 93550
(661) 947-2537
eeg.linde@earthlink.net

Palm Springs

Rose Tijerina-Swearingen
291 E. Camino Monte Vista
Palm Springs, CA 92262-4710
(760) 864-6363

Pasadena

Kent S.Kinzley, MA, MFT
595 E. Colorado Blvd.,
Suite 629
Pasadena, CA 91101-1714
(626) 584-5529 (626) 440-7322

Victoria L. Ibric, M.D., Ph.D.,
  BCIAC
Therapy and Prevention Center
65 N. Madison Avenue, Suite 405
Pasadena, CA 91101
(626) 577-2202

dribric@aol.com
www.neurofeedback-dribric.com

Ann-Marie Stephenson
PSY 13812
Post Office Box 94477
Pasadena, CA 91109
(213) 538-0000
lilah@cheetah.net

Rancho Cucamonga

Ken Olson
Olive Branch Counseling Center
9033 Baseline Road, Suite A
Rancho Cucamonga, CA 91730-
  1214
(909) 989-9030

Marsha Lynn Snow, MS
Olive Branch Counseling Centers, Inc.
9033 Baseline Road
Rancho Cucamonga, CA 91730
(909) 9899030 x14
msneurofeedback@charter.net

Rancho Mirage

Ruth A. Bolton, RN, Ph.D.
Medical Psychology Group, Inc.
39000 Bob Hope Drive, #302
Rancho Mirage, CA 92270-3202
(760) 341-2900

Julie A. Madsen, Psy.D.
42600 Bob Hope Drive
Rancho Mirage, CA 92270
(760) 346-3312
drjmadsen@att.net
jmadsen.eeginfo.com

Redlands

Carol Hindman, RN, MFT
The Center for Wellness
101 E. Redlands Boulevard,
  Suite 251
Redlands, CA 92374-1460
(909) 792-2216

Reseda

Tina VanBenschoten
MM Van Benschoten, OMD, CA,
  Inc. & Assoc
19231 Victory Boulevard, Suite 151
Reseda, CA 91335-6308
(818) 344-9973 (818) 344-9992

Faith D. Sutton-Triandos, AA
M.M. Van Benschoten OMD, CA, Inc.
19231 Victory Boulevard, Suite 151
Reseda, CA 91335
(818) 344-9973
mmvbs2@earthlink.net
www.mmvbs.com

Rocklin

Daniel Jorgensen
3420 Nathan Court
Rocklin, CA 95677
(530) 887-5525 (530) 823-7648

Sacramento

Leonteen Chevreau, MA, BA
Neurofeedback Valley Associates
7501 Hospital Drive, Suite 301
Sacramento, CA 95823
(916) 681-4141
neuroFB@aol.com

Richard Manuel Costa, LCSW
3067 Freeport Boulevard

Sacramento, CA 95818
(916) 361-0440
clinician@comcast.net
www.richardcosta.com

San Diego

Leslie A. Hendrickson-Baral, M.Ed.
California Neuro Education
3636 Fourth Avenue, Suite 210
San Diego, CA 92103
(619) 220-2459
neurobics2000@yahoo.com
lhendrickson.eeginfo.com

Sarah F. Luth, BA
EEG Biofeedback Center
1045 Meade Avenue
San Diego, CA 92116
(619) 296-2895
telenos@aol.com

Judy Phillips, Ph.D.
5230 Carroll Canyon Road,
  Suite 320
San Diego, CA 92121
(619) 220-2525
yehudite@aol.com

Drew Pierson, Ph.D.
Mind Form Institute
5230 Carroll Canyon Road,
  Suite 320
San Diego, CA 92121
(858) 442-1488
list@mindform.org
www.mindform.org

Lisa Tataryn
Center for Neurofeedback and
  Research
3405 Kenyon Street, Suite 105

San Diego, CA 92110
(858) 204-2896
lisatat@hotmail.com

San Jose

Mark Steinberg, Ph.D., M.Ed.
14601 S. Bascom Avenue,
Suite 250
Los Gatos, CA 95032
(408) 356-1002
mark@marksteinberg.com
www.marksteinberg.com

Colin R. Wright, Ph.D.
2101 Forest Avenue,
Suite 222
San Jose, CA 95128
(408) 280-5755
colin@concentric.net

San Juan Capistrano

Joan D. Jackson
31165 Via San Vicente
San Juan Capistrano, CA 92675
(949) 661-2922
dierjoni@aol.com

San Luis Obispo

Janet L. Ingram, MA, Counseling
   Psychology
Neurofeedback Center of San Luis
   Obispo
1012 Pacific Street, Suite B
San Luis Obispo, CA 93401
(805) 543-9301
braintrain@shasta.com
jingram.eeginfo.com

San Mateo

Jane Kingston, Psy.D.
100 S. Ellsworth, #806

San Mateo, CA 94401
(650) 347-5456
jane@igc.org

San Rafael

Julian Isaacs, Ph.D.
The ADD Clinic &
   Neurodiagnostic Brain Imaging
1050 Northgate Drive, Suite 1
San Rafael, CA 94903
(415) 479-7265
julianisaacs@aol.com

Cynthia Kerson, BA
Marin Biofeedback
1050 Northgate Drive, Suite 1
San Rafael, CA 94960
(415) 472-1875
ckerson@pacbell.net
www.marinbiofeedback.org

Santa Barbara

Clark Elliott, Ph.D.
Santa Barbara Neurofeedback
   Center
923 Laguna Street, Suite B
Santa Barbara, CA 93101
(805) 560-7690

Melinda Horn, MA, MFCC
Post Office Box 5843
Santa Barbara, CA 93150

John Broberg, MA
Santa Barbara Neurofeedback
   Center
923 Laguna Street, Suite B
Santa Barbara, CA 93101
(805) 560-7690
neuromail2003@yahoo.com

Kenedy Singer, Ph.D.
413 Paseo del Descanso
Santa Barbara, CA 93105
(805) 448-6689
k.singer@verizon.net

Santa Maria

Frank Schlosser, MFT
1107 So. Broadway
Santa Maria, CA 93454
(805) 922-2989
frankjschlosser@aol.com

Santa Paula

Sandy Talbott, RN
854 E. Main Street
Santa Paula, CA 93060
(805) 701-8884 (805) 525-1610

Tahoe Vista

John Finnick, MA, LEP
Post Office Box 346
Tahoe Vista, CA 96148
(530) 581-1506 (916) 708-3269

Thousand Oaks

Bruce Robert Watson, MSW
Conejo Biofeedback & Counseling
88 Long Ct., Suite C
Thousand Oaks, CA 91360
(805) 526-8534
blwatson@adelphia.net

Torrance

Gary J. Schummer, M.Div., Ph.D.
Attention Deficit Disorder
  Treatment Center
24050 Madison Street, Suite 111
Torrance, CA 90505

(310) 378-0547
addcenters@cs.com
www.Dr-ADD.com

Ventura

Susan Hellman, Ines Monguio,
  Ph.D.
1280 S. Victoria, Suite 230
Ventura, CA 93003
(805) 650-7484 (805) 218-6946

Walnut Creek

Ali Hashemian, Ph.D., BCHT
Center for Attention and
  Achievement
39 Quail Court, Suite 101
Walnut Creek, CA 94596
(925) 280-9100

A. Hashemian, Ph.D. &
  Greg Alter, Ph.D.
Attention and Achievement Center
1600 South Main Street, Suite 260
Walnut Creek, CA 94596
(925) 280-9100
info@idealu.com
www.idealu.com

Nancy B. Larsen, M.Ed. BCIAC,
  CBIS
1301 Ygnacio Valley Road,
Suite 102
Walnut Creek, CA 94598
(925) 934-2399
nancy_l@sbcglobal.net

Carolyn Robertson, MA, MS, ND
Advanced Neurotherapy
31 Panoramic Way, Suite 202

Walnut Creek, CA 94595
(925) 906-0420
ptta@post-trauma.com
www.post-trauma.com

West Los Angeles

Jim Incorvaia, Ph.D.
Reiss-Davis Child Study Center
12401 Wilshire Boulevard,
Suite 306
W. Los Angeles, CA 90025
(310) 204-1666 (310) 393-2626

Thomas Brod, M.D.
12304 Santa Monica Boulevard,
  Suite 210
W. Los Angeles, CA 90025-2551
(310) 207-3337

Westlake Village

Harold L. Burke, Ph.D.
Clinical Neuropsychology
2277 Townsgate Road, Suite 220
Westlake Village, CA 91361
(805) 449-8777 (805) 987-7444

Beverly Cross, MA, MFT
2535 Townsgate Road, #209
Westlake Village, CA 91361-2650
(805) 379-1009

Woodland Hills

Susan F. Othmer, BA, BCIAC
EEG Institute
22020 Clarendon Street, Suite 305
Woodland Hills, CA 91367
(818) 373-1334
sueothmer@eeginstitute.com
www.eeginstitute.com

Yorba Linda

Scott Kambak, MA
Success Unlimited Center For
  Learning
20457 Yorba Linda Boulevard
Yorba Linda, CA 92886
(714) 693-3085
mkambak@hotmail.com
www.successunlimitedcenter.com

COLORADO
Aspen

Joanne Stern, Ph.D.
201 N. Mill Street, Suite 103
Aspen, CO 81611
(970) 925-6072

Littleton

Kay Sheehan, MSW, LCSW, Ed.D.
2305 E. Arapahoe Road, Suite 214
Littleton, CO 80122
(303) 795-1761 (303) 884-3328
drkms@aol.com

Boulder

Louise E. Marks, MS, OTR
ANS Applied Neurophysiology
  Services
3478 16th Circle
Boulder, CO 80304
(303) 546-6639
biomarks@yahoo.com

CONNECTICUT
New Haven

Alan M. Shulik
147 Bishop Street
New Haven, CT 6511
(203) 915-3988

West Hartford

Rae Tattenbaum, MSW, CSW
Inner Act
10 North Main Street
West Hartford, CT 06107
(860) 561-5222 (866) 626-0616
rtinneract@aol.com

Bethlehem

Patti A. Lizotte, RN
Focus, LLC
136 East Street
Bethlehem, CT 06751
(203) 266-5658
pattioldfox@earthlink.net

Stonington

Henry Brower Mann, M.D.
Neurofeedback East
188 Wolf Neck Road
Stonington, CT 06385
(860) 536-6023
hank7503@aol.com

Woodbury

David Pavlick, MSW
Sherman Hill Center
47 Sherman Hill Road,
Suite B-102
Woodbury, CT 06798
(203) 263-8280
dpav@earthlink.net

FLORIDA

Boca Raton

Dr. Wayne Clayman
Florida Mental Fitness Center
19090 Skyridge Circle
Boca Raton, FL 33498
(561) 756-6039

Bonita Springs

JoAnn Blumenthal, MS, MA,
  Clin. Psych.
Biofeedback Center of Florida, Inc.
8850 Terrene Court,
  Suite 107
Bonita Springs, FL 34135
(239) 949-2300
biocenterflorida@aol.com
www.biofeedbackcenter.net

Clearwater

Diana L. Pollock, M.D.
CNS Specialists
1011-A Jeffords Street
Clearwater, FL 33756
(727) 443-3295
drdpowder@yahoo.com
www.pinellas.neurohub.net

Coral Springs

Catalina U. Fazzano, Ph.D.
10167 NW 31st Street, Suite 100
Coral Springs, FL 33065
(954) 341-0660
cataphd@bellsouth.net

Ft. Myers

Barbara K. Carlin, MS
Stress, Pain Management and
  Biofeedback Center
4066 Evans Avenue, Suite 24
Ft. Myers, FL 33901
(239) 768-0821
BCarlin801@aol.com
www.neurofeedbackandbiofeedback.com

Jacksonville

Ann Grenadier, LMHC, CBT,
  CEEG & Ivy Caldarelli, MS
Biofeedback Associates of NE Florida
8130 Baymeadows Circle W., #308
Jacksonville, FL 32256
(904) 733-2038

Maitland

George E. von Hilsheimer, Ph.D.
A-Affiliated Practice
125 S. Swoope Avenue
Maitland, FL 32751
(407) 644-6464
drvonh@mindspring.com
www.drbiofeedback.com

Miami

Samuel E. Roura, M.D.
Dr.'s & Associates
10305 NW 41st Street (Doral
  Blvd.), Suite 205
Miami, FL 33178
(305) 718-9800

Alicia Vidal-Zas, Psy.D., P.A.
10250 S.W. 56th Street, #C102
Miami, FL 33165
(305) 279-0060
arvida712@aol.com

Astrid Schutt-Aine, Ph.D.
9010 S.W. 137 Avenue, Suite 209
Miami, FL 33186
(305) 387-8289
astridsa@bellsouth.net

North Miami Beach

Diana Malca
Healing Through Play. CORP
16300 NE 19th Ave., Suite 233
North Miami Beach, FL 33162
305 945 2774
dmalca@bellsouth.net

Palm Beach Gardens

Leslie Coates, LCSW
Palm Beach Mental Fitness Inst.
600 Sandtree Dr., #206C
Palm Beach Gardens, FL 33403
(561) 799-0088
lcoates@pb.quik.com
www.eegbraintrain.com

Tallahassee

Donna St. Hillier
1901 Maymeadow Lane
Post Office Box 370874
Tallahassee, FL 32303
(850) 847-1107 (850) 224-9959

Linda R.Young, Ph.D.
Family Recovery Resources
219 E. 5th Avenue
Tallahassee, FL 32303-6205
(850) 656-1404

W. Jack Golden, Ph.D.
Mahan Oaks Center
2898 Mahan Dr., Suite 3
Tallahassee, FL 32308
(850) 656-1129
golden263@aol.com
www.drjGolden.com

Venice

Patricia Jo Ryan, Ph.D.
Applied Neurofeedback Associates
333 South Tamiami Trail, Suite 203
Venice, FL 34285

(941) 486-1930 (941) 350-1831
anapjr@acun.com

Lake Worth

Mimi Bailey, RN, B.S. Ed.
Neurofeedback Therapy
1205 No. Federal Highway
Lake Worth, FL 33460
(561) 386-3973
mimipema@bellsouth.net

Melbourne

Henry Owens, Ph.D.
Atlantic Psychiatric and Counseling
  Center
1351 Bedford Drive, Suite 103
Melbourne, FL 32940
(321) 757-6800
drowens@att.net

Sarasota

Jane Kapp
Thinking Cap USA
2426 Bee Ridge Road, Suite B
Sarasota, FL 34239
(941) 927-5953
kappjane@cs.com
www.ThinkingCapUSA.com

South Miami

Mindy Kopolow, Psy.D.
Neuropsychology Associates of
  South Florida
7600 Red Road, Suite 309
South Miami, FL 33143
(305) 663-9180
dockop18@aol.com

GEORGIA
Decatur

Stephen J. Johnson, Ph.D.
The Center for Cognitive
  Rehabilitation
1276 McConnell Drive, Suite C
Decatur, GA 30033-3506
(404) 321-1441 (404) 321-1444

Gainesville

David S. Bailey, Ed. D.
Affiliated Psychological and Medical
  Consultants
200 South Enota Drive, Suite 400
Gainesville, GA 30501
(770) 534-3619
drdavidbailey@aol.com

Roswell

Martin Wuttke, CNP
Neurotherapy Centers For Health
83 Woodstock Street
Roswell, GA 30075
(770) 649-5321
ifw@mindspring.com
www.neurotherapy.us

Thomasville

Catherine B. Howell, Ph.D.
Associates In Wellness
419 N Crawford Street
Thomasville, GA 31792-5128
(229) 228-5192

Woodstock

Richard G. Soutar, Ph.D.
Synapse Neurofeedback Center
9766 Hwy 92, Suite 200
Woodstock, GA 30188

(770) 516-1661
synapse2@bellsouth.net

HAWAII
Honolulu

Amanda S. Armstrong, Ph.D.
EEG Spectrum of Hawaii
1600 Kapiolani Boulevard,
Suite 1650
Honolulu, HI 96814-3806
(808) 951-5540 (808) 236-2563

Honaunau

Jean Cluff, RN, LMT
Ho'oku'u Lomi
Post Office Box 888
Honaunau, HI 96726
(808) 987-5936
genie@hawaii.rr.com

Kamuela

Anita L Gerhard, M.D.
Post Office Box 6705
Kamuela, HI 96743
(808) 885-8989
gerhard@aloha.net

Kaneohe

Peggy S. Hill, MSW
Windward Neurofeedback
  Associates
46-359 Haiku Road, A-6
Kaneohe, HI 96744
(808) 781-3007 (808) 781-3008
pshill555@hawaii.rr.com

Kealakekua

Terry Ann Fujioka, Ph.D.
79-7460 Mamalahoa Hwy., #110

Kealakekua, HI 96750
(808) 324-0434
tokie@gte.net

IDAHO
Coeur d'Alene

Roberta Truscott
3774 N Sutters Way
Coeur d'Alene, ID 83815-9140
(208) 765-3415 (208) 765-0294

Eagle

Joan Odum Ordmandy, MS.Ed.
Idaho Institute Of Biofeedback
593 E State Street
Eagle, ID 83616
(208) 442-4442
joan@biofeedbackworks.net
www.biofeedbackworks.net

Rigby

Fran Bryson
EEG
3881 East 400 North
Rigby, ID 83442-5435
(208) 745-5774

Boise

Sara Denise LaRiviere, Ed.D.
The Brain Training Institute LLC
2503 W. State Street
Boise ID 83702
(208) 331-7711
slarivi@boisestate.edu

ILLINOIS
Champaign

Barbara Blaylock, Ph.D.
206 North Randolph, Suite 3

Champaign, IL 61820
(217) 356-1058

Joanne Gingrich Crass, BSN.,
  MSN.
2718 Valley Brook Drive
Champaign, IL 61822
(217) 352-7654

William Andrew Hogan, Ph.D.
Midwest Neurofitness
313 N. Mattis, Ste. 205
Champaign, IL 61920
(217) 355-4012
andy@midwestneurofitness.com
www.midwestneurofitness.com

Charleston

William Andrew Hogan, Ph.D.
126 Sixth Street
Charleston, IL 61821
(217) 348-1086
andy@midwestneurofitness.com
www.midwestneurofitness.com

Chicago

Ann Richman, MA
Richman Discovery Clinic
6305 North Milwaukee Avenue
Chicago, IL 60076
(773) 774-0910
richmandc@earthlink.net

Deerfield

Joseph Barr, Ed.D.
Biofeedback North
102 Wilmot Road, Suite 140
Deerfield, IL 60015
(847) 444-0704
josbarr@aol.com
www.BFNORTH.com

Glen Ellyn

Ann Louise Stout, MSW
800 Roosevelt Road, #B-104
Glen Ellyn, IL 60137
(630) 858-5105
astout4@aol.com

Highland Park

William Levin, Ph.D.
Rhythmostat Therapeutics
1803 St. Johns Avenue
Highland Park, IL 60035-3298
(847) 432-5270

Hoffman Estates

Alexander Adam Eschbach, Ph.D.
Advanced Biofeedback Center
1000 Grand Canyon Parkway,
  Suite 203
Hoffman Estates, IL 60194-1730
(847) 755-0555

Homewood

Marcia McCabe
South Loop EEG Neurofeedback
2024 Hickory Road, Suite 104
Homewood, IL 60430
(708) 799-4649

Nancy Milnes, LCSW
New Wave Neurofeedback
2024 Hickory Road, #101
Homewood, IL 60430
(708) 798-1886
braintrain@ameritech.net

Matteson

Rosita Butler, RN, NCC, LCPC
Transitions
20320 S. Crawford

Matteson, IL 60443
(708) 748-6000

Northbrook

Joy Ann Lunt, RN, BCIA
Cynthia Kent, MA
EEG Spectrum-Northshore, Inc.
3701 Commercial Avenue, Suite 15
Northbrook, IL 60062
(847) 509-5100
eegjoy@aol.com

Oak Park

Earlene Strayhorn
1022 South Oak Park Avenue
Oak Park, IL 60304
(708) 750-4360

Rockford

Michael S. Logan, MS
Logan Counseling
2233 Charles Street, Suite H
Rockford, IL 61104
(815) 484-0946
mlogan7264@aol.com
www.logancounseling.com

Schaumburg

Joseph N. O'Donnell, Ph.D.
1443 W. Schaumburg Road,
  Suite 205
Schaumburg, IL 60056
(847) 590-0939
phd_60056@yahoo.com

Winnetka

Marty DeBoer
Psychoeducational Services, Inc.
1050 Gage Street

Winnetka, IL 60093
(847) 501-6161 (847) 501-6168

INDIANA
Greenwood

Lise D. DeLong, Ph.D.
Meridian Developmental Center
3100 Meridian Park, Suite 160
Greenwood, IN 46142
(317) 258-7444
drldelong@aol.com
www.DrLDelong.com

Indianapolis

Christine Lannan, RN, MSN
3630 Guion Road, Suite 320
Indianapolis, IN 46222
(317) 613-3064
chrislannan@comcast.net

IOWA
Des Moines

Ladell A. Lybarger, RN
EEG Neurofeedback
1221 Birch Lane
Des Moines, IA 50315
(515) 244-1883
lybargerrn@aol.com

Mt. Pleasant

Rita Davis, RN, MA
REEGeneration
1652 Highway 34 West
Mt. Pleasant, IA 52641
(319) 385-4187 (319) 931-1069
reegener@interl.net

KANSAS
Emporia
Shari Sippola, MA, LPC
Emporia Psychological Services, Inc.
702 Commercial Street, Suite 8
Emporia, KS 66801
(620) 342-1998
shari4@cableone.net

Topeka
Thomas V. Matthews, Ph.D.
Optimum Performance Solutions™
2709 SW 29th Street, Suite 102
Topeka, KS 66614
(785) 273-5373

Lawrence
William Spencer Payne, Ph.D.
901 Kentucky Street, Suite 301
Lawrence, KS 66044
(785) 969-5380
spencerpayne2@aol.com

LOUISIANA
Slidell
Deborah S. Piacsek, APRN, MSN, CS
Center For Better Living
951 Gause Boulevard, Suite 2
Slidell, LA 70458-2937
(985) 641-0505

MAINE
Calais
Scott Withers
Cooper Medical Group
163 Main Street
Calais, ME 4619
(207) 454-8745 (207) 557-6633
coopermedicalgroup@rcn.com

Yarmouth
Cindy Perkins
13 Pennyroyal Court
Yarmouth, ME 4096
(207) 846-3010 (518) 439-6431

MARYLAND
Bethesda
Susan Belchamber
Lifespan Development
7021 Persimmon Tree Rd.
Bethesda, MD 20817
301-767-0261
lifespan-development@starpower.net

Chevy Chase
Michael A. Sitar, Ph.D.
5480 Wisconsin Avenue, #221
Chevy Chase, MD 20815
(301) 718-3588
michaelasitar@cs.com

Ellicot City
Marianne S. Becker, LCSW-C
9051 Baltimore National Pike,
  Suite 3A
Ellicot City, MD 21042
(410) 465-0180 (410) 960-0191
beckermsw@aol.com

Lutherville
Sheldon C. Levin, Ph.D.
The Neuroscience Team
2328 West Joppa Road, Suite 10
Lutherville, MD 21093
(410) 828-7792
slevintnt@aol.com

Olney

Robin Moore, MA
Executive Insights
2707 Olney Sandy Spring Road
Olney, MD 20832
(301) 924-1909
crobinmoore@comcast.net

Rockville

Ann M. Lee, M.Div., LCSW-C
Neurofeedback Associates of
  Maryland
4405 Rex Place
Rockville, MD 20853
(301) 924-2294
amcl5600@aol.com

Towson

Diana L. Walcutt, Ph.D.
7600 Osler Drive, Suite 211
Towson, MD 21204
(410) 337-8883
drwalcutt@comcast.net

MASSACHUSETTS

Andover

Richard N. Shulik, Ph.D. and
  Associates
35 Clark Road
Post Office Box 3067
Andover, MA 01810
(978) 475-3599
shulik@attbi.com

Beverly

Garbis Dimidjian, Ph.D.
119 Cross Lane
Beverly, MA 1915
(617) 628-2929

Brookline

Hannah Levertov, Ph.D.
194 Lancaster Terrace
Brookline, MA 02446
(617) 975-0053
clwshrink@aol.com

Eileen E. Schwartz, Ph.D.
1093 Beacon Street, Suite 1A
Brookline, MA 02446
(617) 731-4141
eschwar2@channel1.com

Great Barrington

Jamie Deckoff-Jones, M.D.
New England Hyperbaric Center
Great Barrington, MA 01230
(413) 528-9977
jdj@newenglandhyperbaric.com
www.newenglandhyperbaric.com

Greenfield

Josephine Queneau, B.S.N.
416 Leyden Rd
Greenfield, MA 1301
(413) 774-4688

N. Falmouth

Paul Goldring, Ph.D.
EEG Biofeedback of Cape Cod
Second Floor
Post Office Box 1901
N. Falmouth, MA 2556
(508) 563-1850 (508) 563-1851

Medford

Georgianna Saba, M.Ed.
EEG Biofeedback Boston - Irlen
  Center
25 A Mabelle Avenue

Medford, MA 02155
(781) 396-3321
eegnfboston@aol.com

Newburyport

Jonathan Davis, Ed.D.
37-A Pleasant Street
Newburyport, MA 01950
(978) 465-8846
ajdavis@ttlc.net

Northampton

Sebern Fisher, MA
34 Elizabeth Street
Northampton, MA 01060-2320
(413) 586-4230

Katharine Hazen, MSW, ACSW,
    LICSW
Brainwave Training
49 Hubbard Avenue
Northampton, MA 01060-2321
(413) 586-8352
khazen@map.com

Catherine Rule, M.Ed., CAGS, CRC
Optimal Brain Institute
16 Center Street, Suite 301B
Northampton, MA 1060
(413) 584-5108 (413) 626-6850

Patricia K. Lyons, RN, MS, CS
16 Center Street, Suite 218
Northampton, MA 1060
(413) 587-0775

Paula Murphy, LCSW
16 Center Street, Suite 301
Northampton, MA 1060
(413) 586-6680 (413) 584-4700

Petersham

Terry Burch, MA., LMHC
Birch Spring Clinical Services
110 N. Main Street
Petersham, MA 01366-9501
(978) 724-0050 (978) 724-8892

Wellesley

Jolene Ross. Ph.D.
Wellesley Neurotherapy
140 Bristol Road
Wellesley, MA 02181-2730
(781) 431-9115

MICHIGAN

Ann Arbor

Eve Avrin, Ph.D.
3300 Washtenaw Avenue, Suite 260
Ann Arbor, MI 48104
(734) 913-9870

Charles F. Spinazola, Ph.D.,
    Director
Licensed Clinical Psychologist
Michigan Neurotherapy Center
2345 S. Huron Pkwy.
Ann Arbor, MI 48108
(734) 761-1757
drspinazola@provide.net
www.eegspectrum.com

Melissa R. Sklar, MS, LLP
EEG Biofeedback of Ann Arbor
    LLC
2311 E. Stadium, Suite 210
Ann Arbor, MI 48104
(734) 302-3330
msklara2@inetmail.att.net
www.eegbioannarbor.com

Dexter

Robert Egri
Counseling Resources of Ann Arbor
2479 Peters Road
Dexter, MI 48130-9454
(734) 665-5050 (734) 665-6924

East Lansing

Martha W. Bristor, Ph.D.
5909 Shadowlawn Drive
East Lansing, MI 48823-2379
(517) 432-3326

Kalamazoo

Patricia T. Williams, CSW
Health Psychology and A.D.D.
  Institute
3335 South 9th Street
Kalamazoo, MI 49009
(269) 375-0624
ptwillcsw@cs.com

Richard R. Williams, Ph.D.
Health Psychology and A.D.D.
  Institute
3335 South 9th Street
Kalamazoo, MI 49009
(269) 375-0624
todocwill@cs.com
www.hp-add.com

Lansing

Lynn Marshall Darling, Ph.D.
RiverWind Psychology Associates, PLC
6639 Centurion Drive, Suite 150
Lansing, MI 48917
(517) 703-0110

RiverWind Psychology Associates
  Licensed Psychologists and
  Certified Social Worker
Kathleen Bowers, Lynn Darling, &
  Richard Dombrowski
6639 Centurion Drive, Suite 105
Lansing, MI 48917
(517) 703-0110
rdphd@juno.com

Northville

Yona Fisher
22020 Garfield
Northville, MI 48167
(248) 349-5950
yona@neuronet.com

Saginaw

Ed Langham, MSW
Child & Family Services
2806 Davenport Avenue
Saginaw, MI 48602
(989) 790-7501 (989) 791-3757
edlangham@att.net
www.ChildandFamilySaginaw.com

St. Joseph

William A. Schnell, MA
Neurofeedback & Counseling
  Center
2517 Niles Avenue
St. Joseph, MI 49085-1936
(616) 983-1600

MINNESOTA
Minneapolis

Michael Joyce, MA, NLP, BCIAC-
  EEG
A Chance to Grow
1800 2nd Street NE

Minneapolis, MN 56418-4306
(612) 521-2266 (612) 706-5551

N. Mankato

Al Mumma, MS
723 Park Avenue
N. Mankato, MN 56003-3634
(507) 388-5224

St. Paul

Gloria Scoonover
Synchrony Biofeedback, Inc.
1885 University Avenue W
St. Paul, MN 55104
(651) 206-9757 (651) 455-7227

Grand Marais

Karl Hansen
Northshore Neurofeedback
Post Office Box 275
703 W. 2nd Street
Grand Marais, MN 55604
(218) 387-2983
solarkarl@boreal.org
www.northshoreneurofeedback.com

Kathleen Stewart
Northshore Neurofeedback
Post Office Box 275
703 W. 2nd Street
Grand Marais, MN 55604
(218) 387-2983
www.northshoreneurofeedback.com

St. Louis Park

John S. Anderson, MA
Minnesota Neurotherapy Institute
3040 Inglewood Ave
St. Louis Park, MN 55416
(952) 915-1206

jsanderson@neurofeedback-
institute.com
www.neurofeedback-institute.com

MISSISSIPPI
Natchez

Terry Rouprich
ADHD Clinic Natchez Regional
Medical Center
54 Sergeant S. Prentiss Drive
Natchez, MS 39120
(601) 443-2282
adhdclinc@natchezregional.com

MISSOURI
Columbia

Wiley Miller, Ph.D.
Hiesberger & Associates
3201 S. Providence, Suite 204
Columbia, MO 65203-3622
(573) 875-0077

Kansas City

Robert L. McRoberts, Ph.D.
222 W. Gregory, Suite 229
Kansas City, MO 64114-1110
(816) 444-4887

St. Louis

John Francis Sheehan, Ph.D., Psy.D.
3601 Lindell Boulevard
St. Louis, MO 63108
(314) 977-2588
sheehasf@slu.edu

MONTANA
Dillon

Geri Godecke, MFT
4000 Hwy 91 S

Dillon, MT 59725
(406) 683-6676
godecke@mcn.net

Great Falls

Audrey Thompson, Ed.D., LCPC
2300 12th Avenue S., Suite 14
Great Falls, MT 59405-5017
(406) 761-5671

Missoula

Z'eva Singer, MA
Singer Associates, P.C.
5190 Old Marshall Grade
Missoula, MT 59802
(406) 721-3351
singer@montana.com

Robert A. Velin, Ph.D.,
 Mary K. Bartch, MS
Montana Neurobehavioral Specialist
900 N. Orange, Suite 101
Missoula, MT 59807
406-327-3384
RVelin@mtneuro.com

Whitefish

Clare Chisholm, MA, LPC
The Neurofeedback Clinic
244 Spokane Avenue, Suite 3
Whitefish, MT 59937-2600
(406) 863-9767

NEBRASKA
Crete

Dixie (Ruthann) Maresh Placek,
 MA, LMFT, CNP
The Affiliates
995 East Highway 33, Suite 1
Crete, NE 68333

(402) 826-5858
affiliates@alltel.net
www.crete-ne.com/business/affiliates

Hastings

Virginia K. White, RN, MSEd.
Professional Counseling Associates
The Burlington Village
208 South Burlington, Suite 106
Hastings, NE 68901
(402) 461-4917

Lincoln

BJ (Elizabeth) Wheeler, Ph.D.
The Quest - Connections in Mind
 and Body
6759 South Bermuda Drive
Lincoln, NE 68506
(402) 484-6759

Rick J. Windle, M.D.
Train Your Brain
2221 South 17th, Suite 203
Lincoln, NE 68502
(402) 476-6630 (402) 430-6425
rwindle@neb.rr.com

Eileen M. Curry MS, LMHP
Great Plains Family Counseling
315 So. 9th, Suite 12
Lincoln, NE 68508
(402) 474-5858 (402) 474-5859
eecee1244@aol.cm

Sandy Lamberson, RN, MA
First Step Wellness
1919 South 40th Street, Suite 211
Lincoln, NE 68506
(402) 441-9280
slamberson@neb.rr.com

Andrea Joy Sime, MSW
First Step Wellness Center
1919 South 40th Street, Suite 212
Lincoln, NE 68506
(402) 441-9280
asime@inebraska.com
www.firststeprecovery.com

Broken Bow

Patricia Ann Smith, MS
New Potentials Counseling &
  Biofeedback Center
Post Office Box 38
510 S. 10th Street
Broken Bow, NE 68822
(308) 872-6651
npc@inebraska.com

NEVADA
Henderson

Judith DeGrazia Willard, Ph.D.
Associated Neuro & Psych
  Specialties
1701 E. Green Valley Parkway
Building #2, Suite A
Henderson, NV 89014
(702) 650-0590

Carson City

Jerry Cinani, MS
Sierra Counseling & Neurotherapy
2874 N. Carson Street, Suite 215
Carson City, NV 89706
(775) 885-7717
jcinani@sierracounseling.com

NEW HAMPSHIRE
Londonderry

Edward Jacobs, Ph.D. & Associates

12 Parmenter Road
Londonderry, NH 03053
(603) 437-2069 ext. 10
ehjpsych@aol.com

NEW JERSEY
Atlantic Highlands

Betty Jarusiewicz, Ph.D., CADC
Atlantic Counseling Center, Inc.
51 Memorial Pkwy (Hwy 36)
Atlantic Highlands, NJ 07716
(732) 872-8700 (732) 801-4505

Morristown

Jill Sharon Broderick, MS, OTR
20 Community Place, 4th Floor
Morristown, NJ 07866
(973) 586-6554
jscb058@aol.com

Princeton

Les G. Fehmi, Ph.D.
Princeton Biofeedback Center
317 Mt. Lucas Road
Princeton, NJ 08540
(609) 924-0782
lesfehmi@ix.netcom.com
www.openfocus.com

Tenafly

Anya Luchow, Ph.D.
Neurodynamics
111 East Clinton Avenue
Tenafly, NJ 07670
(201) 569-4585
aklphd@aol.com

South Plainfield

Kirtley Elliott Thornton, Ph.D.

Neurotherapy Center
2509 Park Avenue, Ste. 2A
South Plainfield, NJ 07080
(908) 753-1800
ket@chp-neurotherapy.com
www.chp-neurotherapy.com

NEW MEXICO
Santa Fe

Carolyn Earnest,
   Clin. Nurse Spc., BCIA
The Neurotherapy Center
1448 S. St. Francis
Santa Fe, NM 87505
(505) 989-7259
neurotherapy@mindspring.com

NEW YORK
Astoria (New York City)

Vaia Delidimitropulu, Ph.D.
Aristotle's Psychological &
   Biofeedback Serv.
31-87 34th Street
Astoria, NY 11106
(718) 726-0842
efrosini_k@hotmail.com

Baldwinsville

James E. Terry
Pathway Counseling Center
8174 Speach Drive
Baldwinsville, NY 13027
(315) 635-7483
mosesjet@aol.com

Bronx (New York City)

Julie Weiner, MS
Biofeedback Learning Center
5997 Riverdale Avenue

Bronx, NY 10471
(718) 601-4569
jweiner1@netzero.net
www.biofeedbacklearning.com

Delmar

Cindy Perlin, CSW
13 Willow Drive
Delmar, NY 12054
(518) 439-6431
cperlin@nycap.rr.com

Fayetteville

Dr. Jean Cohen
Cohen Chiropractic
7313 Highbridge Road
Fayetteville, NY 13066
(315) 637-2225 (315) 863-5479

Hampton Bays

Christine Coolidge, PH.D.
Hampton Pain and Stress Center
186 W. Montauk Hwy., D-1
Hampton Bays, NY 11946
(631) 728-2000

Ithaca

Judith Abrams, LAC, PAC
Judith Abrams Acupuncture
342 DeWitt Building
Ithaca, NY 14850
(607) 277-7713
jask@clarityconnect.com

New York City (Manhattan)

Merlyn Hurd, Ph.D., BCIAC-EEG
88 University Place, 8th Floor
New York, NY 10003-4513
(212) 807-8690 (212) 243-4867

Katherine Leddick, Ph.D., BCIAC-EEG
164 West 80th Street, Lower Level
New York, NY 10024
(212) 787-8155

Laurence R. Lewis, Ph.D.
155 East 38th Street, Suite 2C
New York, NY 10016
(212) 697-5990
llewis@nyc.rr.com

Daniel Kuhn, M.D.
Integrative NeuroPsychiatric
  Services of New York
30 West 63rd Street, Suite 26-O
New York, NY 10023
(212) 315-1755
dankuhn@mindspring.com
www.integrativeneuropsychiatry.com

Deborah Pines, CSW
275 Central Park West, Suite 1F
New York, NY 10024-3035
(212) 579-3888

Kamran Fallahpour, CSW, Ph.D.
The Brain Resource Company -
  New York
315 West 57th, #306
New York, NY 10019
(212) 977-0178
kf@neurcog.com
www.neurocog.com and
www.neuro-feedback.com

Alfred Kleinbaum, Ph.D.
11 Riverside Drive
New York, NY 10023
(212) 861-5269
alfred@alfredkleinbaum.com
www.alfredkleinbaum.com

J. Lawrence Thomas. Ph.D.
19 West 34th Street, Penthouse
New York, NY 10001
(212) 268-8900
nurosvcs@aol.com
www.addadults.com

Round Lake

Arlene Nock, M.D.
Brain Topics
PO Box 740, 320 Ruhle Rd. So.
Round Lake, NY 12151
(518) 899-6500
arlene1@nycap.rr.com

Saratoga Springs
Kathy Zilberman, Ph.D.
4 Franklin Square, Suite D
Saratoga Springs, NY 12866
(518) 587-4350

Suffern

Mary Jo Sabo, Ph.D.
Biofeedback Consultants Inc.
191 Route 59
Suffern, NY 10901
(845) 369-7627
saboeeg@aol.com
www.TheRippleEffect.Org

Shortsville

Joseph R. Duba, M.D.
Neurofeedback Center of Shortsville
8 West Main Street
Shortsville, NY 14548
(585) 289-9160
docduba@brain-waves.com
www.brain-waves.com

Warwick

Don Wilde, Ph.D.
28 Railway Avenue, #2C
Warwick, NY 10990
(845) 987-9960
drwilde@warwick.net

Williamsville

Judy N. Chiswell, Ed.D.
Hemispheres
6511 Main Street
Williamsville, NY 14221
(716) 634-4313
hemispheres@adelphia.net

NORTH CAROLINA

Asheville

Phil Ellis, Ph.D.
Focus: Center for Neurofeedback
189 Chestnut Street
Asheville, NC 28801
(828) 281-2299

Ed Hamlin, Ph.D.
The Pisgah Institute
158 Zillicoa Street
Asheville, NC 28801
(828) 254-9494 (828) 254-3045

Thea Schulze, LCSW
31 Clayton Street
Asheville, NC 28801
(828) 251-2681
sthea@bellsouth.net

Boone

Ed Castro, M.D.
High Country Enhancement Clinic
245-C Winklers Creek Road
Boone, NC 28607

(828) 268-0010
thehcec@charter.net

Charlotte

Kent Crawford and Iris Prince
Charlotte Neurofeedback Associates
1819 Sardis Road North, Suite 360
Charlotte, NC 28212
(704) 844-8317
kent@carolina.rr.com

Greensboro

Gail Sanders Durgin, Ph.D.
Neurofeedback Associates
2311 West Cone Blvd., Suite 227
Greensboro, NC 27408
(336) 540-1972

Greenville

Judy M. Carlson-Catalano, Ed.D.,
  APRN, BCIAC
Health Innovations
2415 Charles Boulevard
Greenville, NC 27858
(252) 353-8022
healthinnovations@earthlink.net
www.healthinnovationsinc.com

Murphy

Mary A. Ricketson, MAEd.
Post Office Box 742
Murphy, NC 28906
(828) 837-4107
maryricketson311@hotmail.com

Tryon

Susan Lynne Ford, BAEEG
Centre For Neurofeedback
2512 Lynn Road, Suite 1
Tryon, NC 28782

(828) 859-1220
sueford@earthlink.net

OHIO
Akron

Keith Ungar
Center for Natural Medicine
2828 S. Arlington Road, Suite 100
Akron, OH 44312
(330) 644-7246 (330) 495-1111

Chagrin Falls

Mark C. Brown, Ph.D.
The Center for Better Living
7160 Chagrin Road, Suite 105
Chagrin Falls, OH 44023-1100
(440) 247-7465

Alan Bachers, Ph.D.
Center for Better Living
7160 Chagrin Road, Suite 106
Chagrin Falls, OH 44023
(440) 247-7465
abachers@apk.net

David Brinkman-Sull
7160 Chagrin Road, Suite 150
Chagrin Falls, Ohio 44023
(440) 247-7465

Centerville

Fred Sinay, M.Ed.
Centerville Counseling and ADHD
  Clinic
18 South Main Street
Centerville, OH 45458
(937) 434-4882
fsinay@msn.com

Cincinnati

Justine Ritter, Ph.D., RN
Cincinnati Neurotherapy Center
149 Siebenthaler
Cincinnati, OH 45215
(513) 521-5483
wandjritter@earthlink.net

William Michael Wing, Ed.D.
Rodney E. Vivian M.D.
8000 Five Mile Road
Cincinnati, OH 45230
(513) 232-3070
psychmanw@hotmail.com

Cuyahoga Falls

Rita Cowan, Ph.D. & Associates, Inc.
1900 23rd Street
Cuyahoga Falls, Ohio 44223
(330) 971-7152
cowanr@summa-health.org

Dayton

Rosemary E. Herron, M.Ed.
Dayton Biofeedback Center
2301 Far Hills Avenue
Dayton, OH 45419
(937) 298-9011
daytonbiocenter@worldnet.att.net

Elyria

Elaine Thompson
Associates in Adoptive/Foster
  Family Psych
1041 Rosealee Avenue
Elyria, OH 44035
(440) 365-6629 (440) 365-3786

Gahanna

Larry R. Schollenberger, MA

Neurotherapy of Central Ohio
769 Tim Tam Avenue
Gahanna, OH 43230
(614) 323-9421
ischollenberger@netwalk.com

Piqua

Carla Bertke
Brain Wellness Center
850 S. Main Street
Piqua, OH 45356
(937) 779-7630
neurofeedbac@nls.net

Westlake

George F. Houck, Ph.D.
Center for Individual & Family
  Therapy
24500 Center Ridge Road, #125
Westlake, OH 44145
(440) 871-8102
ghouck@ameritech.net

OKLAHOMA
Ada

Dana Hargus, M.Ed., LPC
Biofeedback & Counseling, Inc.
2100 N. Broadway
Ada, OK 74820
(580) 436-7120 (580) 310-5969

Lawton

Dane Nielsen, MS, LPC
Brainwave Feedback
144 NW Red Bud Road
Lawton, OK 73507
(580) 512-6064
cir@ionet.net

Kenneth Jones, MS
Mental Fitness Center
102 S.W. 12th Street
Lawton, OK 73501
(580) 250-1545
kjones1277@sbcglobal.net

Oklahoma City

Anne Barker, LCSW
3120 West Britton Road
Oklahoma City, OK 73120
(405) 570-2581
ambarker@telepath.com

Vicki Harris Wyatt
The Wyatt Group
Post Office Box 1947
Oklahoma City, OK 73101
(405) 232-1000 (405) 514-4880

Norman

Sally Church, Ph.D.
1300 McGee Drive, Suite 101A
Norman, OK 73072
(405) 360-0048
swmlc1@aol.com

OREGON
Ashland

Susan C. BerryHill, MA, MPH, LPC
Potential Unlimited
376 B Street, Suite 1
Ashland, OR 97520
(541) 482-2780

Phil Miller, MS
Potential Unlimited
376 B Street
Ashland, OR 97520
(541) 482-2780
philmiller@eegpower.com

Klamath Falls

Chauncey E. Farrell, MS
Mind Body Connection
1310 McClellan Drive
Klamath Falls, OR 97603
(541) 883-3485

Eugene

Matthew J. Fleischman, Ph.D.
Center for Attention & Learning
915 Oak Street, Suite 300
Eugene, OR 97401
(541) 343-9221
matt541@qwest.net
www.attentionlearning.com

Lebanon

Lila McQueen, Ph.D. and
  Associates
1711 S. Main Street
Lebanon, OR 97355-3111
(541) 259-5400

Portland

Kayle Sandberg-Lewis, LMT, MA
1433 SE Tolman Street
Portland, OR 97202-5421
(503) 234-2733
stressless@att.net

Nora Teresa Gedgaudas
Northwest Neurofeedback
1920 NW Johnson Street, Suite 100
Portland, OR 97209
(503) 274-7733
eegnora@earthlink.net
www.northwest-neurofeedback.com

Kana Suppaiah, PMHNP PMHNP
Advance Neurofeedback Clinic
2301 Northwest Thurman Street,
  Suite A
Portland, OR 97210
(503) 243-7907
kana@nurofeed.com
www.nurofeed.com

Salem

Jeremy T. Davis
4164 Sunray Avenue South
Salem, OR 97302
(503) 375-3638 (541) 812-2738

PENNSYLVANIA
Carlisle

Henry M. Weeks, Ph.D.
211 Echo Road
Carlisle, PA 17013-9510
(717) 249-8382 (717) 243-3164
hweeks@epix.net

Chester

Frank Masterpasqua, Ph.D.
Widener Uninversity
One University Place
Chester, PA 19081
(610) 499-1234
frank.j.masterpasqua@widener.edu

Downingtown

Kathleen J. West, Ph.D.
506 E. Lancaster Avenue Lower
  Level West
Downingtown, PA 19335
(610) 518-6020
kathleenwestphd@brokenhillfarm.com

Exton

Barbara Pennington Tury, MA
Community Clinical Counseling
Neurofeedback & Counseling
  Connection, P.C.
47 Marchwood Road, Suite 2-H
Exton, PA 19341
(610) 280-9555
btury@aol.com
www.neurofeedbackonline.com

Lafayette Hill

Marvin H. Berman, Ph.D.
Quietmind Foundation
600 Germantown Pike,
  Suite A
Lafayette Hill, PA 19444
(610) 940-0488
marvinberman@quietmindfdn.org
www.quietmindfdn.org

Plymouth Meeting

Domenic Greco, Ph.D.
NeuroDynamix - www.nrdx.com
531 W Germantown Pike – #201
Plymouth Meeting, PA 19462
(610) 940-2233
Marlton, NJ office:
(856) 988-0707
neuro1@netreach.net
www.nrdx.com

Philadelphia

Marged Lindner, Ph.D.
633 West Rittenhouse Street
Philadelphia, PA 19144
(215) 849-0735
ged.lin@verizon.net

Swarthmore

Kathryn N. Healey, Ph.D.
Inst. Grad. Clinical Psych.
c/o Frank Masterpasqua
211 Park Avenue
Swarthmore, PA 19081-2418
(610) 499-1234

Trooper

Mitchell M. Sadar, Ph.D.
Sadar Psych. Services
124 Woodlyn Avenue
Trooper, PA 19403
(610) 933-9440

Valley Forge

Angelika Y. Sadar, Ph.D.
Valley Forge Road Suite 72
  (mail not received here)
Valley Forge, PA 19482
(610) 933-9440
mitch@sadarpsych.com
www.sadarpsych.com

West Chester

Bob Patterson, BS, LPT
The Neuro-Enhancement Center
790 East Market Street, Suite 300
West Chester, PA 19382
(610) 431-9509 (484) 354-0169
bob@instituteforchildren.com
www.instituteforchildren.com

Yardley

Barry Belt, Ph.D.
Attention Deficit Specialists
Floral Vale Professional Park
503 Floral Vale Boulevard
Yardley, PA 19067
(215) 497-0240 (215) 497-0258

PUERTO RICO
Ponce
Carmen L. Maldonado, Ph.D.
Centro de Psicoterapia y
  Neuroterapia
Jardines Fagot Avenue Fagot N-4
Ponce, PR 00716
(787) 848-4720
basimaldonado@hotmail.com

San Juan
Carlos E. Rios, MA, MS
EEG Neurotherapy Center
RR 2 Box 9
San Juan, PR 00926
(787) 748-9252
carlosrios33@hotmail.com

RHODE ISLAND
Narragansett
Peter Seuffert, MS, LMFT
23 Lauderdale Drive
Narragansett, RI 2882
(401) 782-2980

Barrington
Joseph Crane, MA
East Bay Neurofeedback
15 Juniper Street
Barrington, RI 02806
(401) 247-9369
josephcrane@cox.net

Providence
Laurence M. Hirshberg, Ph.D.
The NeuroDevelopment Center
Two Regency Plaza,
  Suite 15
Providence, RI 02903
(401) 351-7780
lhirshberg@cox.net

SOUTH CAROLINA
Mt. Pleasant
Dr. Michael C. Mithoefer
Neurofeedback Associates
208 Scott Street
Mt. Pleasant, SC 29464-4345
(843) 849-6899

Beaufort
Royce Vernon Malphrus, Ph.D.
Sea Island Pain and Stress Clinic
989 Ribaut Road, Suite 260
Beaufort, SC 29902
(843) 522-8569
malph@hargray.com

TENNESSEE
Franklin
Carole Kendall, Ph.D.
1107A Lakeview Drive
Franklin, TN 37067-1302
(615) 791-1332

Germantown
Cliff Heegel, Ph.D.
Stress, Trauma, and Biofeedback
  Clinic
2199 S. Germantown Road
Germantown, TN 38138
(901) 753-0381
cheeg@askdrcliff.com
www.askdrcliff.com

Memphis
Dale S. Foster, Ph.D.
Memphis Counseling Center

950 Mt. Moriah, Suite 201
Memphis, TN 38117
(901) 682-3371
dfoster1@midsouth.rr.com

TEXAS
Allen

Sherene McGee, RN
The Fit Mind
1212 Bel Air Drive
Allen, TX 75013
(972) 727-8102 (214) 577-3118
fitmind@swbell.net

Austin

Neil C. King, MSW
4131 Spicewood Springs Rd., Suite Q2
Austin, TX 78759-8665
(512) 338-4095

Lynda Kirk, MA, LPC
Austin Biofeedback Center/Optimal
  Performance Inst
3624 North Hills Drive,
  Suite B-205
Austin, TX 78731
(512) 794-9355
lkirk@austinbiofeedback.com
www.austinbiofeedback.com

Al Mustin, Ph.D.
Jan Ford Mustin, Ph.D.
4407 Bee Cave Rd, #411
Austin, TX 78746
(512) 347-8100
akm@mustin.com
www.mustin.com

Corpus Christi

Burton Kittay, Ph.D.

Psychological Wellness Center
5350 S Staples Street, Suite 200
Corpus Christi, TX 78411-4654
(361) 992-2244

Dallas

Marvin W. Sams, N.D.
Neurofeedback Centers of America
16990 No. Dallas Parkway,
  Suite 120
Dallas, TX 75248
(972) 247-6796
drmsams@aol.com

Denton

Robert Lawson, MS
200 West Collins St.
Denton, TX 76201
(940) 387-5941
robert.lawson@augustmail.com

Houston

Michael Keppler, MS, LPC-I
3334 Richmond Avenue, Suite 121
Houston, TX 77098
(713) 928-2925 (713) 878-1983
mskep@hotmail.com

Carol J. Kershaw, Ed.D.
Institute for Family Psychology
2012 Bissonnet Street
Houston, TX 77005
(713) 529-4589 (832) 545-4812
hypnopsych@aol.com
www.mhehouston.com

Samuel Sims, R.PSGT.
Sims Management, Inc.
8102 Wateka
Houston, TX 77074

(832) 816-2856
ssleep6@aol.com

Nancy White, Ph.D.
The Enhancement Institute
4600 Post Oak Place, Suite 301
Houston, TX 77027
(713) 552-0092
nancy@enhancementinstitute.com
www.enhancementinstitute.com

Plano

John H. Millerman, Ph.D.
Achievement Plus
1825 E. Plano Parkway, Suite 110
Plano, Texas 75074
Phone # (972) 422-1399
drjohnm@earthlink.net
www.neurofeedbackcenters.com

San Antonio

Michael Hoffmann, CNP
Neurofeedback Center of
  San Antonio
6836 San Pedro Avenue, Suite 103
San Antonio, TX 78216
(210) 930-9205 (210) 827-0377
mhoffmann@austin.rr.com

Randall R. Lyle, Ph.D.
Ecumenical Center
8310 Ewing Halsell Drive
San Antonio, TX 78229
(210) 616-0885 (210) 431-2001

UTAH
Salt Lake City

Steve Szykula, Ph.D.
Comprehensive Psychological
  Services

1200 East 3300 South
Salt Lake City, UT 84106-2522
(801) 483-1600

D. Corydon Hammond, Ph.D.,
  QEEG-D
University of Utah School of
  Medicine, PM&R
30 No. 1900 East
Salt Lake City, UT 84132-2119
(801) 581-5741
D.C.Hammond@m.cc.utah.edu

South Ogden

Heber C. Kimball, Ph.D.
Neurofeedback Center
5898 So. 1050 East
South Ogden, UT 84405
(801) 725-7118
khc5@comcast.net

VIRGINIA
Abingdon

Robert W. Hill, Ph.D.
The Oaks
Post Office Box 2077
16501 Jeb Stuart Way
Abingdon, VA 24210-2077
(276) 628-1378

Ronald W. Brill, Ph.D.
Tamarack Center, Inc.
390 Commerce Drive, Box 8
Abingdon, VA 24210
(276) 628-1496
rwbrill@naxs.com

Alexandria

William A. Decker, Ph.D.
BioPsych Services

300 S. Washington Street,
 Suite 300
Alexandria, VA 22314
(703) 836-3678
wdecker1@cox.net

Deborah Anne Stokes, Ph.D.
Neurofeedback Consultants, Inc.
2121 Eisenhower Avenue, Suite 200
Alexandria, VA 22314
(703) 684-0334
dstokes3@cox.net
www.neurofeedbackconsult.com

Arlington

Dan Dinsmoor, Ph. D.
2504 N. Ohio Street
Arlington, VA 22207
(703) 966-1693
ddinsm@co.arlington.va.us

Burke

Martha Susan Lappin, Ph.D.
Alternative Health Care Research,
 Inc.
10841 Split Oak Lane
Burke, VA 22015
(703) 250-4695
marlappin@aol.com

Herndon

Stacie Clark Masters
The Brain Haven Neurofeedback,
 LLC
489 Carlisle Drive, Suite A
Herndon, VA 20170
(703) 707-0125
stacie@thebrainhaven.com
www.TheBrainHaven.com

McLean
Joan Bullard, Ph.D.
6845 Elm Street, Suite 710
McLean, VA 22101
(703) 734-3545

Newport News

Adrianne Ryder-Cook, LLD, ML,
 MCL, MS.JD
Riverside EEG Biofeedback Services
11815 Rock Landing Drive
Newport News, VA 23061
(757) 594-3399

Lanny Fly, Dmin
Family Therapy
718 J Clyde Morris Boulevard
Newport News, VA 23601
(757) 873-8565
lanny@flyconsulting.com
www.flyconsulting.com

Laura L. Nichols BA (psychology)
Family Therapy
718 J. Clyde Morris Boulevard
Newport News, VA 23606
(757) 873-8566
lanierfly@yahoo.com

Reston

William R. Chatlos, Ph.D.
11333 Sunset Hills Road
Reston, VA 20190
(703) 437-9103
rudychat@aol.com

Richmond

Glenn Weiner, Ph.D.
Dominion Behavioral Healthcare

703 N. Courthouse Road,
  Suite 101
Richmond, VA 23236
(804) 794-4482 (804) 379-4090

Carol C. Hughes, Ed.D.
1506 Willow Lawn Drive,
  Suite 200
Richmond, VA 23230
(804) 798-2555
hugh303@erols.com

Roanoke

Brenda R. Baird, Ph.D.
Neuro Scan LLC
5330-D Peters Creek Road
Roanoke, VA 24019
(540) 563-9500
neuroscan@eeg-biofeedback.com
www.eeg-biofeedback.com

Springfield

Lorraine F. Faherty, B.S.
8916 Cromwell Drive
Springfield, VA 22151
(703) 425-3438 Home
rainrainlp@aol.com

Warrenton

Linda F. Harrover, RN
The Harrover Group, Inc.
7296 Forrest Road
Warrenton, VA 20187
(540) 349-1415
frankhar@erols.com

WASHINGTON
Bainbridge Island

Judy Peters, Ph.D., BCIAC
Neurofeedback Clinic
15420 Smoland Lane
Bainbridge Island, WA 98110
(206) 855-9265
drpeters211@aol.com

Bellevue

Steve Rothman, Ph.D.
1800 112th Avenue NE, #240W
Bellevue, WA 98004-2934
(425) 454-4266 (425) 747-9020

Bellingham

Greg Sharp
Colville Healing Arts Center
4140 Guide Meridian, Suite 200
Bellingham, WA 98226
(360) 676-4325

Edmonds

Stephanie Harris, RN
Biofeedback Clinic of Edmonds
8523 224th Street SW
Edmonds, WA 98026
(425) 672-1677
C3Beta@MSN.com

Kirkland

Jeanne Anne Craig, Ph.D.
Neuro Education Center
1118 First Street
Kirkland, WA 98033
(425) 822-8159
drja2@aol.com

Mt. Vernon

Rosemary P. MacGregor, CRN, MS
Stress Management Biofeedback
  Center
2114 Riverside Drive, #205
Mt. Vernon, WA 98273
(360) 428-0135
rosemary@rockisland.com

Richland

Lynn M. Orr, Ph.D.
1901 George Washington Way,
  Suite A
Richland, WA 99352
(509) 946-0984
desertwarriors@msn.com

Seattle

Thomas DuHamel, Ph.D.
ABCD, Inc.
2611 NE 125th Street, #225
Seattle, WA 98125-4357
(206) 361-6884 (206) 361-0132

Elizabeth Walker, Ph.D.
5134 S. Willow Street
Seattle, WA 98118
(206) 725-6926

WISCONSIN
Oconomowoc

Anne Felden, Ph.D.
Oconomowoc Developmental
  Training Center
36100 Genesee Lake Road
Oconomowoc, WI 53066-9201
(262) 569-5515

Wauwatsa

Peter J. Hansen, Ph.D.
Family Care Psychological Services
2500 N. Mayfair Road, Suite 560
Wauwatosa, WI 53226
(414) 771-5002

WEST VRGINIA
Bluefield

Teresa Paine, Ph.D.
New Horizons Comprehensive
  Counseling
311 North Street
Bluefield, WV 24701
(304) 327-8362

WYOMING
Casper

Bruce Leininger, Ph.D.
420 West 12th Street
Casper, WY 82601
(307) 473-7925
bcleininger@juno.com

ARGENTINA
Buenos Aires

Ester Romero Tannenhaus
Rosario 478- 2nd Floor
Buenos Aires 1424
Argentina
54 11 4901 8911

AUSTRALIA
NEW SOUTH WALES
Artarmon

Jan Osgood
Action Potential Neurotherapy
25 Onyx Road
Artarmon NSW 2064

02 9419 6683 0410 686 929
josgood@ozemail.com.au

Bass Hill

Rosemary Boon
Learning Discoveries
104 Chester Hill Rd.
Bass Hill
New South Wales 2197
02 9727 5794
rboon@one.net.au

Bowral

Geraldine Mary Knights, RN, Enpc
Advance, Learning & Behaviour
  Solutions
Unit 2 / 371 Bong Bong St
Bowral 2576
NSW Australia
02-48624482 04-1271-3338
gknights@acenet.com.au
www.acenet.com.au/~gknights

Charlestown

Sr. Patricia Wilson
Stroke & Disability
17 James Street
Charlestown 2290
NSW Australia
02-4943-9786

Fairfield

Terry Cook, M.D.
8/14-16 Court Road
Fairfield NSW 2165
02 7257088

Milton

Jon Richard Hegg, MA, Psych
South Coast Neurotherapy Services

137 Princes Hwy
Milton NSW 2538
02-4455-5971 0419-241-421
jonhegg@bigpond.com

Merrickville

John Criticos
79 Silver Street
Merrickville NSW 2204
02-9349-7802

St. Leonards

Alex Sevitt, Psychologist
National Diagnostic Services
Level 1, 48 Albany Street
St. Leonards NSW 2065
011-61-2-9437-5071
rolex@geko.net.au

Sydney

Dana Adam, MA, M.Appl. Psych
Active Support Centre
Level 5
149 Castlereagh Street
Sydney South NSW 1235
02 9262 9408 0417 664 882

Wollongong

Geraldine Mary Knights, RN, Enpc
Advance, Learning & Behaviour
  Solutions
Suite 15B, 157 Crown St
Wollongong NSW 2500
Ph 0412713338
gknights@acenet.com.au
www.acenet.com.au/~gknights

Wentworthville

Angelo Schibeci, Ph.D.
Health Plus

52 Dunmore Street
Wentworthville NSW 2154
02 9604 6937 02 9604 6937

QUEENSLAND
Newmarket

Tamara Lorensen, Psychologist
The Neurotherapy Centre
Newmarket
Australia
07 3352 7755
tamara@tpgi.com.au

Buderim

Mark Darling B Soc Sc (Hons)
  (Psych)
Mark Darling Neurotherapy
Lakeshore Medical Centre,
  Lakeshore Avenue
Buderim Qld 4556
Australia
07 5476 8899
mdarling@powerup.com.au

Cairns

Rob Buschkens
The Neuro Training Clinic
Post Office Box 7993
29 Headrick Street
Cairns QLD 4870
Australia
07 40417516
eegspectrum@austarnet.com.au

Coorparoo

Brian O'Hanlon
Post Office Box 313
Coorparoo, QLD 4151
Australia
07 3397 8250 041 930 2173

Gympie

Don Brinkworth
Informere Pty Ltd
37 Tamaree Road
Post Office Box 728
Gympie QLD 4570
Australia
07 5482 9298

Del Sherlock, Ph.D.
Management and Psychological
  Services
37 Tamaree Road
Gympie, Queensland 4570
Australia
017 482 9298

Robina Gold Coast

Pamella Anne Pope Applied Science
  Psychology
Innersense Psychology
214 Ron Penhaligon Way
Robina Gold Coast Queensland 4226
Australia
07 5591 9773
innersense4u@yahoo.com.au

Rockhampton

Alan Keen
A & M's Psychological Services
123 Denham Street
Rockhampton, QLD 4700
Australia
07 4927 2153
a.keen@cqu.edu.au

VICTORIA
Doncaster

Jacques Duff
Behavioural Neuotherapy Clinic

Suite 2, 314 Manningham Road
Doncaster Victoria 3108
Australia
039 842 0370

Leopold

Dennis Shum
15 Ferguson Road
Leopold, Victoria 3224
Australia

South Caulfield

Moshe Perl, Ph.D.
Clinical & Forensic Psychologist
650 Glenhuntly Road
So. Caulfield Victoria 3162
Australia
03 9571 9933 0412 299 099
mperl@ozemail.com.au

WEST AUSTRALIA
Como

Roger P. Lavell, MAPS, Clinical
  Psychologist
Suite 2, Como Corporate Centre
11 Preston Street
Como WA 6152
Australia
08-9367-0610 04-1114-6620

Cottesloe

Kerry Monick MBBS, DPM,
  FRANZCP.
Suite 10 - 136 Railway Street
Cottesloe
West Australia
08 9384 8595 08 9384 8535

Fremantle

Denis L. McCarthy Master Applied
  Psych (Clinical) , BA Hons
  (Psych)
Denis McCarthy & Associates
Post Office Box 789
12/158 High Street
Fremantle W. Australia 6959
Australia
08 9430 7777
info@int-a1.com
www.int-a1.com/dm

Joondalup

Ramakrishna Naidoo Consultant
  Pediatrician
Jonndalup Health Campus
Suite 204 - Specialist Medical
  Center
Joondalup 6027
WA Australia
08-9400-9911
West Australia Cottesloe

Leederville

Carol Smith
7 Rosslyn Street
West Leederville 6007
Western Australia
08 8212 4005 0417 849 458

SOUTH AUSTRALIA
Adelaide

Tim Hill
86 South Terrace 1
Adelaide, SA 5000
Australia
08-8410-6500

Stephen Dunstone, BSc BDS Dip
  APP Psych Grad Dip A p p Psych
Dr Stephen Dunstone
41 George Street Norwood
Adelaide 5066
South Australia
08 83645342
dunstone@senet.com.au

Peter Thomas
48 Carrington Street
Adelaide 5000
South Australia
08 8212 4005 0417 849 458

Greg Ireland, M. Psych.
Registered Psychologist
U of So. Australia School of
  Psychology
GPO Box 2471
Adelaide 5001
South Australia
618 302 2468
greg.ireland@unisa.edu.au

Greenwith

Ed J. Zahra
  B.Com.,Dip.App.Psych.,M.App.P
  sych.,M.A.S.H.
Access Psychology
43 Reordan Drive
Greenwith 05125
South Australia
08 8289 7766
ed@accesspsychology.com.au
www.accesspsychology.com.au

AUSTRIA
Donau

Gerfried Schenner

12/1/B A-3370
A-3370 Ybbs a.d. Donau
Austria
43-699 100 56428

Volders

Dietmar Kamenschek
Begleitung, Integration, Toleranz
Kirchgasse 6
Volders 6112
Austria
011-43-5224-51055

BOLIVIA

La Paz
Patricia Wiener
Av. Montenegro
Edificio An Miguel Arcangel
La Paz
Bolivia
591-2-2-796899

CANADA
Surrey

Susan Diamond
13768 32nd Avenue
Surrey BC V4P 2B8
Canada
(604) 541-9350

Ontario / Russell

Janet MacMillan
Brain Wave Therapy
159 Forced Road
Russell Ontario K4R 1A1
Canada
(613) 445-4514

Vancouver

Virginia Martin, MSLP
108 W48th Avenue
Vancouver B.C., V5Y3R1
Canada
604-876-7286
ginnymartin@shaw.ca

CHILE

Santiago

Jane Crossley
Fernando Morgado, M.D.
Apoquindo Medical Building
Apoquindo 4100. Of. 1009
Santiago
Chile
011-562-212 9011

Fernando Morgado, M.D.
Neurofeedback Clinic
Apoquindo Medical Building
Apoquindo 4100, Room 1009
Santiago 6760355
Chile
011-562-212-9011

COSTA RICA

Francisco Jimenez Marten
Latin American Institute of
  Neurotherapy
Plaza Cristal, 100 Mts South
50 West 25 South Curridabat
San Jose FL 33102-5216
Costa Rica
506-224-61-76

CZECH REPUBLIC

Praha

Ing. Josef Tomek

Tak Co, Ltd.
Holandska 1
101 00 Praha
Czech Republic
(420) 272-4187

Prague

Jiri Tyl, Ph.D.
AAPB / Biofeedback Institute
  Czech Republic
Evropska 94
Prague
Czech Republic
+420 602 224 964
biofeedback@vol.cz
www.eegbiofeedback.cz

GERMANY

Altotting

Dr. Ronald Schmidt
Sozialpadiat6risches Zentrum Inn-
  Salzach
Vinzenz-von Paul Strabe 10
84503 Altotting
Germany
06 71 509 247

Thomas Fuchs
Zentrum fur Kinder und Jugendliche
Kreiskrankenhaus
Altotting 84503
Germany
086 71 / 5 09 246

Allentown

Avi Sonnenschein
Ludwigkirchstrasse 10A
Allentown 10719
Germany
011-49-30881-5620

Munchen

Wolfgang Keeser, Ph.D.
Leopoldstrasse 59 D-80802
Munchen
Germany
089 38977 0

INDONESIA
Jakarta

Yu Wei Shin
Nanyang Technological Univ.
Pusat Terapi Alami Spektrum
Kimplek Mega Glodok
Pluit, Jakarta
Indonesia
62 81 6660319

ISRAEL
Haifa

Ernesto Miselevich, M.D.
1, Litanis Street
Post Office Box 6490
Haifa, 31064
Israel
011-972-48375748 011-972-052-
    539831

Jerusalem

Naomi Palmor
Or Shraga 17/2
Jerusalem, 00000
Israel
011-9722-587-2424
brain@actcom.co.il

KOREA
Seoul

Sooyoung Kim, M.D.
International Clinic

737-37 Hannam-Dong
Yong San-Ku Seoul 140-212
Korea
011-82-2- 790-1857

Kim Keum Jun
Bio Comp Clinic
576-6, Dasol Bldg.
Shinsa-dong, kangnamgu
Seoul 135-120
Korea

Hyung Bae Park
Mind Symphony Clinic
724 Rosedale Blvd., 2F 201
Suseo Dong
Seoul
Korea
82-2-3411-8878

Cheolhwan Kim
108 Pyung-Dong Jongno-Ku
Seoul 1107
Korea
82-2
kchosh@samsung.co.kr

MEXICO
Mexico City

Georgina de Blasquez, Psychologist
    and Family Therapist
Crece Neurofeedback S.C.
Tesoreros 86
Tlalpan, 14000
Mexico City
Mexico
(525) 666-1593 (525) 652-1700

Cuernavaca, Morelos 62157
Mexico
52-7-3-13-9410

Gabriela Michaca
CIANPP
Centro Integral de Atención
  Neuropsicopedagógica SC
Crepúsculo no. 47
México D.F. CP 04530
52 55 50 33 64 60
52 55 50 33 64 61
www.cianpp.com

Cuernavaca

Ron Wynne
CNC Spectrum
Avenue Palmas 811-2

NEW ZEALAND
Wellington

Jan Bowers, BA (psyc/educ),
  NZRN, MNZAC
Audra Ctr Health Profes.
75 Guznee Street
Level 6
Wellington 6006
New Zealand
011-64-4-801-7780 011-64-4-801-6610
janbowers@xtra.co.nz

NORWAY
Ulvik

Jonelle Villar
Paradis
5730 Ulvik 5730
Norway
47 56 52 65 55

Geir Flatabø, M.D.
Ulvik Neurofeedback Senter
Brakanes
Ulvik Hordaland N-5731
Norway
+47 5652 6505
geirf@ulvik.org

Toensberg

Mette Tveten, RN, Psychiatric
  Nurse
Medicus
Oevre Langgt. 44
N-3110 Toensberg
Norway
011-47-33-31-37-80

Arne Tveten, M.D., Psychiatrist
Medicus
Mollegt. 8
Toensberg 3111
Norway
011-47-33-31-37-80

Oslo

Oystein Larsen
Ungplan as
Gjerdrumsvel 12a-f
0486 Oslo
Oslo 486
Norway
23008530 47 90143389

SINGAPORE

Kenneth Kang, Ph.D.
Spectrum Learning Pte. Ltd.
583 Orchard Road
#16-01/17-01 Forum Singapore
  23888

Singapore
65-6834-9476
contact@spectrumlearning.biz

SPAIN
Madrid

Ana Diez Bolanos, Psy.D.
EEG Biofeedback Services
Centro de Neuroposicologia
  Cibernitica
Isabel 11, n 10, 2, Izda
Madrid
Spain
011-34-942-364-241

Sevilla

Luise F. Jaki, MS
Valparaiso 21, Pl.4, B-3
Sevilla E-41013
Spain
011- 34-95-4232 872

SWITZERLAND
Zurich

Gierin Foppa
308 Schaffhauserstrasse
Zurich AK CH-8050
Switzerland
0041-1310-29-23

Maximilian Teicher
Limmatquai 70 CH-8001
Zurich CH8001
Switzerland
011-411 262-85-85

Chur

Dr. Andreas Muller
Schulpsychologischer Dienst
  Graubunden

Quaderstrasse 15
Chur 7000
Switzerland
0041 81 257 27 42

Thalwil

John Styffe
Weberstrasse 8
Thalwil 8800
Switzerland
011-411-722-1828 411 771 34 62

THE NETHERLANDS
Hardenberg

W.D. van der Zwaag, MA, Clinical
  Psycologist/Psychotherapist
Hardenburg Medical Centre
Hardenberg 7770AA
The Netherlands
00-31-523-287878

Zilvermeeuw

Johan Fekkes, MA, Clinical
  Psycologist/Psychotherapist
Medische Psychologie
Twenteborg General Hospital
Zilvermeeuw 1 Almelo AK 7555
The Netherlands
031- 546-833240

Meppel

Bjorn van Twillert, MA, Health
  Psychologist
Koestraat 25A
Meppel
The Netherlands
00-31-522-233354

Ben Reitsma, Ph.D.
Pain Expertise Centre

University Hospital Groningen
Department of Medical Psycology
9700 RB
The Netherlands
(31) 50-3614133 31 5036 141 33

UNITED KINGDOM
Cambridgeshire

Beverly Steffert
Dyslexia Associates
35 Madingley Road
Cambridgeshire PE19 3JR
United Kingdom
011-44 01284 724 301 44-1284-
724301

VENEZUELA
Caracas

Sarita Kramer, Clinical Psycologist
Centro Clinico Profes Caracas
Ave Panteon San Bernardino
Conultorio Caracas 412
Venezuela
58 2 574 2853

Pedro Delgado, Psychaitrist
Humana
Res. Esmeralda San Bernardino
51 Memorial Pkwy Hwy 36
Caracas 1010
Venezuela
58 212 5500425/0829 58 14 3 28
7414

Alvaro Villegas, M.D.
Clinica Santa Maria
A. Calle Geminis
Qta. La Negra
Caracas 1061
Venezuela
58 212 232 2421 58 416 625 1662

ADDENDA

ARIZONA
Scottsdale

Robert Gurnee, MSW, DCSW,
  BCIA:EEG, QEEG/Diplomate
A.D.D. Clinic
8114 E. Cactus Rd., #200
Scottsdale, AZ 85260
(480) 424-7200
bob@add-clinic.com
www.add-clinic.com

MAINE
South Portland

Elizabeth Millett, MS
Bridgeside Counseling &
  Neurofeedback
13 Ocean St.
South Portland, ME 04106
(207) 767-0117
emillet2@maine.rr.com
www.maineneurofeedback.com

On the Authors

Mark Steinberg, Ph.D. is a practicing licensed psychologist in Los Gatos (San Jose), California with over 29 years of experience in clinical, educational, and neuropsychology. He has worked extensively with children and families, and with educational agencies and businesses. He has taught graduate school in psychology at several universities. His specialties include EEG neurofeedback, Voice Technology, mental fitness training, peak performance, cognitive retraining, and technology-assisted learning therapy for individuals with academic, motivational, and neurological problems. Dr. Steinberg has made numerous appearances nationally on television and radio, including TV appearances on ABC, NBC, CBS and FOX. He is often consulted and invited for studio appearances as a medical expert by NBC. He was voted Educational Psychologist of the Year in 1993 by a professional peer organization and Best Child Therapist in 2000 by Bay Area Parent magazine.

Siegfried Othmer, Ph.D. is the Chief Scientist at the EEG Institute of the Brian Othmer Foundation in Woodland Hills (Los Angeles). This foundation is dedicated to research, education, and clinical services in the field of neurofeedback. Dr. Othmer is also the Founder of EEG Spectrum (1988), which rapidly became the largest neurofeedback service delivery organization in the world. He is a physicist who has spent most of his career in aerospace research. However, two children with neurological impairments, and a third with ADHD, moved his attention forcefully to this emerging technique of neurofeedback. Dr. Othmer and his wife, Susan Othmer, have introduced several thousand professionals into the field of neurofeedback. The story of these developments is told in the book, *A Symphony in the Brain*, by New York Times Science writer Jim Robbins.